Napoleon's Purgatory
The Unseen Humanity of the "Corsican Ogre" in Fatal Exile

Thomas M. Barden

Introduction by
J. David Markham,
President of the International Napoleonic Society

Vernon Series in World History

VERNON PRESS

Copyright © 2017 Vernon Press, an imprint of Vernon Art and Science Inc, on behalf of the author.

All rights reserved. No part of this publication may be reproduced, stored in a retrieval system, or transmitted in any form or by any means, electronic, mechanical, photocopying, recording, or otherwise, without the prior permission of Vernon Art and Ascience Inc.

www.vernonpress.com

In the Americas:
Vernon Press
1000 N West Street,
Suite 1200, Wilmington,
Delaware 19801
United States

In the rest of the world:
Vernon Press
C/Sancti Espiritu 17,
Malaga, 29006
Spain

Vernon Series in World History

Library of Congress Control Number: 2017932339

ISBN: 978-1-62273-243-2

Product and company names mentioned in this work are the trademarks of their respective owners. While every care has been taken in preparing this work, neither the authors nor Vernon Art and Science Inc. may be held responsible for any loss or damage caused or alleged to be caused directly or indirectly by the information contained in it.

Cover image used with permission of Rare Historical Photos.

This book is dedicated to the memory of Betsy Balcombe, whose youthful, caring, and loving heart helped to ease the pain and sorrow of a great man who not only lost his Empire, but also his wife, son, mother, and family. May she always have known that he cherished her company, games, mischievous smile, and her innocent and non-judgmental heart. For it was Betsy who was mainly responsible for revealing the human side to Napoleon Bonaparte.

Table of Contents

List of Prominent Individuals — 7

Illustrations — 9

Introduction — 11

Preface — 17

Chapter 1 — Flight Or Fight — 25

Chapter 2 — "This Cursed Rock" — 47

Chapter 3 — Betsy And Boney — 71

Chapter 4 — "This Is My Sure Test" — 111

Chapter 5 — Torment By Vexation — 157

Chapter 6 — "The Soul Is Beyond Their Reach" — 185

Chapter 7 — Digging The Ground — 233

Chapter 8 — Purification Through Suffering — 265

Chapter 9 — A Temporary Resting Place — 291

Chapter 10 — Absolution And The Journey Home — 299

Author's Note — 305

Index — 309

Endnotes — 313

List of Prominent Individuals

1. Napoleon Bonaparte – Emperor of the French
2. Josephine Bonaparte – Napoleon's first wife and Empress
3. Marie-Louise Bonaparte – Napoleon's second wife and Empress
4. King of Rome / Napoleon II – Napoleon's son with Empress Marie-Louise
5. Madame Mere – Napoleon's mother
6. Queen Hortense – Josephine's daughter, Napoleon's stepdaughter
7. Grand Marshal Henri Bertrand – Napoleon's distinguished officer
8. Madame Bertrand – wife of Grand Marshal Bertrand
9. General Baron Gourgaud – Napoleon's general
10. General Charles-Tristan de Montholon – Napoleon's general
11. Madame Montholon – wife of general Montholon
12. Count Emmanuel de Las Cases – Secretary to Napoleon
13. Louis Marchand – most trusted valet to Napoleon
14. Cipriani Franceschi – longtime friend and servant of Napoleon
15. St. Denis (Ali) – valet to Napoleon
16. Francesco Antommarchi – Corsican doctor to Napoleon
17. Abbe Vignali – priest to Napoleon
18. Abbe Buonavita – priest to Napoleon
19. Barry O'Meara – Napoleon's English doctor
20. Admiral George Cockburn – British Admiral and first Governor of St. Helena
21. Admiral Sir Pulteney Malcolm – British Commander of Cape Station (St. Helena to Cape Town, South Africa)
22. Sir Hudson Lowe – British officer and second Governor of St. Helena
23. William Balcombe – purveyor on St. Helena, owner of The Briars and pavilion
24. Betsy Balcombe – daughter of William Balcombe, friend to Napoleon
25. Captain Poppleton – British orderly officer in charge of supervising Napoleon daily on St. Helena

26. Count Balmain – Russian Commissioner on St. Helena
27. Count de Montchenu – French Commissioner on St. Helena

Illustrations

Many of the illustrations used in *Napoleon's Purgatory* have long been in the public domain due to their age. Others come from the author's personal collection unless otherwise noted. The photographs in and around Longwood (10-14) are courtesy of Margaret Rodenberg, www.findingnapoleon.com.

1. Napoleon Bonaparte
2. Count Las Cases
3. Grand Marshal Bertrand
4. General Montholon
5. General Gourgaud
6. Dr. Barry O'Meara
7. Governor Lowe
8. Napoleon dictating to General Gourgaud
9. Betsy Balcombe Abell's dedication to Lady Malcolm's son
10. Longwood, featuring the windows of Napoleon's bedroom
11. Longwood, front view
12. Napoleon's bedroom
13. Napoleon's camp bed, featuring his death mask
14. Bust of the King of Rome
15. Napoleon on his deathbed

Introduction

'What a novel my life has been,' Napoleon famously said while in exile on St. Helena. Truer words were never spoken. When Napoleon stood astride Europe like a colossus, who could have guessed how it would all end. But like any novel, it is the end of the story that reveals much about major characters and, in some ways, comes to define the protagonist. Such is the case with Napoleon Bonaparte.

The story of the end of Napoleon's career, his exile to the remote island of St. Helena and his death there is one of his fascinating life's most interesting sagas. It is a story of pathos, politics, intrigue and, sometimes, fun.

It is also the story of three, perhaps four, islands.

The story really begins on the island of Elba, a few miles off the coast of Italy in the Mediterranean. There, in 1814, Napoleon was sent into exile as Emperor of that island. He ruled it peacefully, making substantial improvements, and living a comfortable life, often with family around him. But political intrigue in the capitals of the allied forces who defeated him led him to fear for his life. In a bold gamble, he returned to France and once again became Emperor of the French. But those same allies would have nothing of it, and they began to move their armies against the man they now declared an international outlaw. In yet another bold gamble, Napoleon moved north to face the British and Prussian forces, with Waterloo as the result.

Napoleon understood that his time was up, and was determined to either retire in style in England (as other deposed monarchs had done) or—and this was his decided preference—move to the United States, where much of his family could join him. But he delayed too long in Paris, delayed again on his trip south to Rochefort, and delayed there as well. He stayed on his second island of this story, the Ile d'Aix. A British blockade prevented his escape to the United States, so he surrendered to Captain Maitland of the Bellerophon, expecting to be allowed to retire comfortably in England. He was taken to Plymouth Sound (thus England being the possible fourth island, though he never set foot on it). After two weeks, Napoleon and his entourage were transferred to the Northumberland, which took him, over his furious objections, to his last island, St. Helena.

There are many first-hand sources of information on Napoleon's time on St. Helena, a time spent in large part trying to establish and shape his legacy. Some of them are quite reliable, others less so, but all contribute to a better understanding of Napoleon the man, the main purpose of this book.

Upon arrival to Jamestown, St. Helena, Napoleon quickly desired to live outside the city and its curious eyes. His future home, Longwood, was not yet ready. But he had a very pleasant visit to the home of William Balcombe, who offered Napoleon his pavilion known as The Briars. The setting of the Briars was, in the words of Balcombe's daughter Betsy, 'a perfect little paradise—an Eden blooming in the midst of desolation.' He moved in on 18 October, and would stay for about two months. William Balcombe was superintendent of public sales for the East India Company.

The entire family was nice, but the star, at least for Napoleon, was fourteen-year-old Betsy. The two of them hit if off extremely well. She was young enough not to cause a scandal (though some have tried), and her easy-going nature gave her excellent access to Napoleon, even over the objections of some of his staff. He became something of a kindly uncle, constantly teasing her. In his eyes, she could do no wrong and was a very welcome relief from the otherwise rather dreary existence facing him. The two would have long talks about Napoleon's life, and she got insight that few others could match.

A falling out with the island's governor, Sir Hudson Lowe, led to the Balcombe's departure from the island in 1818. Some years later, she published a memoir of her time with Napoleon on St. Helena. It is one of the most poignant—and important—of the St. Helena memoirs.

As important as Betsy's memoirs are, there are plenty of other people who wrote of their time on the island and their observations of Napoleon, as well as his dictation of his own memoirs. Here are some of the more important.

As Thomas Barden rightfully points out, probably the best of the rest is Napoleon's personal valet, Louis Marchand. He was with Napoleon during some of his most private moments, and was known for his absolute loyalty to his Emperor. His ties to the Emperor were substantial. His mother served as a nurse to Napoleon's son, generally known as the King of Rome. He was the executioner of Napoleon's will and was present at the exhumation of Napoleon's body in 1840. In 1869, Napoleon III made him a count.

Introduction

Napoleon had a number of doctors while on St. Helena. His last was Dr. Francesco Antommarchi. He was practicing in Corsica when word came that Sir Hudson Lowe was anxious for Napoleon to have a doctor of his choice. Napoleon's uncle, Cardinal Fesch, and his mother, Letezia, chose Antommarchi to be that doctor. He was there from September of 1819 until Napoleon's death in 1821. Napoleon had little use for him. He conducted the post-mortem exam, but refused to sign the official report that indicated stomach cancer as the cause of death. In 1825, he published his memoirs of his time on St. Helena, *Last Moments of Napoleon*.

Another doctor who saw Napoleon was Dr. Archibald Arnott, one of several British doctors. The two of them had a very good relationship. Indeed, Napoleon gave him an endowment and a gold snuffbox. He also participated in the post-mortem exam. In 1822 he wrote *An Account of the Last Illness of Napoleon*, whose conclusions upset Sir Hudson Lowe.

Marie Joseph Emmanuel Auguste Dieudonné, comte de Las Cases is one of the most known of those who wrote of their time on St. Helena. Las Cases served Napoleon in a variety of capacities. He accompanied Napoleon to St. Helena and spent much of his time taking dictation from Napoleon. He was not very popular with the others there and eventually seems to have arranged to be exiled from the island. He wrote several accounts of his time there, most notably *Memorial de Sainte Hélène*. His books were best sellers.

Charles Tristan, Comte de Montholon was a generally undistinguished general who had been an aide-de-camp to several superior generals and later as an Imperial Chamberlain. He was an aide to Napoleon at Waterloo, and he and his wife went with Napoleon to St. Helena. He also became quite close to Napoleon. Some say too close, as he is often a suspect of those who feel Napoleon may have been poisoned. After Napoleon's death, Montholon wrote his memoirs, *Memoirs of the History of France During the Reign of Napoleon, Dictated by the Emperor at Saint Helena to the Generals Who Shared His Captivity; and Published from the Original Manuscripts Corrected by Himself*. While useful, some historians downplay its accuracy.

Dr. Barry Edward O'Meara was a last minute selection to accompany Napoleon when his personal doctor declined to go into exile with him. He also became too close to Napoleon to suit Lowe and was replaced in July of 1818. He took countless notes on everything

Napoleon did. His book, *A Voice from St. Helena,* provides extensive and useful information on Napoleon's exile.

There are numerous other people who have written about their time on St. Helena, and Thomas Barden includes a nice selection of them in his telling of the tale.

Napoleon's time on St. Helena provides a fascinating look into the nature of Napoleon, and Barden gives us excellent insight into that nature. He completes Napoleon's 'novel' very nicely.

J. David Markham
President of the International
Napoleonic Society

"Now thanks to my misfortunes, one can see me naked as I am."

Napoleon

Preface

For more than two centuries, historians have devoted their entire careers to constructing a comprehensive history of the life and reign of Napoleon Bonaparte. Hundreds of works have been published focused on the same significant and well-documented periods of his life: his military conquests, coup d'etat, reign as Emperor, decline after the Russian debacle, and most of all, his climatic defeat and ruin on the battlefield of Waterloo. In each work, these historians labored with the utmost intensity to discover that one unique aspect of his character that might place their evaluations and analysis above the others.

Volumes have been published analyzing his military tactics and his diplomatic strategy against enemies, potential enemies, and even friends. Even more works have been published documenting his legislative agenda and governance. However, a considerable number of historians choose to end their historical assessments with his defeat at Waterloo. Once exhausting this topic, and observing that Napoleon's days were numbered in Europe, these writers bring closure to their works with a few brief pages pertaining to his final and permanent exile to the island of St. Helena. There are only a few prominent historians who have dedicated extensive examinations into Napoleon's time there.

But why is it that many Napoleonic historians view Waterloo as the last important phase of Napoleon's historical life? Is that where his history ends? Did Napoleon Bonaparte merely sail to St. Helena and drift off into the sunset or fall from the face of the earth? Is that recording true history? Does one's removal from the world's stage as a major player in world politics, governance, and war cause events, time, and history to cease? Certainly not. Napoleon was feared even in death. The casket and choice of his final resting place could have brought Europe to war again. His name, legend, and character were enough to bring even members of the Old Guard Of Napoleon's Army to their feet.[1] There was a lingering fear and prospect that Napoleon would rise like a phoenix from the ashes to once again ravage a now 'peaceful' Europe. The Emperor's successful flight and return to power from his first exile on the island of Elba in 1814 is a perfect example.[2]

But why should these six years of exile be included into his history in such an expanded detail? What do they contribute to the overall interpretation of the life and career of Napoleon Bonaparte? How does this exile to the island of St. Helena fit into the history of not only this influential figure but into European history as well?

First, and foremost, it completes the history of Napoleon Bonaparte. By including details of his years in exile into the works of Napoleonic studies, a historian puts forth a work that actually spans all the years of his life. Though it is correct to state that Napoleon's rise to power, his role as General and Emperor, and his fall at Waterloo seems to be more appealing to readers of history, military strategists, and enthusiasts than his final years and death, St. Helena represents the 'last hurrah' or closing chapter of his life. The memoirs and journals of those in the Emperor's entourage and others close to him on the island contain countless personal reflections about his past victories and defeats, his successes and failures, and opinions about the future history of France, Europe, and most importantly, his legacy. To leave out a section of an individual's life, particularly his own reflection on it, which is so important in history, is like leaving out the last piece of a puzzle or a final link in a chain; one does not see the complete picture. As in the case of Napoleon, by leaving out the history of his last exile readers and scholars do not see the complete person. They cannot fully grasp the magnitude and influence of Napoleon Bonaparte without examining his entire life.

Secondly, Napoleon had one luxury that most leaders in world history lacked: he survived the fall from power. Leaders of nations both before and after Napoleon often had their rule extinguished by the sharpness of a blade, the piercing of a bullet, the brutality of a revolution, or by their own hand on their own terms, Julius Caesar or Czar Nicholas being prime examples. These rulers' authority ended when their lives did. For those rulers who died of natural causes during their reign, it was virtually impossible to honestly reflect on past actions during their reign and admit failures, mistakes, and defeats, without leading their subjects to question the legitimacy, abilities, and power of their leader.

Honesty is born from the realization that one has nothing to lose. Consequences of a ruler's actions have already taken place through the act of falling from power. In all reality, at that point, there is nothing left to lose through reflection. What Napoleon realized in exile was that through his reflections, he had everything to gain. He was able to seize upon this fact. Napoleon was in his mid-forties upon arriving at St. Helena and could possibly have lived for another twenty years. European history may have been quite different if he had.

Through reflections recorded by those who shared his exile, there are descriptions of Napoleon giving numerous discourses regarding his career. He provides detailed and personal reflections upon past triumphs and defeats. The journal entries also record the Emperor assessing what he could have or should have done to win lost battles or continued his hold over the lands and leaders of the European continent. Though for the first few years of exile, Napoleon believed he would be invited back to Europe, he eventually realized that this goal was not realistic. Therefore, if Napoleon were to die on St. Helena, he had one last battle to win: lay the blame of his death on the English and ensure that his blood stained their coat.

Because Napoleon had reached this point in his life, and his future was uncertain, it was only natural for him to look to the past. It was a time for the Emperor to reexamine his past successes and defeats, to provide answers where there were questions, to answer criticisms with reasons, to dispel myths with facts, and to defend and mold a legacy shaped by the very hands of Napoleon himself.

Napoleon was quite aware that all who came close to him, whether French or English, would record everything they witnessed and heard for posterity. He capitalized on this human weakness and used them to his advantage to not only craft his legacy but to influence public opinion in Europe and the rest of the world.[3] He did not guard his speech. He did not keep himself or his words hidden from those around him. Though his temper would flare and his depression became obvious, his destiny would lay in the words of those around him, and his true judge would be history.

In all of the journals and memoirs that came from those six years of exile on St. Helena, Napoleon reflected upon numerous events and actions in his life that so many Napoleonic historians have examined, analyzed, and interpreted throughout their works. In these journals and memoirs, the Emperor dispelled the myth that he ordered the execution of his own soldiers who were stricken with the plague. He admitted his mistakes in the Russian Campaign. He explained his planning of the coup d'etat. He described his eternal love for his first wife, the Empress Josephine. He provided impressions of the leaders of Europe. Perhaps most importantly of all, he addressed his mistakes and reassessed the battle of Waterloo.

The selection of St. Helena as Napoleon's final place of exile itself provides another reason why his exile should be examined more closely and added to the analysis of his life. The choice of this island reveals a great deal about how he was viewed and feared in Europe and the lack of trust that the leaders of the continent had in believing the Emperor would remain in exile. His first exile on the island of Elba, just a few hundred miles from France, proved to be ineffective considering he escaped after being there barely one year. The effects of his return were catastrophic in these leaders' minds. Napoleon could not be trusted to remain in exile. His supporters must not be able to rescue or aid him in another escape.

The European powers also had to be quite careful in the handling and treatment of their new prisoner. Napoleon's charismatic character gave him the power to win over people in just one conversation, so it was important to keep him isolated from all but a few of his French companions. Winning the minds of some British citizens could place them in a situation where he could convince them to help him in an attempted escape.

Executing Napoleon would have been dangerous and quite possibly have sparked another bloody revolution with the possibility of spilling into neighboring countries. Keeping him alive would at least prevent a French revolt against the Allies who occupied the fallen nation. To mistreat him in exile would have been to risk the loss in the battle for public opinion and create a martyr. The worshipping of a 'tortured' or 'sacrificed' martyr could be almost as dangerous to England and the rest of Europe, if not more, than a swift execution of the prisoner. Exile would have to be the solution to put a permanent end to the ambitions of Napoleon Bonaparte: an exile that was far enough away to ensure that Europe would never have to worry about him again.

The island of St. Helena was remote, over one thousand miles away from the nearest continent, surrounded by ravaging ocean water, and easily guarded by naval ships due to its mountainous structure. A rescue was virtually impossible for there was only one port on St. Helena where a ship could anchor. An escape would also be impossible for the same reasons. News of anything in Europe would reach the island at least two months after the event had happened. To an Emperor accustomed to the rigors of battle and with a mind that constantly turned and processed information, St. Helena was a humdrum; a virtual Hell on Earth for him. This is precisely what the European powers wanted: punishment without the obviousness of brutality.

There is no doubt of the historical importance of Napoleon's exile to St. Helena. Besides the invaluable personal reflections and dialogue, and with the Imperial and militaristic aspects aside, who was the Napoleon that was now faced with the end of his career and very possibly his life? A man who ruled over much of Europe was being sent to a tiny island off the western coast of Africa. With nothing left to conquer and nothing left to rule, what did Napoleon do on St. Helena for almost six years?

When one examines the journals and memoirs of those who shared the exile with Napoleon, they find that each opens a different portal into the complex and sophisticated mind of the fallen Emperor. However, a deeper look into the words in these memoirs reveals a completely different side of the Emperor that was overshadowed by his military genius, his Imperial presence and had remained hidden.

When the conquest has been taken away from the conqueror, what is a general to do? When might and power are no longer within his grasp, what is a man of prominence to do to bide his time? When the empire is removed from the Emperor, who does he become? Napoleon Bonaparte had everything taken away from him upon his exile to St. Helena, including his wife and son. When everything that constitutes such an Imperial and militaristic individual is lost, there is only one thing left for him to become: human.

During the six-year exile that Napoleon spent on the island of St. Helena, his character and presence as an Emperor and master of the art of war remained with him until the day life left his body. But at the same time, his 'human' side began to show itself more and more. What began to emerge out of the rubble of defeat were the emotions of a father, a husband, a grandfather, a friend, a 'playmate,' and sadly enough, a prisoner.

Through the detailed memoirs of the members of the Emperor's suite who shared his exile and other English individuals on the island, this human side to Napoleon was revealed for the reader to observe. From his shaving and eating habits to his laughter and love of children, practically everything the man did and said on the island was recorded in their journals. Besides reliving the past, these works put forth descriptions concerning Napoleon as a human being.

In describing the 'human side' to Napoleon Bonaparte, their observations record not only the warm, caring, loving, and gentle aspects of his personality, but also his temperament, frustrations, anger, and most of all, his agonizing struggle to cling to life as it slipped through his fingertips. This formidable man long sustained through control and command was now faced with two forces he could not govern; time and death.

Numerous journal entries by Napoleon's generals, valets, secretaries, and others around him during his exile reveal his sense of humor, his love for children, his grief and depression over being separated from his wife and son, and even his revelations concerning his deep and eternal love for Josephine. Other entries paint in exquisite detail his anger and frustration at being considered a prisoner by England and, most of all, his hatred for the English Governor of St. Helena, Sir Hudson Lowe.

Why examine this side of Napoleon Bonaparte, especially at the end of his life? What benefit does it have to the study of his career to learn about his characteristics as a mere person? Napoleon was a man who battled to present and maintain an appearance of unwavering determination, confidence, and success. This human side was never a focal point of the written history of any of his followers, soldiers, generals, or government officials. His reign, battles, victories, and legislation were the pinnacle of his existence. Many historians gravitate to these characteristics of Napoleon's history out of interest. The human side to Napoleon as explained by his followers on St. Helena is just as interesting if not more so.

Pulling back the curtain of power allows the true persona of Napoleon to be seen in the light of day. Among his entourage in exile, the Emperor was no longer as self-guarded about himself out of concern that a weakness might be revealed publically. On the contrary, he was quite open with them. Emotion and caring are two of the greatest qualities of a person. In exile, Napoleon truly revealed both as part of his genuine character.

There are two memoirs that truly capture the human side of Napoleon Bonaparte while in exile. The first is a memoir by Betsy Balcombe, written during her later years as Mrs. Abell, which provides numerous accounts, stories, and tales of her humorous escapades with the Emperor when she was fourteen years old during his stay at their home on St. Helena and later at his permanent residence, Longwood. A sincere friendship emerged between the two. The playful, caring, and mischievous side of Napoleon was given full reign in his interactions with the innocent, carefree, and non-judgmental young girl who was not bound by imperial etiquette and military protocol. Betsy witnessed Napoleon in a state in which he threw aside all inhibitions and shared in the joys and laughter of a child.

The memoirs of Louis Marchand are invaluable in that he served as the personal valet to the Emperor. He was with Napoleon during Napoleon's least guarded moments, sometimes dressing and shaving him or even when cleaning the vomit from his face or changing his soiled bed sheets during the final days before his death. Marchand witnessed Napoleon in moments of loneliness and depression as well as during his bursts of laughter and humor. He listened as the Emperor longed for news of his wife and son, and shared in the despair when he was denied it. The young valet saw Napoleon explode in anger at being treated like a common prisoner and later held the hand of the mere man who was both an Emperor and a father figure as he struggled for each strenuous breath during his last days.

The purpose of this work is to reveal this human side of Napoleon through the words of those who were with him on St. Helena. The goal in much of the following pages is to allow their words to speak to the reader and to permit them to breathe life again into a man who has been dead for more than one hundred and ninety years. Their words let the true person who was Napoleon reveal himself through their memories of him. For one must realize, if Napoleon never wanted this human side to him to be exposed, he would have kept it permanently hidden. He would have ordered the valet or secretary to remove those entries from their diaries. He did not. Therefore, through their words, the true Napoleon emerged.

The following pages are Napoleon Bonaparte; the human being.

Chapter 1

Flight Or Fight

There he sat, exhausted, confused, and mentally alone. The face flushed and dry, his hair thinning with age. The lingering expression told of nothing but absolute defeat. The sounds of warfare echoed in his ears. The glory and reign of the 100 days was now over for the great Emperor of the French. The future of this newly fallen leader would depend upon his next decision. Any hope of regaining the throne of France for the third time was beyond impossible.

He was now running out of time.

Napoleone Buonaparte, better known as Napoleon Bonaparte, had been forced to abdicate the throne of the French Empire for the second time. Just days before, Napoleon had ruled the Empire as the crowned Emperor and commanded every inch of its territory with the vast and dedicated army of his creation. But that was before, and history can deal many prominent figures a difficult hand to play. The hand that Napoleon was now dealt proved to be unplayable and worthy of being folded. Unfortunately, when at the helm of an Empire such as France, it was just not that simple.

It is now June 1815, and as the sounds of Waterloo still echoed in the ears of Europe, the Allies Powers began converging on Paris. The vast armies that had defeated Napoleon and his troops at Waterloo were laboring to quickly tighten the noose around the French capital in the hopes of eventually strangling its Emperor. To make matters even worse, the Bourbon King Louis XVIII and his English escort were just hours away from arriving in Paris themselves.

Realizing that his choices were quickly vanishing, the Emperor abdicated his throne to his infant son, Napoleon II, referred to by his father as the King of Rome. The Allies gladly accepted the abdication, but the passing of the crown, they did not accept. Napoleon sent word to the Council of Five Hundred that he would lead the Paris garrison against the approaching Allies as 'General' and not 'Emperor.' But Napoleon's own Minister of Police Joseph Fouche refused and 'suggested' he leave the capital for the benefit of France. The Emperor's time and options for 'survival' were quickly running out.[4]

Taking rest at the Elysee Palace in Paris, Napoleon still sought options for remaining in the capital city for her defense. Though many soldiers vowed loyalty to the death, it was not enough to protect the Emperor from the wrath of the Allies who were fast approaching. It was time to go. But where to seek refuge? Napoleon knew exactly where he wanted to go. The Emperor was now leaving his beloved capital for the last time. The next time Napoleon would be in Paris, it would be while inside a coffin.

To help disguise himself for the carriage ride from the Elysee Palace, the Emperor wore a long brown coat and a round hat.[5] The man who had commanded armies and put fear into millions of enemy troops was now hiding in the clothes of a commoner. Rumors of oncoming Allied troops, assassination attempts, and potential kidnapping were running rampant throughout the streets of Paris. The Emperor's entourage could not take any chances. Surrounded by a number of his devoted Marshals, other officers, hundreds of troops, and his most trusted servants, Napoleon sought temporary sanctuary at the Chateau de Malmaison; the final home of the deceased ex-Empress, Josephine.

For a number of years, this had been the home of Emperor Napoleon and his beloved Empress Josephine.[6] It was in her bedroom at the mansion where Josephine had died almost a year earlier. Napoleon could not be with her during her last moments. He had been on the island of Elba, in exile for the first time. When news reached the island of her death, Napoleon was completely devastated and grief-stricken.

Though divorce in 1810 had stripped her of the title of Empress of the French, Josephine was supported financially until her death by Napoleon. Napoleon loved her with every ounce of his being. It was an eternal love that stayed with him until his death. But due to her inability to produce an heir to the throne because of her age, Napoleon was forced to divorce his beloved Josephine and marry a much younger woman. His family absolutely despised Josephine and saw her as nothing but a whore. When Napoleon fell in love with Josephine, she was the mistress of a member of the French Directory named Paul Barras. Napoleon's family believed Josephine had attached herself to the young, successful Napoleon as a way to advance herself and provide for her children. Napoleon had fallen in love with her the moment he saw 'Rose' those many years before. But Napoleon felt that the name 'Josephine' was a more beautiful name, which perfectly fit her attractiveness. From that day, Napoleon had his Josephine.

He now found himself in her bedroom, the very place where her soul had left the world. And there he sat.

Josephine's daughter Hortense followed the Emperor to Malmaison to be with him in those desperate hours. She knew that he would want to be in the place where Josephine had been. Hortense was immensely loyal to Napoleon. French General Montholon wrote of her devotion when he recorded in his memoirs that her "*devotedness to the Emperor was unbounded...There never was seen so complete a disregard of personal interest. Her affectionate soul could not comprehend that she could have any other wish than to give her father, when in misfortune, proofs of her filial love and duty.*"[7] Napoleon sent for Hortense and asked her to walk with him in the gardens. Though facing the most difficult moment of his life, his mind still turned to Josephine. Hortense wrote of his expression of sadness:

> *Poor Josephine! I cannot become accustomed to this place without her. It always seems as though I were going to catch sight of her behind the next hedge, picking the flowers she loved so dearly. Poor Josephine!...It is true she would be very sad if she could see the way things are going at present. There was only one subject we ever disagreed about, her debts. How I used to scold her about them! She was certainly the most charming person I have ever known. She was a true woman with all the qualities that word conveys, quick, lively and so good-hearted. Have another portrait made of her for me. I want it as a medallion.*[8]

But the real world around the Emperor could not wait while his heart raced back through time. Word had come to Malmaison that a Provisional Government had formed and that the Emperor had been ordered to stay at the Chateau. The following day, General Becker arrived with orders from the Provisional Government to stay and protect Napoleon.[9] No one actually believed he was there to 'protect' the Emperor. Napoleon's servant, St. Denis - who he often referred to as 'Ali,' - was certain that General Becker was there "*to keep watch on his* [Napoleon's] *actions if there should be need.*"[10] St. Denis was quick to observe that Becker "*had ears to hear and a tongue to speak. He was an agent of the provisional government, and particularly of Fouche.*"[11]

The Emperor sent word to the Provisional Government that if he could not stay in Paris to protect the people of France, then his wish was to go to the United States to live out the rest of his days.[12] The Provisional Government granted his request and gave orders in writing "*for two frigates to be prepared at Rochefort, to convey Napoleon Bonaparte to the United States.*"[13] Napoleon was concerned about his safety while traveling to the coast. He again sent word to Fouche that he would be willing to command the troops to protect the capital. Fouche declined and stated that Napoleon's offer "*could not be accepted and that it is most necessary that he should immediately set off for Rochefort, where he will be safer than in the neighborhood of Paris.*"[14] The Provisional Government was giving the Emperor a head start.

Still, Napoleon hesitated, almost acting as if this was all a dream and that the Provisional Government and the people of his beloved France would come to him one more time seeking rescue from their enemies. He was still searching for the right option.

The Emperor sought the counsel of his family at Malmaison, including his mother, Madame Mere, and his brothers Joseph, Lucien, and Jerome.[15] Still, he hesitated. Napoleon spent those days at Malmaison rehashing the past, contemplating the present, and preparing for the future, the latter being the most uncertain and frightful. Hortense was struck by Napoleon's predicament; "*I felt we were really prisoners, and exclaimed sadly: "Whoever could have imagined that some day the Emperor would be the prisoner of Frenchmen at Malmaison!*"[16] Unfortunately, that is exactly what had happened. Time was running out and a certain horrific fate was coming closer in sight. "*At Malmaison, Napoleon lived the hours of his Gethsemane.*"[17]

Knowing that his window of opportunity to escape France was getting smaller by the moment, Napoleon made the decision to quit France and make for the coast where the two frigates awaited his arrival to transport him to America. But he hesitated once again. The Emperor had two adolescent visitors, both of whom held striking resemblances to himself.

*   *   *

The question of the Emperor's second wife, the Empress Marie-Louise, joining him on his trek to the coast was out of the question. His father-in-law, Austrian Emperor Francis, had made sure that not only would his daughter not go into exile with Napoleon the first time to the island of Elba, he made sure that she would not be following him anywhere ever again. When Napoleon was sent to Elba, the Empress was taken under her father's care. Even more difficult for Napoleon, was the fate of his son, the King of Rome. Against Napoleon's wishes, the young boy had gone with his mother and was under his grandfather's care. If Emperor Francis had his way, his grandson would never see his father, Napoleon, again.

The absence of his son, the King of Rome, was another cross that was extremely difficult for Napoleon to bear. Difficult not because of the King of Rome being the heir to the throne or the continuation of Napoleon's legacy, but because this was his flesh and blood; his son.

These two young boys who now stood in waiting at Malmaison were there to say their 'hellos' as well as their goodbyes; goodbyes, that is, to their father.

Like many other Emperors and monarchs of the day, Napoleon had mistresses outside his marriage. Some of these liaisons produced illegitimate sons. Hortense was taken by how the Emperor reacted to first meeting one of the boys during those chaotic moments at Malmaison on June 28th.

> *At noon one day the Emperor sent for me. He was in his private garden with a man I did not know and a young boy who seemed to be about nine or ten years old. Taking me aside the Emperor said, "Hortense, look at that child. Whom does he resemble?"*
>
> *"Your son, Sire. He is the very image of the King of Rome."*
>
> *"You think so, do you? Then it must be true. I did not believe that I had a sensitive nature, but the sight of him made a deep impression on me. You seem to know who he is. How did you find out about it?"*

"Sire, the public has spoken a good deal about the matter, and this close resemblance proves that people were not mistaken."

"I admit that for a long time I doubted he was really my son. Nevertheless,

I had him educated in a boarding-school in Paris. The man in whose charge

I had placed him wrote me asking what my intentions were in regard to his future. I wished to see him, and like you I was struck by his resemblance to my son."[18]

Though a military General and an Emperor in the strongest sense, Napoleon was always taken with children. He found amusement in their playfulness, their laughter, and their innocence. Seeing the spitting image of his son, in the face of another son, went right to his heart. But another boy was still waiting to see his imperial father.

Countess Walewska, Napoleon's Polish mistress, had also come to Malmaison to present her son to the Emperor. Hortense wrote that the Countess "*had made her farewells to the Emperor...She was all in tears. I shared her grief and invited her to stay and lunch alone with me so that people might not see her in such a state.*"[19] Though touched by the sight of his two sons, Napoleon still longed to see his royal heir, the King of Rome, one more time. That was not going to happen.

*   *   *

It was time. The Emperor had made his decision. He would make his way to the coast with his entourage and board the two frigates to live out the remainder of his life in America. As Napoleon was preparing for his departure, the silence was disrupted by the cheering of a crowd. Making his way to a window of the Chateau, the Emperor witnessed several hundred soldiers who had made their way to their leader cheering. Hortense recorded that the "*enthusiasm they displayed for the man who was obliged to leave them made a deep impression on all those present. The Emperor seemed touched by it. "It is not cheers but acts which I need," he said, and at once withdrew to his study."*[20] Even at that late moment, it is almost as if Napoleon was still holding out for an opening that would leave him with an opportunity to defend the nation, that the call would be put out for his return to the capital to lead his men one more time. That call never came.

Napoleon's mother and the rest of his family had come to bid their farewells to their Emperor, brother, and son. Madame Mere promised that she would join her son in America when he would permit it.[21] Napoleon was very attached to his family, even trusting them more than they returned in loyalty to him. He sought the counsel of his brothers, he doted on his sisters, he provided for the comfortable living of his mother, but there were countless times they had let him down, disobeyed his wishes, and in some cases challenged him on his decisions. No one did that to the Emperor, except for his family. If there was one fault that Napoleon Bonaparte had, it was that his love of family often clouded his judgment.

The Emperor went to bid Adieu to his adopted daughter and the flesh and blood of his beloved Josephine. Hortense was in tears. She gave him a string of diamonds that he had given to her years before. "*He consented to take one string worth about two hundred thousand francs. He insisted on giving me a note for this amount although I obstinately resisted his doing so, regretting bitterly to be able to do so little for the man to whom I owed everything.*"[22]

Napoleon sat with Hortense on a bench in the garden and quietly looked around the grounds of Malmaison in deep reflection. "*Ah, how beautiful Malmaison is! Surely, Hortense, we should be happy if we might only remain here.*"[23] She was overcome with emotion, but captured the moment and what the Emperor faced when she wrote:

> *I could not reply. My voice would have betrayed my emotion. It was the first time I had ever known him to care for any particular place. I was the more surprised because I had never imagined such things would affect him. When men start to desert us we turn instinctively to Nature, who does not deceive. For who is there who can without emotion leave a spot where he has been happy and which he will never see again, a spot*

associated in his mind with so many visions of success, fame, fortune and happiness, a spot where so many hearts have submitted to his spell, whence he has set forth to conquer the world, and where now he is spending the last few days that he is allowed to live in his own country, before setting out alone, banished from his native soil, to face whatever uncertain fate awaits him overseas?[24]

The Emperor changed from his military uniform and put on a gray dress-coat.[25] With threats still being made against his person and with Minister Fouche possibly setting a trap, Napoleon could not be too careful. The Emperor left with a portion of his entourage of Generals and Secretaries and headed down one road en route to the coast to board the frigates for America. The rest of his group followed another road with plans to meet Napoleon at the shore. He was leaving Malmaison forever and was now on the run.

Napoleon Bonaparte was forty-five years old.

*   *   *

Leaving the Chateau of Malmaison on June 29, 1815, the Emperor and his entourage reached the coast on July 3 and stayed in Rochefort. Count Las Cases, one of Napoleon's trusted secretaries, was with the Emperor and recorded much of what transpired while on the journey to Rochefort.

During the whole of the journey – not a word either of his wife or son. From time to time he took a pinch of snuff from General Becker's box, and as the box happened to be adorned with a portrait of Marie Louise, the Emperor once took it into his hands, looked at it for a moment, and returned it without uttering a syllable.[26]

It must have been agonizing for the Emperor to not have his wife and son with him during these trying days. The thoughts that must have been going through his mind are almost unimaginable. Worse yet was the realization that his wife, the Empress, the mother of his son, was not doing everything in her power to be with him. The truth was Empress Marie Louise did not want to go with Napoleon. Her father, the Emperor Francis, had helped see to that. Francis would also ensure that Napoleon's son would be brought to his palace in Austria. And in Austria is where the King of Rome would remain.

Once the Emperor and his entourage reached Rochefort, they took another small vessel to the Isle of Aix near the mouth of the Gironde River. There awaiting the Frenchmen were the two French vessels; the *Saale* and the *Medusa* as promised by the Provisional Government.[27] But that was not all. Surrounding the two French vessels were countless British warships. England had doubled the number of ships on the coast since Napoleon's failure at Waterloo. There was no way out. The Emperor was trapped.[28]

The legendary mind of Napoleon was again put to the test. He had to quickly decide his next move, for there is no doubt that from that moment on, any action taken by the Emperor could very well be his last. He had to consider his options.

Various scenarios were suggested to Napoleon as to how he could escape the British blockade and reach the United States. His older brother, Joseph, offered to disguise himself as the Emperor and hand himself over to the British thus allowing Napoleon to escape to America. *"The Emperor embraced him and rejected this proposal while saying goodbye and urging him to look after his own safety."*[29] He certainly did not want his history to end with him captured in a manner that made him appear desperate.[30]

Generals Montholon and Gourgaud favored Napoleon attempting to escape the British ships by boarding the frigates offshore and making a break for America.[31] The Captains of the two frigates reassured the Emperor that they could outrun the British warships, but Napoleon refused that offer as well for fear of the safety of the women and children that comprised part of his entourage.[32] Plus, penetrating the British blockade en route to America would practically be suicide. Even if the frigates were successful in getting through, his ship would be no match against the firepower of the British naval vessels. Being captured while attempting to 'run away' was not something the Emperor would entertain as an option. Though he preferred to spend the rest of his life, if need be, in the United States, his quickly realized that this would not be possible.

Grand Marshal Bertrand and Las Cases believed it would be best for the Emperor to board the British ship, *HMS Bellerophon*, "*having first sent an aide-de-camp, who should be dispatched to England with an autographed letter from the Emperor to the Prince Regent.*"[33] This seemed like a good possibility, for it would provide Napoleon an opportunity to negotiate with England's Prince Regent to allow his passage to the United States.

It is interesting to see into the counsel that the Emperor received from his advisors when faced with a decision that could decide his fate. Though providing Napoleon with a wide array of choices, some members of the entourage knew that the Emperor might listen to some more than others.

> *Unhappily, Gourgaud and myself [Montholon] were very young and we had to contend against influences of long standing, well deserved, and justified, it must be acknowledged, by years of noble devotedness and the exercise of the highest functions of the state. The attempt to make our opinion prevail over that of the Duke of Rovigo and the grand marshal, was a different thing; we were beaten, and ought to have been so.*[34]

Napoleon knew that his only choice was either to turn back and return to Paris to accept defeat and defend the nation, or to surrender himself to one of the Allied nations that had just extinguished his Imperial reign on the fields of Waterloo. However, he believed that returning to the capital and placing himself at the mercy of the Bourbon King Louis XVIII would be nothing but foolish. The newly restored King was not likely to waste any time on ridding himself of this troublesome Corsican. Twice before, Napoleon seized the throne from the Bourbons. They would no doubt not permit it to happen a third time.

But Louis XVIII was not an ignorant man. He certainly could not condemn Napoleon to death in Paris because Louis XVIII was now on the path of ruling a country that was still somewhat loyal to their former Emperor. Executing him would only divide the people and create a potential violent uprising. Louis XVIII knew how this scenario could play out all too well having witnessed the nightmare of the French Revolution and the execution of his brother Louis XVI. Jailing Napoleon in Paris would make him an even larger icon and could foster countless attempts at rescue. The King's already low popularity could not withstand either choice. If the Bourbon monarch followed one of these paths, he too could find himself running for his life, again.

Napoleon's other option of surrendering himself to one of the Allied nations seemed almost as dreadful. To whom should he surrender? Given the number of times Napoleon had ravaged the Austrian countryside with his Grand Army, Napoleon was not entirely confident that his father-in-law, and the grandfather of his son, would welcome him with open arms.

Russia was a possibility, but the Emperor's relationship with Czar Alexander had been strained considerably. The French Invasion of Russia a few years earlier had practically severed the diplomatic ties that the two Emperors once shared between their Empires. If he surrendered to Czar Alexander, Napoleon was not confident in what fate might await him. That left only one country: England.

Napoleon expressed his viewpoints on the subject to Hortense back at Malmaison when he stated "*Give myself up to Austria, never! – she has seized upon my wife and son! Give myself to Russia, that would be to a single man; but to give myself up to England, that would be to throw myself upon a people.*"[35] The Emperor believed that England would be the most merciful, honorable, and humane of all his enemies. He felt confident that he would be safe and treated well in their hands. After all, he never directly invaded their homeland, unlike the other Allies. Perhaps they would respect his choice in surrendering to their care and allow him to proceed to the United States. England could even allow the fallen Emperor to come to London. Napoleon believed if he had to lay his life before another country, England would treat him with the most respect. He could not have been more mistaken.

*   *   *

Anchored off the coast was the *HMS Bellerophon*, which was under the command of Captain Maitland. Napoleon sent the Duke of Rovigo and his English-speaking Secretary, Count Las Cases, on board the vessel to discuss terms with the Captain. They asked if the Captain would take Napoleon to England and eventually to America if the Emperor agreed to place himself aboard the *Bellerophon*.

As discussions commenced, Las Cases allowed the Duke of Rovigo to state in French that the pair did not understand English, though Las Cases was quite fluent in the language. This way Napoleon's secretary could understand the whispering and casual talk among the English officers without their knowledge that he could understand all that they discussed.[36]

The French representatives of the Emperor also expressed to Captain Maitland their concerns over the safety of Napoleon if he were to board the British vessel.

> *The Captain told us...that if the Emperor would embark immediately for England, he had instructions to convey him thither. He farther declared it as his private opinion, and several captains who were present expressed themselves to the same effect, that there was not the least doubt of Napoleon's meeting with all possible respect and good treatment: that there neither the king nor his ministers exercised the same arbitrary authority as those of the Continent: that the English people possessed a generosity of sentiment, and liberality of opinion, superior to sovereignty itself.*[37]

Napoleon would discover quite abruptly that this was not the case. In reality, the English government held no sympathy towards the 'fallen' Emperor.

Las Cases and the Duke of Rovigo took this information back to the Isle of Aix to inform the Emperor. Napoleon realized that his safest choice was to board the *Bellerophon* and send a representative to the Prince Regent to express his wishes. He ordered Las Cases and General Gourgaud to return to the British ship and inform Captain Maitland that the Emperor would be surrendering himself the following day with the understanding that he could seek refuge in England while waiting for passage to the United States. Las Cases was to meet with Maitland to arrange the surrender, while Gourgaud boarded the *Slaney* to continue on to London to meet with the Prince Regent.[38] In his hand, General Gourgaud carried a written declaration from the Emperor himself that was to be personally delivered to the Prince Regent in London:

> *Your Royal Highness, faced with the factions that divide my country and the enmity of the greatest powers in Europe, I have ended my political career, and I come like Themistocles to sit by the hearth of the British people. I place myself under the protection of their laws, which I request from Your Royal Highness, as the most powerful, the steadiest, and the most generous of my enemies.*[39]

The allusion to the Greek General Themistocles by the Emperor was by no means a mere incidental reference. Even in surrendering, Napoleon knew how to tap into the soul of even his enemies. "*The Greek general forced into political exile after he had defeated the Persians was granted asylum by his enemies.*"[40] This French 'General' was hoping for the same treatment.

For the members of the Emperor's entourage who stood in that room, they thought such a day would never come. To see the Great Napoleon surrender to the English would never happen. In their minds and in their dreams, they wanted to see their Emperor call up the army, march back into Paris, defend the Empire, and sit upon the throne of France again. If not, they wanted Napoleon to give a valiant effort and crack through the British blockade. This was Napoleon Bonaparte. This is what he had always done. It was his destiny to win. He must battle to the finish...wouldn't he do that now?

The Emperor explained to Grand Marshal Bertrand that "*it is not without risk to put yourself in the hands of your enemies, but it is better to trust their honor than to fall into their hands as a rightful prisoner.*"[41] Part of Napoleon's decision to surrender to the English was due to the fact that he was convinced they would allow him safe passage to the United States. There, he could do no harm to the European continent. He would be far away from the theater of war and politics and there were no loyal soldiers in America for him to call upon to whisk him back to Europe even if he wanted to return. If the Emperor was not allowed to seek self-imposed exile in America, what was he to do? Would Napoleon settle for life in England?

*   *   *

July 15, 1815, Napoleon Bonaparte kept his promise. At six in the morning, the Emperor boarded the brig *L'Epervier* under the flag of truce to be presented to the English on board the *Bellerophon*.[42] Napoleon's most trusted valet, Louis Marchand, described the agonizing sadness that was felt by those who had followed their Emperor all those years:

> *The deepest sadness showed on every face, and when the British gig approached to take the Emperor on board, the most heartrending cries were heard: officers and sailors saw with despair His Majesty trust his fate to the generosity of a nation whose perfidy they well knew. Having said goodbye to the crew and cast a final look on this beautiful France whose destiny he was abdicating, the Emperor climbed into the gig. Cries of Vive l'Empereur! mixed with sobs accompanied him until he arrived on board the Bellerophon. Despair was so great among some that they pulled their hair out, while others trampled their hats with their feet, out of rage.*[43]

Formerly the most powerful man in Europe, Napoleon now stood on board this small vessel as it gracefully cut through the waves, making its way towards the *Bellerophon*. In just a few minutes, the moment that these English soldiers were breathlessly awaiting would finally come. The Corsican upstart who was viewed by the English as "*the ogre of our popular fables, living upon human flesh*" was now about to appear right before their eyes.[44] No paintings, no political cartoons, no written descriptions in newspapers: it was Napoleon Bonaparte alive and in person. Their hearts raced in suspense as anticipation filled their veins.

Suddenly, the loud command of the British officer put the soldiers at attention. The only sounds heard on the ship at that very moment were waves crashing against the sides of the vessel, the heavy breathing of the nervous soldiers, and the footsteps of the new prisoner of the British Empire.

And there he stood.

The man who had brought the continent of Europe to her knees now stood before them. Napoleon was in full military uniform and bearing the medal of the Legion of Honor, an honor created by the Emperor based on merit, not aristocratic birth, a fulfillment of the French Revolution. Upon his head, lay the famous hat. Draped over his uniform was a long, heavy, gray coat opened at the front as to not hide his prestigious medal.

Surrounded by some of the most important members of his entourage as well as their families, Napoleon walked over to Captain Maitland and stated in French and thus translated, "*I come on board your ship, to place myself under the protection of the laws of England.*"[45] The Captain graciously answered Napoleon with a bow of respect and "*took him down to the main stateroom, where a few moments later the ship's officers were introduced to him.*"[46] Throughout the journey to Plymouth and while on board the *Bellerophon*, Captain Maitland remained quite respectful to Napoleon, even referring to him as 'Sire' or 'Your Majesty.'[47]

As the pleasantries were being made, the British vessel began its voyage to the English port of Plymouth. When the introductions were complete, Napoleon went up on deck and stood quietly as the shores of France slowly faded away. He gazed across the water, hands clasped behind his back and said nothing. His French officers were just behind to give their Emperor his moment and his time alone. The British soldiers and sailors watched in sheer fascination as if this was not real. Without moving or muttering a word, the Emperor gazed towards the horizon laying his eyes upon the land of France. Napoleon Bonaparte would never return to France again while there was still breath in his body.

Though the British façade of hospitality was still waiting to subside, the people of England and their viewpoint upon the 'Corsican Ogre;' that was a completely different story. As the *Bellerophon* was making her way towards Plymouth, the vessel made short stops at a few ports along the English coast. It became quite evident that news had traveled fast and that the English had already learned of

Napoleon's presence aboard the *Bellerophon*, for as they arrived at each port, hundreds of small boats, loaded to the brim with people, filled the waters. For his own 'protection,' the English had arranged for the ship to remain anchored out in the bay upon reaching Plymouth. The French aboard the ship were amazed at the crowds of English. All wanted a glimpse of this man who had terrorized Europe for almost two decades. But therein lay a crucial point; how would the people of England receive him? Were these welcoming crowds or were these angry mobs of the masses seeking revenge for the wars against their people?

While anchored at the port of Torbay, General Gourgaud came on board the *Bellerophon* to inform the Emperor that he was denied permission to set foot on English soil to deliver Napoleon's note to the Prince Regent.[48] "*The captain of the Slaney, upon which he [Gourgaud] was embarked...informed General Gourgaud that his orders were not to allow him to communicate with shore, and that he himself would deliver the letter Gourgaud was carrying to London.*"[49] This was not welcomed news to the Emperor.

On July 26, the Emperor reached Plymouth and the *Bellerophon* anchored in the bay. The crowds of English onlookers who had rowed boats out to the ship astonished Napoleon and his entourage. The crowds were not just there to view the Emperor with their own eyes; they were there to cheer for him. And the cheers were overwhelming. Marchand recorded the scene:

> *A large number of boats carrying a population anxious to see him were gathered around the ship. The Emperor, approaching the side, saluted them, and was answered with cheers...The sea was obstructed by them out to a great distance; it was easy to see, through the welcome the Emperor received when he showed himself, that interest was mixed with curiosity on the part of the multitude. No doubt it was feared that it might become greater, for orders were given to push these boats some distance away from the vessel. The people in charge of the task did so with revolting brutality, showing no concern whatever for the accidents that might result from the impact of*

> their own boats against those they were ordered
> to push back, full of men, and children all crying
> out in terror.[50]

In a horrific scene, Marchand's fears became a reality for a cutter that had been circling the *Bellerophon* had sunk a boat filled with spectators, and a number of them drowned.[51]

Napoleon's valet, St. Denis, recorded similar scenes of crowds cheering Napoleon as he took his daily walks on deck. On one occasion, he was stunned to observe a boat filled with English officers that drew close to the ship. St. Denis recorded that he "*saw a boat containing several officers come pretty near, and these officers took off their hats and made profound bows. At that moment if all those people had been masters of the Emperor's person they would have taken him to London, drawing his car like that of a conqueror. One might say that by his presence alone the Emperor had won the sympathy of the English people.*"[52]

Napoleon took quite a liking to the women who were scattered amongst the boats. Montholon remembered the "*endless spectacle of beautiful and elegant women, who saluted us with their pocket-handkerchiefs and shawls, which they transformed into flags as evidences of their sympathy. This revived our hopes that the national feeling would open the gates of England for our reception, or at least force the ministers to allow us to proceed to America.*"[53] Napoleon made sure to take off his hat at recognition of their kindness.

On another occasion, a woman in one of the crowded boats lifted her child up high for Napoleon to see. Due to the movement of the boat, the child fell into the water and was rescued by sailors who had jumped in to save the youth. The toddler was brought upon the *Bellerophon* and was safe. Napoleon was dramatically affected by the suffering and possible drowning of this child.[54]

But neither the Emperor nor any member of his entourage was allowed to set foot on shore. Gourgaud was denied permission and sent back to the *Bellerophon* and the entire French suite sat on the ship anchored in the bay waiting. What were the English doing? Why was Napoleon not allowed to continue onto America if he was not allowed to set foot on English soil? The Emperor knew exactly why.

Throughout Napoleon's life, he had always remained one step ahead of his enemy. Though in the hands of the English, this would be no exception. The Emperor had been secretly working with an

English lawyer who was guiding him on how to protect himself under English law. If Napoleon had set foot on English soil, he would have been entitled to the *Writ of Habeas Corpus*. That is, he would have been entitled to a trial to decide his fate. Therefore, he could not be executed, imprisoned, or exiled a second time. This is precisely why the English kept Napoleon and his suite out in the bay. In fact, Lord Liverpool wrote to Lord Castlereagh warning him of the dangers of allowing Napoleon to come to the shore when he said, "*We are all of the same opinion: we must not let Napoleon reside in this country. The very delicate legal questions that would be raised on this subject would be highly embarrassing.*"[55]

Napoleon became angered with the delay that was being caused by the English Ministers. "*The Emperor immediately dictated a protest and memorandum to Count Las Cases. A sailor, who was a good swimmer, conveyed it to Plymouth by night, and on the next day it was in London, in the hands of a celebrated advocate; and we began again to hope!*"[56] In fact, a writ was obtained by a lawyer on July 31 and was en route to be delivered to the Emperor. The purpose of the Writ was to "*claim the person of the Emperor in the name of the laws or of some competent tribunal.*"[57] Out of growing concern, Liverpool wrote again to Castlereagh explaining that "*Bonaparte is giving us a great deal of trouble in Plymouth.*"[58]

The mere presence of Napoleon offshore residing on board a British vessel was causing greater problems for the English than they had anticipated. He needed to be removed soon. The longer he remained within sight of the mainland, the more he won over the hearts and minds of those who were coming in droves to observe and cheer him. The more people arrived, the more the British had to push them back. Marchand began to worry about his Emperor.

> *These precautions had their reason: the faces around us had changed, the name of Saint Helena was being heard. Two honor guards had been stationed on either side of the dining room door since the Emperor came on board; one of these, an Irishman by birth, at a moment when he believed he was not being watched, crossed himself to let me understand he was a Catholic and said to me in a low voice: "No good for Emperor Saint Helena."*[59]

But the Emperor and his entourage still heard nothing official from the English Ministry. They still had to wait to hear of the fate of Napoleon. During that time, the Emperor conversed with all of the Englishmen on the ship, officers and soldiers alike. Napoleon was intrigued with everything around him on board the *Bellerophon*, and, in turn, the English were fascinated with him.

> *In the brief two weeks he had been in their custody, the English had seen all too much the evidence of Napoleon's magnetic personality: in the tourist boats clustered around the Bellerophon as the government deliberated his fate and, perhaps even more, in the remarkable impact he had had on the ship itself. Within days Napoleon had come to dominate life on the Bellerophon. Master of politics as well as war, he had set out to show the English that the Corsican Ogre was in fact very much human. He was unfailingly courteous to all, and maintained an outward show of good spirits...His curiosity was insatiable. He questioned the officers about their war experiences, and especially about English ways...He watched the ship's personnel at work, asked them about their duties, and commented on the differences between English and French practices...Many of the English spoke some French or Italian, Napoleon's two languages, and if not it did not seem to matter: a young midshipman would recall with some delight years later how, when he gaped at the Emperor, "the great Napoleon" smiled at him, cuffed his head lightly, and pinched his ear.[60]*

But the fragile optimism that filled the hearts and minds of the French suite was smashed to pieces when England's Lord Keith came aboard. The Viscount Lord Keith had been recently promoted to be the commander-in-chief of the English Navy along the English Channel. The Prince Regent bestowed upon Lord Keith the duty to notify Napoleon of what his official fate was to be. Lord Keith entered the temporary chambers of the Emperor on board the *Bellerophon* and read from the official document of the British Government deciding the fate of their captive as Las Cases translated it to the Emperor. It was a fate that the Emperor would never accept.

> *As it is appropriate for General Bonaparte to learn, without any further delay, the intentions for the British government toward him. Your Lordship (Admiral Keith) conveyed the following information to him: It would be little in keeping with our duty toward our country and the allies of His Majesty that General Bonaparte retain the means or opportunity to again disturb the peace of Europe. This is why it is absolutely necessary that he be restrained in his personal freedom, insofar as this primary and important goal requires. The island of Saint Helena has been chosen as his future residence; the climate is healthy and its location will allow him to be treated with more indulgence than would be possible elsewhere, in view of the mandatory precondition that would have to be employed to secure his person. General Bonaparte is authorized to choose among the people who accompanied him to England – with the exception of Generals Savary and Lallemand – three officers, who along with his surgeon and twelve servants will be permitted to follow him to Saint Helena, and will never be allowed to leave the island without the approval of the British government. Rear Admiral Sir George Cockburn,[61] who is named commander in chief of the station at the Cape of Good Hope and the adjacent oceans, will take General Bonaparte and his retinue to Saint Helena, and will receive detailed instructions governing the execution of*

this duty. Sir George Cockburn will probably be ready to leave in a few days, therefore it is desirable that General Bonaparte immediately chose the people who were to accompany him.[62]

Napoleon listened with no emotion and without interruption. But the island of St. Helena was not a place over which the French suite could rejoice. The island was located off the west coast of South Africa and was a 'floating rock' in the middle of the Atlantic Ocean south of the Equator. It was used as a place to resupply British vessels for the voyage to and from India. At the prospect of going to St. Helena, General Montholon wrote, "*St. Helena appeared nothing less than a burning tomb in the midst of the Atlantic.*"[63] So remote was St. Helena that during his reign, Napoleon toyed with attempting to conquer the small island once, but changed his mind. That tiny island was now to become his permanent home.

When Lord Keith had completed reading the declaration, the Emperor's rage began to come forth when he stated, "*I am the guest of England and not its prisoner; I came freely to place myself under the protection of the British law. The government has violated the laws of its country, the rights of the people, and the sacred rights of hospitality in regard to me. I protest and appeal to the British honor.*"[64] Lord Keith explained that he would relay Napoleon's words to the appropriate ministers of the government. There was very little empathy in the words and actions of Lord Keith towards the Emperor's plight.

For Napoleon, final defeat had come. Instead of succumbing to the army of a superior nation or general, Napoleon Bonaparte was defeated by a 'floating rock' in the Southern Atlantic that he had yet to see.

Chapter 2

"This Cursed Rock"

The English were left with little choice in their selection of exiling Napoleon to St. Helena. To allow him to continue on to the United States left the fallen Emperor's fate and 'mobility' out of their control. There were many possibilities for Napoleon in America. Would he honestly just retire to the countryside of upstate New York? Would not the American military want his advice and expertise on their own increasing military strength? The British had just reached a stalemate with the young nation across the ocean and did not wish to have further wars against them. Permitting this wealth of military expertise into their grasp would be a foolish action by the British government. What would prevent Napoleon from slipping out of the country and ending up back on French soil? He had escaped once, he most certainly could do it again.

Why not allow him to remain in England? What would be the harm? Would it not be easier to keep an eye on their new prisoner? To the British government, nothing good could come of keeping Napoleon Bonaparte on British soil. The scenes at the bay of Plymouth were proof enough that the fallen French Emperor would turn into a celebratory figure to whom countless more English would flock, just to get a glimpse. England could even find droves of international visitors yearning to pay homage to the 'great Napoleon.' This could not be permitted.

Why not just put Napoleon on trial for war crimes against the British Empire and execute him when convicted? The tyrant would be disposed of and the threat would be extinguished. Simple in action, deadly in its long-term consequences. The French nation may have been defeated at the Battle of Waterloo and its Emperor dethroned, but many Frenchmen were still very loyal to his name, his honor, and now his memory. Spilling his blood in retribution for past wars would only ensure that the French would pick up their weapons again to defend the Emperor who had instilled their hearts with pride and respect based on a system of merit and not birth; a system that favored the common man and was created by the mind of Napoleon. Even if execution took place, the question would remain as to what to do with Napoleon's body. But the English would find out soon enough how difficult it was just to possess the remains of Napoleon Bonaparte.

There is no doubt that trial and execution were out of the question. The Prince Regent's only recourse was to send the man as far away from the European continent as possible and to ensure that a means of escape did not exist. The island of St. Helena would fulfill both these needs.

That evening, Napoleon dictated an official response to Las Cases, who gave it to Admiral Cockburn so that he could submit it to London.

> *Milord, I have carefully read the extract of the letter you sent me. I have informed you of my protest: I am not a prisoner of war; I am the guest of England. I came to this country on the British vessel Bellerophon, after having informed its captain of the letter I was writing to the prince regent, and having received from him the assurances that his orders were to receive me on board and transport me to England with my retinue, if I so requested, Admiral Hotham has since reiterated the same assurances; from the moment I was freely received on the Bellerophon, I have found myself under the protection of your country's laws. I wish to freely live in England, under the protection and supervision of the laws, taking all engagements and measures, which might be deemed appropriate. I do not wish to have any correspondence with France, or partake in any political affairs. Since my abdication, my intention has always been to reside in the United States or England. I flatter myself that you, Milord, and the undersecretary of your government shall make a faithful report of these facts. It is the honor of the prince regent and the protection of your country's laws that I have place, and place my trust.*[65]

But the Emperor's plea was to no avail. The decision was made and it would be kept.

Napoleon was beyond annoyed and frustrated. Following the dictation of this letter to Admiral Keith, the Emperor stood up and began to undress for bed. After placing his uniform on the chair and putting on his white gown, Napoleon got into his military camp bed and pulled the curtain shut, separating himself from his valet, Marchand. Because Napoleon was used to sleeping on his military camp bed during all of his battles, he could not rest comfortably on anything else. Marchand would set up two different camp beds because the Emperor would quite often get up in the middle of the night and switch to the other bed. No matter how hard he tried, comfort was a necessity for Napoleon that he could never fully achieve.[66]

"Read." The Emperor ordered.

Marchand picked up the book entitled, *Lives of Illustrious Men*, from the table and began to read at the spot where he had left off. Word after word, page after page, the valet read from the text for over a half an hour, ending with the death of Cato. To Marchand, the *"memory of the death of Cato could not be applied to the position of the Emperor who, a new Prometheus, was sailing to Saint Helena."*[67]

Not only did the decision and treatment he received by this declaration of exile enrage him, Napoleon was also much infuriated by being referred to as 'General' and not 'Emperor' by the English government. To him, this was purposeful disrespect to someone who had been crowned by the Pope and Vicar of Christ in the Cathedral of Notre Dame.[68] In his eyes, his coronation placed him on par with that of the crowned heads of Europe. Many of the Kings who doubted Napoleon's legitimacy actually had the soil of treachery and deceit on their hands as well as they ascended their thrones. In fact, Czar Alexander I of Russia was rumored to have had his own father murdered so that he could obtain the throne. Many historians believe this guilt remained with him for the entire period of his reign.

So who were the English to deny his legitimate title now? Had he not been Emperor of the French for over a decade? Had he not waged war and negotiated with the heads of Europe on equal terms? Many of those heads of state had respected his title as they sat across from Napoleon at the bargaining table following defeat.

However the English never officially recognized Napoleon's reign as Emperor of the French and therefore referred to him by the title he held before his ascension: the title of General.[69] Though irritated by the slight, Napoleon responded saying, *"they may call me whatever they choose, but they cannot prevent me from being 'myself.'"*[70] As another means of insult to Napoleon, the British refused to spell his last name 'Bonaparte' as Napoleon had changed it early in his career. The British continuously spelled it 'Buonaparte' which was the original Italian spelling of the name. Napoleon would remain bitter and angered by the disrespect that these two actions by London represented.

*   *   *

As one would well expect, the members of the Emperor's entourage were not enthusiastic about their new 'home.' Madame Bertrand, the wife of Napoleon's Grand Marshal, dropped to her knees and begged Napoleon not to permit her husband to follow him into exile. As the Emperor tried to console her, she leaped to her feet and ran from the room. Napoleon was shocked by her emotion and said to Las Cases, *"Can you comprehend all this? Is she not mad?"*[71]

> *A moment afterwards loud shrieks were heard, and every body seemed to be running towards the stern of the ship. Being desired to ring the bell, and to enquire the cause, I found that Madame Bertrand, on leaving the cabin, had attempted to throw herself into the sea, and was prevented with the greatest difficulty. From this scene it is easy to judge of our feelings!*[72]

Marchand recorded that this act of desperation and attempted suicide by Madame Bertrand gave *"a measure of the more or less strong internal agitation felt by each of us."*[73] There was no doubt amongst the members of the Emperor's suite that spending perhaps years on the island of St. Helena would become not only Napoleon's Hell on Earth but theirs as well.

But Napoleon was not only angry, he too was filled with anxiety and what some would call fear. He considered suicide as he expressed to his secretary,

> "My friend," continued the Emperor, "I have sometimes an idea of quitting you, and this would not be very difficult; it is only necessary to create a little mental excitement, and I shall soon have escaped! – All will be over, and you can then quietly rejoin your families. This is more easy, since my internal principles do do not oppose any bar to it: - I am one of those who conceive that the pains of the other world were only imagined as a counterpoise to those inadequate allurements which are offered to us there. God can never have willed such a contradiction to his infinite goodness, especially for an act of this kind; and what is it after all, but wishing to return to him a little sooner?"[74]

In this time of emotional strain, Napoleon was providing to Las Cases a glimpse into his feelings, his stressful thoughts, his hope that this fate could somehow be removed from its reality. The secretary listened with tears in his eyes searching for some sort of words that would convince the Emperor that exiting this world by his own hand was not the option he needed to take. Napoleon continued to reveal his thoughts when he asked Las Cases, "*but what can we do in that desolate place?*"[75]

> "Sire," I replied, "we will live on the past: there is enough in it to satisfy us. Do we not enjoy the life of Caesar and that of Alexander? We shall posses still more, you will re-peruse yourself, Sire!" "Be it so!" rejoined Napoleon; "we will write our Memoirs. Yes, we must be employed; for occupation is the scythe of Time. After all, a man ought to fulfill his destinies; that is my grand doctrine. Let mine also be accomplished."[76]

The secretary succeeded in bringing the Emperor out of his depression, for the moment.

As the private emotional moment subsided with the encouraging words of Las Cases, Napoleon soon returned to a state of anger at his exile. On August 4, 1815, the Emperor wrote a final stinging complaint against the treatment and decision of the English Crown. The official declaration contained similar protests to the ones detailed in Napoleon's first response letter, but with the exception that this one was more aggressive and laced with accusation.

> ...If the [English] government in giving orders to the captain of the Bellerophon to receive me and my retinue had only wanted to set a trap for me, an ambush, it has forfeited its honor and blemished its flag. If such an act were consummated, it would be in vain for the British in the future for their loyalty, their laws, and their freedom; British faith would be lost with the hospitality of the Bellerophon. I appeal to history; it shall say that an enemy who made war for twenty years against the British people came freely, in his misfortune, to seek shelter under their laws – and what greater proof could he give of his esteem and trust? But how did England reply to such magnanimity? She pretended to extend a hospitable hand to this enemy and, when he gave himself up in good faith, she slaughtered him.[77]

But again, the Emperor's protest fell on deaf ears. The decision had been made, and the decision would be kept. Left with no other choice but to accept what was happening, Napoleon began to choose those who would follow him into exile.

The first of the three officers was Henri Bertrand, Grand Marshal of the Palace. He was the officer most devoted to Napoleon, serving alongside him at Waterloo, and he had shared his exile on the island of Elba. Bertrand would again wholeheartedly follow his Emperor into exile along with his wife and their children.[78] Though Madame Bertrand had earlier expressed her 'dissatisfaction' with going to St. Helena, her husband convinced her that this was his duty to the Emperor.

The second officer was General Baron Gourgaud, who after learning that he was not originally chosen to go to St. Helena, became emotional and begged the Emperor to let him serve him in exile, to which Napoleon agreed. Gourgaud had fought at the battle of Waterloo, boasting that he had saved the Emperor's life there. He would brag about a great many things while on St. Helena to the annoyance of all those present amongst the Emperor's entourage. Always feeling slighted and self-consciously unappreciated, Gourgaud would spend his time on St. Helena battling for the attention of Napoleon. He would go to St. Helena alone, without family.[79]

The final officer was Count Charles-Tristan de Montholon, who before this time had not served very close to the Emperor. He served the Empire in various capacities and eventually became a marshal in 1814. In 1812, while in Moscow, Napoleon sent orders to Paris condemning Montholon's marriage to Albine Vassal citing that the marriage was "*incompatible with the honorable functions entrusted*" him. After the defeat at Waterloo, Montholon was successful in attaching himself to the Emperor's suite. He followed Napoleon into exile with his wife and son.[80]

After the tantrum by Gourgaud at potentially being left behind, Napoleon petitioned the English government to allow him to bring another officer so that he could include Las Cases, but the request was denied. The Emperor instead listed him as his personal secretary. Count Emmanuel de Las Cases was a former emigrant who was a "latecomer" to the Imperial Court. He had been from the old nobility and had spent time in England during the heart of the French Revolution. He returned under the reign of Napoleon and was commissioned as a secretary. Also known as a successful author, Las Cases and his fifteen-year-old son followed the Emperor into exile.[81]

The rest of Napoleon's entourage consisted of his personal valets and other servants. His three main valets were with the Emperor practically twenty-four hours a day, Marchand in particular. Louis Marchand was in his early twenties and always slept in a room adjacent to Napoleon's. He was absolutely dedicated to the Emperor. As a young and unattached man, he would be giving up the best years of his life to work as a servant for the fallen Emperor while on St. Helena. Most men his age would be frolicking around the salons of Paris in search of the most beautiful and eligible women in the hopes of finding a lasting bride. Loyalty was an understatement when it came to Louis Marchand's relationship with Napoleon. He would dress the Emperor in the morning and read to him as he fell asleep. He heard almost every word spoken by Napoleon. He witnessed the Emperor's anger, pain, sadness, joy, amusement, and eventually his suffering. It would be Marchand's memoirs that would later reveal so many personal and warm aspects about the human side of Napoleon.[82]

One of Napoleon's most trusted servants and aides was a man by the name of Cipriani Franceschi. He had been with Napoleon since the early days in Corsica. He was exceptionally loyal to the Emperor who was heavily relied upon to act as his spy to obtain whatever necessary information Napoleon needed. Cipriani never let him down. It was he who had been sent near the Congress of Vienna while Napoleon was in exile on the island of Elba. He would report back to Napoleon that the Congress was potentially examining the option of moving him from the island to a more 'remote' location. This information very well may have played into his decision to flee Elba and attempt to regain his throne in 1814. Cipriani's resemblance to the Emperor was also striking. On a number of occasions, Cipriani would serve as the Emperor's body double, protecting him from assassination threats. Cipriani would also go into exile with his beloved Emperor and friend.

One of the most interesting members of the Emperor's entourage to St. Helena was an Irish doctor by the name of Barry O'Meara. He was the *Bellerophon's* doctor and spoke Napoleon's native Italian. They had many conversations together while en route to Plymouth. When it came time for Napoleon to choose a doctor to follow him into exile, the Emperor extended the invitation to O'Meara, who was quite flattered by the request. The doctor gladly accepted upon approval by the English government and with the condition that he would retain his rights as an Englishman. Surprisingly, London did not object to the Emperor's request. How valuable it would be for them to have a 'spy' in the very bedroom of their new prisoner. That is as long as the English government could keep O'Meara loyal. Napoleon's personality could be quite captivating.[83]

The remaining members of the Emperor's entourage consisted of the following people, St. Denis – valet, Noverraz – valet, Santini – usher, Archambault – groom, Archambault (brothers) – groom, Gentilini – footman, Pierron – butler, Lepage – cook, Rousseau – steward.[84]

During the first days of August 1815, the *HMS Northumberland*, two frigates and several brigs filled with British troops anchored by the side of the *Bellerophon*.[85] It would be this larger vessel of the *Northumberland* that would transfer Napoleon to his new home. The *Bellerophon* was an older ship that could not make the long voyage to the island of St. Helena. Aboard the *Bellerophon* were reported to be a total of *"1,080 persons on board, including two companies of picked men, and the staff officers of the 53rd foot."*[86]

Before the Emperor was to embark onto the *Northumberland*, Lord Keith paid him a final visit. Accompanying Keith was Admiral George Cockburn who was presented to the Emperor as the officer in charge of not only conveying Napoleon to St. Helena, but to serve as a temporary governor of the island as well. Keith explained to the Emperor that he had orders from Lord Bathurst to inspect the luggage of the French and that they were to surrender all monies, gold, silver, and firearms that they had smuggled out of France and onto the British vessel.[87] Though some money and valuables were handed over, the French were able to keep *"secret about 400,000 francs in gold, from 3 to 400,000 francs in valuables and diamonds; and letters of credit for more than 4,000,000 francs."*[88]

But the scene that was to take place next was almost unbearable to witness by the members of the Emperor's suite.

> *General Gourgaud remained by the starboard guns, prepared for any event. The Emperor, a few feet in front of us, appeared to expect that he had only to receive their adieus, when Lord Keith, at length resigning himself to the execution of an order which was at variance with the whole of his long and brilliant military career, approached the Emperor, and said in a voice subdued by lively emotion – "England demands your sword." The Emperor by a convulsive movement placed his hand upon that sword, which an Englishman dared to demand – the terrible expression of his eye was the only reply; never had it been more powerful or more penetrating. The old admiral was astounded, his tall figure shrunk,*

> *his head, white with years, fell upon his breast like that of a criminal shrinking before the sentence of his judge. The Emperor retained his sword.*[89]

When it was finally time for the French suite to board the *Northumberland*, Admiral George Cockburn recorded in his journal the moment that transpired when the Emperor first set foot on the ship. He captured the ease and charisma of this 'despised' enemy of the British; an enemy that none of those British soldiers had ever seen with their own eyes.

> *On reaching the deck the General said to me, 'here I am, General, at your orders.' He then asked to be introduced to the Captain; enquired the names of different officers and gentlemen upon deck, and desired to know in what countries they were born; and then asked various other questions of trifling import.*[90]

This was a characteristic of Napoleon's personality. He would converse with anyone and question him or her on various topics important in their own lives. By taking an interest in his enemy's personal life and concerns, Napoleon was disarming his opponent. In doing so, the connotation of Napoleon being the enemy quickly begins to fade. When the political barrier of the enemy is gone, a personal friendship can begin. One's previous hatred or anger for that enemy soon turns to empathy and respect. The title of 'enemy' or 'prisoner' gradually becomes that of 'friend.' Napoleon knew this all too well. It was what made his personality so captivating, persuasive, and magnetic.

Admiral Cockburn witnessed the persuasive character of Napoleon almost immediately, especially when it came to deciding where his quarters would be aboard this vessel that was to deliver him into exile.

> *When I had shown him the cabin which I had appropriated for his exclusive use, and requested him to sit down in the great cabin, he begged me to cause the Lieutenants of the ship to be intro-*

> duced to him. As, however, by this time his own followers had come to take leave of him, I thought it best to retire for a short time; but I found, soon afterwards, that advantage was taken of this for him to assume exclusive right to the after or great cabin. When therefore I had finished my letters, I went into it again with some of my officers, and desired M. de Bertrand to explain to him that the after cabin must be considered as common to all of us; and that the sleeping-cabin, which I had appropriated to him, could alone be considered as exclusively his. He received this intimation with good humour, and soon afterwards went on deck, where he chatted in a very good natured mood with everybody.[91]

Though a mechanical bed had been provided for him, Napoleon preferred to sleep on the camp-bed that he had used throughout the numerous military campaigns that he had led over the decades. "*During the whole time of his sojourn in St. Helena, the Emperor never slept on any other bed.*"[92] Napoleon would die in this very bed.

It was now August 9, 1815, and the time had come. After settling into his quarters aboard the *Northumberland*, the 'fleet of exiles' began its journey to the wretched rock of St. Helena in the Atlantic. As the shores of France again came into view as they exited the English Channel, "*the Emperor, who was on deck, removed his hat and remained motionless, saying with intense emotion in his voice; "Adieu, land of the brave! Adieu, France! Adieu!"*"[93] Napoleon would never again see the shores of France.

* * *

The journey to the island of St. Helena would not be a quick one. A total of ten ships would make this voyage. Napoleon and his entourage would sail aboard the *Northumberland*, while the possessions of the French suite and the necessary British troops to guard the Emperor were placed on the nine other ships. It would take the ships nearly two months to complete the trip to this destination of exile.[94] Boredom reigned supreme on board the *Northumberland.*

Napoleon tried to maintain his regular routine while en route to St. Helena. The Emperor chose to wear the green uniform of the chasseurs of his guard and ate dinner meals with the British officers on board. They were not particularly accustomed to the Emperor's dining habits. He rarely sat long enough to eat his meal, let alone digest it and remained at the table for light conversation. When he was finished eating, Napoleon would abruptly push away the plate and rise from the table long before the rest of the people seated and he would go out on the deck of the ship to converse with a member of his entourage or with members of the ship's crew.[95] Admiral Cockburn was very observant of Napoleon's habits.

Buonaparte, since on board the Northumberland, has kept nearly the same hour: he gets up late (between 10 and 11) has his breakfast (of meat and wine) in his bedroom, and continues there in his dishabille until three or four in the afternoon, when he dresses for dinner. He then comes out of his bed-cabin, and either takes a short walk on deck, or plays a game of chess with one of his Generals, until the dinner hour (which is five o'clock.) At dinner he generally eats and drinks a good deal, and talks but little. He prefers meats, of all kinds, highly dressed, and never touches vegetables. After dinner, he generally walks for about an hour and a half, and it is during these walks, that I have the most free and pleasant conversations with him. About eight he quits the deck; and we then make up a game at cards for him, in which he seems to engage with considerable pleasure and interest, until about ten, when he retires to his bed-room, and I believe goes almost immediately to bed.[96]

This was a nightly ritual for the Emperor and he would walk on deck until dark. He would "*take eight or nine turns the whole length of the deck...he would seat himself on the second gun from the gangway on the larboard side. The midshipmen soon observed this habitual prediction, so that the cannon was thenceforth called the 'Emperor's gun.'*"[97] The sailors were incredibly taken with the Emperor and his openness with them. Napoleon "*doubly obtained the respect and admiration of all the English who had the honour to approach him; not one of them could resist the magical influence of his actions and words...*"[98]

In terms of the Emperor's hand at the game of chess, that was also something of a sort of intrigue for those that took up the challenge. Sometimes he would win and other times he would lose and this was an issue that Napoleon addressed with humor.

> *The Emperor was an indifferent [chess] player, he gained with some and lost with others, a circumstance which one evening led him to say, "How happens it that I frequently lose with those who are never able to beat him who I almost always beat? Does that not thus seem contradictory? How is this problem to be solved? Said he, winking his eye, to shew that he was not the dupe of the constant politeness of him who was really the best player.*[99]

To help pass the time as well, Las Cases would read the English papers to the Emperor. Napoleon was always fascinated not only with the English in terms of their daily customs and habits, but he was interested in learning the English language and inquired to whether Las Cases could teach him. The secretary "*promised him that in a very few lessons he would be in a position to read these public documents himself. An hour each day was assigned to this lesson, which also served to fight boredom during this long journey.*"[100]

But this lack of physical activity was not something to which the Emperor was accustomed. He was known for taking to horseback for hours a day as well as for long walks. Being confined to a ship inside claustrophobic cabins without the ability to go for horseback rides was something that began to worry the members of Napoleon's suite. It also began to concern Admiral Cockburn. As someone who had just begun to witness the Emperor's daily habits, he quickly observed that this type of routine could be detrimental to Napoleon's health. He felt that "*such a life of inactivity, with the quantity and description of his food, makes me fear that he will not retain his health throughout the voyage; he, however, as yet, does not appear to suffer any inconvenience from it.*"[101] Later in the voyage, the Admiral recorded that Napoleon's health remained quite well throughout the voyage. He observed that "*General Bonaparte, himself, is certainly fatter, and looking better than when he first came on board the Northumberland. I must acknowledge, that he has, throughout, shown far less impatience about the wind or the weather, and made fewer difficulties, than any of the rest of the party.*"[102]

Napoleon's physical stamina was an amazement to many. Whether on the field of battle, on the long journey en route at the head of the army, to dictating to numerous secretaries on various subjects at the same time, Napoleon had the mental and physical capabilities of five men. But placed under these circumstances and with the mental punishments that he will soon face on St. Helena, even the strongest man could break.

*   *   *

Being a military man of high rank himself, Admiral Cockburn observed some of Napoleon's actions as an attempt to prove his stature and Majestic fortitude. The Admiral would often find humor in seeing these displays.

> *Our trade-wind continued, until about four in the evening, when we experienced a very heavy rain...To my great surprise, after General Buonaparte had eaten his dinner, he got up to take his walk as usual. Upon my remarking to him that it was still pouring with rain, and therefore advised him not to go out, he treated it lightly, and said it would not hurt him more than the sailors, whom he observed at the time catching water, and running about in it. Of course I no longer opposed his whim, and out he went in the rain, accompanied by two of his French friends, who,*

> *though obliged to attend him, seemed by no means to enjoy the idea of the wetting they were doomed to get par complaisance. I have no doubt General Buonaparte intended that this dash of his, should give us a great idea of his hardiness of character. As however no particular notice was taken of any of us, and finding it, I suppose, more unpleasant than he expected, his walk was of very short duration. Being, as was unavoidable, perfectly wet through, he immediately, on quitting the deck, went into his own cabin, from whence he did not rejoin us during the evening.*[103]

But there came a point where Admiral Cockburn could see directly into the persona of Napoleon Bonaparte. Almost as if he had broken himself from the attraction of Napoleon's spell. The Emperor was captivating and engaging and could charm even his worst enemies. As the Admiral in charge, Cockburn knew that this could be dangerous for his other officers and crew. Allowing the Emperor to win too much favor with the British crew could perhaps lead them to aid the prisoner in potential mischief; a plan that Napoleon had actually used on many occasions and would put into effect on St. Helena. Admiral Cockburn realized that this had to be controlled.

> *Immediately after dinner to-day, the General got up rather uncivilly, and went upon deck as soon as he had swallowed his own coffee, and before all the rest of us were even served. This induced me to request particularly the remainder of the party to sit still; and he consequently went out attended only by his Mareschal, without the slightest further notice being taken of him. It is clear he is still inclined to act the Sovereign occasionally; but I cannot allow it, and the sooner therefore he becomes convinced it is not to be admitted, the better.*[104]

Though steadfast in his orders to prevent Napoleon from attempting to project his Majestic persona, Admiral Cockburn did cast aside all apprehensions about avoiding controversial subjects with his new prisoner. During their numerous conversations while on board the *Northumberland*, the Admiral freely asked Napoleon questions on a variety of controversial topics that not many people would dare pose to the disposed Emperor. Admiral Cockburn asked Napoleon why he did not throw himself to the generosity of his father-in-law, the Emperor of Austria. He asked Napoleon if he really poisoned his own troops instead of allowing them to be tortured by the Muslim fighters during the Egyptian campaign. The Admiral asked him if he ordered the execution of the Duc d' Enghien, the heir to the Bourbons. It is amazing to see that Napoleon gave him truthful answers.

Many of these issues had been discussed in the salons of France and the taverns of England, even by members of the English Parliament. But no one close to the Emperor would have posed such questions in casual dinner conversation or during walks along the deck unless the Emperor chose to share the information. The frankness of Admiral Cockburn to probe such questions is both incredible as it is bold. What is even more astonishing is that Napoleon freely shared his reasoning with the British officer. The Emperor did not hold back and simply stated the rationale for his actions.

Napoleon was not engaging in this personally detailed conversation for the sake of discussion, but rather he was molding his history. There were not many disposed Kings who were in a position to discuss the reasoning of their actions post sitting on the throne. British Kings did not have this option. King Louis XVI of France certainly did not. Looking farther into the past in terms of historical leaders, Alexander the Great and Julius Caesar certainly did not have the opportunity to reflect following their reign. Napoleon Bonaparte did and he used it to his fullest advantage.

Napoleon knew that whomever he conversed with would most certainly record the discussions into their own diaries and then relay his words to others. He was well aware that people were intrigued by him and had their own preconceptions and judgments regarding his actions and what they perceived to be his actions. By telling people his version of events and knowing that they would be recording and printing his words, Napoleon was stealthily able to spread his version of his history and reign. He was able to counter the negative histories being written of him without having to publish his accounts himself. The person speaking with him and writing down his every word was, in fact, doing this for him. If there could be any advantage to his exile, instead of an execution, this would be it.

On one occasion Admiral Cockburn witnessed a sense of grief come over Napoleon. The *Northumberland* was approaching the islands of Porto Santo and Madeira and the Admiral assumed that the Emperor would come out on deck as usual to observe the land. He recorded that Napoleon "*appeared thoughtful, and out of spirits, as if the passing of the island made him reflect the more strongly on the little chance he had of ever seeing Europe again.*"[105] There is no doubt that times would arise where Napoleon was painfully reminded of his situation. Observing an island that may resemble his place of exile could do nothing to lighten his spirits. Even though he sat upon the throne of France as a Sovereign, his human heart reminded him that he was now a prisoner.

There were a number of moments when Napoleon's insatiable appetite for knowledge and his sense of humor would show itself again while on the voyage to St. Helena. Over the course of a few days, some of the sailors noticed a large group of dolphins swimming along side the ship. A few of them were caught and eaten by the British men. The Emperor was quite curious to taste the meat and upon eating some he "*found the flesh quite good, but that was not the case with shark meat, which he found disgusting.*"[106]

In another instance, the Emperor became very interested when he was informed that a sailor had just caught another shark and had it on the deck weighing one hundred and eighty pounds. Marchand recorded in this memoir that Napoleon "*wished to see it and took pleasure in the struggle that it was waging against the sailors. They began to skin it, and the tail thrashing against the deck was so frightening that the Emperor, who had moved in a little too close, was almost wounded. Inside this young shark were found remnants of human clothing.*"[107] Las Cases recorded that the shark was so large and moved so violently that it "*knocked down four or five sailors, and had well nigh broken the Emperor's legs.*"[108] Upon returning to the Emperor's cabin, Las Cases viewed blood on Napoleon's leg and thought that he had truly been injured. After further examination, it was concluded that Marchand was quite correct when he stated that the Emperor had gotten too close to the shark, for the blood on his leg was that of the shark.

As the *Northumberland* began to get closer to St. Helena, the ship eventually crossed the Equator on September 23. A celebration ensued onboard the vessel. The French referred to this momentous event as the celebration of "Old Man Equator," whereas to the British it was "the Great Beard." When the ship crossed the line, "*the oldest of the sailors becomes Neptune, and those who make up his retinue, in the most ridiculous of dress, carry him on a seat made of a gun carriage decorated with draperies.*"[109] Neptune's job was to ask each of the people on the ship if they have been initiated or not. When this character came to Napoleon, the Admiral merrily stated that he had in which the Emperor, in turn, gave Neptune five hundred napoleons through the Grand Marshal.[110] Napoleon did so joyfully "*in order that he [Neptune] and all his court might drink to his health; this was a signal for deafening hurras and cries of "Long live the Emperor Napoleon!"*"[111]

Ironically, Admiral Cockburn did not record this event in his diary the same way, as did Montholon and Marchand. The British Admiral wrote that he refused to allow Napoleon to give the money to Neptune or sailors as he considered "*this to be an attempt of the General, to avail himself, with his usual finesse, of a plausible excuse to distribute such a large sum among the seamen, solely with a view of rendering himself popular with them. I of course not only refused my assent to this request, but pointedly prohibited it.*"[112]

It is interesting to see such varying accounts juxtaposed. The Frenchmen may have been exaggerating the story to present Napoleon as being generous and kind, but at the same time, they both recorded the same facts, thus potentially giving them validity to some extent. The Admiral may be recording it factually, or he may be changing the account as well to protect himself from later criticism for allowing such an act by a 'prisoner.' The chronicling of history quite often lies in the eye of the beholder, and frankly, in the pen of the person who is trying to preserve their perspective upon it.

*   *   *

One lasting characteristic of Napoleon's personality was that he never hesitated in conversing with someone that others found distasteful or an outcast. He sought throughout his life to give recognition to those based on merit, not hereditary class. He looked for determination of character that would lead to success, not just alluding to name recognition to seek the respect of others. Respect, advancement, and character were earned in his eyes. If he came upon someone that others scorned, he would give them the opportunity to prove otherwise. This is the same Napoleon that once addressed people stricken with a contagious disease, when others warned of the dangers to his person. It was this aspect of Napoleon's personality that led him to converse with an 'outcast' aboard the *Northumberland*. One evening on the 25th of September, Napoleon went out on deck for his usual walk.

> *The first person he saw there was the clergyman – a kind of original, whom the young people amused themselves by turning into ridicule: the Emperor sent for him – spoke of religion to him, and placing him thus on the field of his true worth, found some pleasure in changing his questions into regular controversy. From that day forward no one ventured to ridicule the poor man; the Emperor had raised him in the eyes of all, and thenceforth his theological knowledge compensated for the absurdity of his face and manners.*[113]

Now that the voyage had been at sea for over a month, the sense of boredom and the onset of time became elements that were too powerful to be conquered by the Emperor and the members of his suite. The French exiles were beginning to see these effects on the Emperor. Napoleon's legs were beginning to swell and cause him considerable discomfort.

> *This crossing was becoming tedious for the Emperor who, accustomed to much exercise, could not find an opportunity to take any; a few dictations to General Gourgaud or to Count de Las Cases were the only distraction during the day, and even then he was not set up well for this type of affair. He was anxious to arrive in the place of his exile, no matter how sad the scene might be.*[114]

The Emperor did not have to wait too much longer for his 'wish' to come true. After nearly seventy days since their departure from England and one hundred and ten days after their flight from Paris, the exiles reached their new home on October 15, 1815. With a friendly pinch on Marchand's ear to wake him from his sleep, Napoleon grabbed his field glass and made his way to the deck. The entire French suite soon followed and all were on deck to observe the 'floating rock.'[115]

As the lens reflected the light, the Emperor got a glimpse of his new home. Rising out of the think fog materialized a steep rock fortress. In the middle of one side of the solid land mass was a road winding left and right until it reached what appeared to be the peak of a great mountain. St. Helena looked like a lifeless rock located at the edge of the earth. As the *Northumberland* sailed closer to the island, a tiny port could be seen along the shore. The port of Jamestown would be the place where the Emperor would first feel the soil of St. Helena beneath his feet.

None of the exiles were pleased with their first glimpse of St. Helena. Marchand referred to the effect of his first sighting as being only able to greet the island "*like a grave.*"[116] Las Cases was more emotional stating that their initial view of their prison was "*the first link of the chain that was to bind the modern Prometheus to his rock.*"[117] Another member of the French suite proclaimed that "*the devil must have shit this island as he flew from one world to the other.*"[118] General Gourgaud recorded hearing Napoleon remarking upon seeing the island for the first time that "*it is not a pretty place to live. I would have done better to stay in Egypt. By now, I should be Emperor of all the East.*"[119] And with that, he turned around and went back to his cabin.

The Emperor obviously was not expecting to be sent to a land as beautiful as Paris. But if a country rich and glorious with people who praised his name and who would build him a grand palace was his ideal Heaven, then St. Helena truly was his complete Hell on Earth. Napoleon could not turn back. This was his reality.

*   *   *

The Portuguese discovered St. Helena in 1502, but in 1815, the English East India Company controlled it. The island is located 1,750 miles from Cape Town, South Africa, 1,800 miles from South

America, 4,000 miles from England. The nearest land is Ascension Island, some 700 miles away, and was uninhabitable. The civilian population of St. Helena was around 3,000 consisting of roughly 800 Europeans, and the rest being made up of Africans, Chinese and Lascars.[120] Three-fifths of the Africans were slaves. St. Helena was located on the sea route from England to South Africa and India.[121]

As many of the Emperor's entourage would soon discover, the climate of St. Helena was not something to which they were entirely accustomed. Montholon described the climate of the island as *"in general unhealthy"* and continued that there was *"no instance of a native or a slave having reached the age of sixty years. Dysentery and hepatitis rage during six months of the year..."*[122] Las Cases labeled the island *"a true Siberia: the only difference is its limited extent, and the climate being warm instead of cold."*[123]

As the English ships carrying the exiles came closer to the Port of Jamestown in which they were to anchor, it became apparent that the residents of St. Helena were quite aware of the cargo that the British ships were carrying.[124] Hundreds of people crowded onto the tiny beach that lay at the base of the never-ending rock. Marchand recorded that *"for two days the inhabitants remained on the piers, waiting to see the Emperor at the moment he disembarked. Each evening at sundown they would go back home, disappointed in their expectations."*[125] Numerous little boats, packed with the curious, attempted to row as close to the *Northumberland* as possible. All of them were there to get a glimpse of the 'Corsican Ogre.'[126]

Observing the number of people crowded on the waterfront, the Emperor expressed to Admiral Cockburn his desire to go on shore at night so that he would not be a spectacle. Accommodating the Emperor's wishes as much as possible, Admiral Cockburn ordered that Napoleon and the members of his entourage would go on land at 6:00 pm on October 17. But the time made no difference. The people remained on the beach during the day and lit torches to light the shore at night so as to ensure a good view of the English prisoner.

Admiral Cockburn had gone onto the island earlier on the 17th to locate a suitable residence for Napoleon in Jamestown while his permanent residence of Longwood was being renovated. It was decided that he would stay in the home of a Mr. Porteus in town.[127] The Admiral returned to the *Northumberland* accompanied by the Governor of the island, Colonel Mark Wilks. Admiral Cockburn would be replacing Wilks as Governor once the Emperor was settled on the island. Wilks knew more about the island than Cockburn because he had been there for a number of years. Once aboard, both men immediately went to the Emperor's cabin to discuss the island of St. Helena.

As the crowds continued to remain on shore waiting for the arrival of Napoleon and unable to delay the moment any longer, the Admiral boarded a smaller boat with the Emperor and Grand Marshal Bertrand and went ashore. Napoleon was dressed in his famous hat, a long black coat covering his uniform, with the Legion of Honor pinned to a satin band tied around his chest. Rows of soldiers lined a path for the men to follow, but the crowds began to swarm the path making it difficult for the men to proceed. British sentries were then ordered to *"stand with fixed bayonets at the entrance from the lines to the town, to prevent the multitude from pouring in. Napoleon was excessively provoked at the eagerness of the crowd to get a peep at him, more particularly as he was received in silence though with respect."*[128]

The first signs of Napoleon Bonaparte's presence on the island of St. Helena were left for all to see as footprints along the shore of the port. The markings of St. Helena lay stained upon the soles of his boots. Unbeknownst to Napoleon, and hidden within that mob of spectators stood a scared, adolescent girl, who would soon change this man's life, and bring forth in him, a human side that would change Napoleon forever.

How many superior men are children oftener than once a day!

Napoleon

Chapter 3

Betsy And Boney

After setting foot upon St. Helena for the first time, the Emperor and his entourage took up residence in Mr. Porteus' home in Jamestown. The residence called Longwood, which would function as Napoleon's permanent home, was being further remodeled to accommodate the Emperor and his suite. Longwood was a structure farther inland and at a higher elevation on the island and would serve as Napoleon's permanent home. It was a renovated barn that had been converted into the summer residence for the lieutenant Governor, Colonel Skelton.[129] This was quite a different scene for Napoleon who was used to the halls of palaces like those of St. Cloud, Versailles, Malmaison, and Elysee.

The next morning at 8 o'clock, Admiral Cockburn came to Mr. Porteus' home to escort the Emperor to inspect the progress being made at Longwood. A horse was brought for Napoleon to ride, but he did not trust the unknown animal. Napoleon ordered his servant St. Denis to first ride the horse to ensure that it was safe for him to ride. After St. Denis made a few circles with the horse proving its ability, Napoleon mounted the animal and proceeded to follow the Admiral to Longwood.[130] The Emperor was accompanied by Grand Marshal Bertrand and St. Denis. The later described this ride as a journey to "*the spot chosen by the admiral to be the prison of the illustrious captive of the Holy Alliance.*"[131]

On the way to Longwood, the Emperor spotted a lovely house that possessed a small pavilion behind the home. The place caught his eye as a more comfortable and suitable place for him to stay. He found the pavilion to be both "*rustic and charming*" and wished to visit the place on their return from Longwood.[132]

Once the group arrived at Longwood, the Emperor was taken aback by his new 'home.' The rooms were still not finished, and the smell of newly applied paint filled the air. He saw that the house "*enjoyed no shade or water, and was exposed to the southeast wind that prevailed there constantly, and was quite strong at that time. He immediately realized all the work remaining to be done before he could take up residence there, and therefore paid little attention to everything the admiral would say regarding construction projects and improvements."*[133] The Emperor explained that he could not live in the dwelling until it was aired out thoroughly. The Admiral responded by stating that he would have to remain in town then until Longwood was complete.

When Napoleon's servant, Marchand, made the trek to Longwood for the first time, he looked around at what was to become their new home. The servant quickly realized that St. Helena and this building in particular *"had become the state prison for the Emperor, as well as his grave."*[134]

What disgusted the members of Napoleon suite, even more, was the fact that there was a beautiful home that was well situated on the island called 'Plantation House.' This was the home of the present Governor and would have been perfect for Napoleon and his entourage to live during his exile.[135] It was an elegant home located in a more pleasant location on the island where the weather would not have been so brutal to the exiles. But then again, that is probably precisely why the British chose Longwood over Plantation House. Marchand believed the goal of the British Crown was to shorten the Emperor's life by choosing Longwood, *"they wanted the severity of the climate to extinguish it as quickly as possible. Eternal shame upon the British government!"*[136]

Though the Admiral had insisted that Napoleon remain in town until Longwood was complete, the Emperor reminded him about the pavilion that they had seen earlier in the day. He found it to be quite superior to the shabby house he was presently staying in, and the pavilion's isolated location from curious onlookers made it even more appealing. Remaining in Jamestown would have caused the Emperor to be viewed by the town's inhabitants like a caged animal. At the pavilion, he could be left alone. Napoleon inquired as to who lived there. The Admiral responded that the house was called 'The Briars' and that the Balcombe family resided in the main house. Intrigued with the pavilion, Napoleon asked whether he could live there temporarily until Longwood was ready. Admiral Cockburn found no threat in the location compared with Jamestown, and he responded that he would inquire whether this arrangement would be satisfactory to Mr. Balcombe.[137]

The Emperor, the Admiral, and the other two men rode their horses down the path that brought them to The Briars. Admiral Cockburn dismounted and conversed with Mr. Balcombe who had now come outdoors to meet his guests. After hearing the request of the Admiral on behalf of Napoleon, Mr. Balcombe graciously agreed and offered the main house to the Emperor instead of the smaller pavilion.[138] The Emperor conveyed his appreciation but did not wish to impose saying that he would occupy the pavilion separated from the main house with pleasure, on condition that the family's habits would not be disrupted.[139]

William Balcombe was a naval agent and purveyor for the East India Company. He lived at The Briars with his wife, their two daughters and two sons. Mr. Balcombe made a steady and profitable income working for the Company and had servants and slaves that worked at The Briars. The two sons were William and little Alexander,[140] both of which were under 8 years of age. The two daughters were Jane, who was sixteen-years-old and Betsy who was only fourteen-years-old. They had spent some time at school in England where Betsy, in particular, had studied the French language.[141]

Because of its small size, the pavilion in the back yard of the main home would not house all of the members of the Emperor's entourage. The structure itself consisted of one large square room. Marchand, St. Denis, and another servant named Noverraz would sleep on the floor next to the Emperor's camp bed while Las Cases would sleep in the loft overhead.[142] When Napoleon heard that Las Cases thought it was better to leave his son in Jamestown, the Emperor disagreed saying *"I do not wish to separate those who are close: go send for young Emmanuel."*[143] Napoleon was very fond of Las Cases' son and was often playful with him: teasing, lifting his hair, or pinching his ear.

While staying in the pavilion, Admiral Cockburn was still not about to take any chances. He ordered British soldiers to live in The Briars to keep guard of Napoleon. *"Artillery Captain Greatly moved into The Briars with two orderlies to keep an eye on the Emperor."*[144] Greatly was in command of the guns on the *Northumberland*, which were brought on the island to defend it against a 'rescue' expedition.[145] Much more would be done to ensure that this one man did not leave the island and return to Europe ever again.

Once the orders were given by Admiral Cockburn for Napoleon to temporarily reside at The Briars, the pavilion was prepared for Napoleon to begin his stay that night.

> *As soon as the things had arrived, we took care of assembling his bed; the table was placed in the*

> middle of the room with a rug. It was to serve as desk and dining room table, just as the room itself was to be bedroom, study and dining room. It was impossible to be more confined than the Emperor was, but he was free to move about and the rest could be forgotten. A dresser was offered to me with so much insistence on Mr. Balcombe's part that I had to accept. I spread out on it the Emperor's travel kit which, once opened, decorated the room a little...Portraits of the King of Rome and Empress Marie-Louise were hung on the wall, and a few pieces of cloth stretched on ropes across the windows completed the furnishings of the room.[146]

When this preparation of the pavilion was complete, it was time for the full Balcombe family to meet their new visitor. They all assembled in front of the home to watch the Admiral and his prisoner arrive. One can only imagine the concern, nervousness, and perhaps fear that the family felt knowing that Napoleon Bonaparte himself was coming to stay at their home. What makes this even more extraordinary is the fact that he technically was not coming as a guest for dinner, but rather, as the prisoner of the English government.

Upon dismounting their horses, they approached the family. The Admiral introduced the Emperor and after greeting Mr. Balcombe again, he instantly went over to Mrs. Balcombe and complimented her on her beauty. Next to her were the two boys to which Napoleon playfully pinched their noses and rustled their hair. Being little children, they took little notice and continued playing with their toys. To them, this famous figure was just another man in a military uniform. Jane curtsied to the Emperor and he remarked about her beauty as well. But the younger Betsy, she was an entirely different story.

Betsy was a young girl who was at the state between childhood and womanhood. She was young enough to enjoy Napoleon's games but old enough to laugh at his childish ways. Betsy had been taught to fear the 'Corsican Ogre' since early childhood; he was "...*a huge ogre or giant, with one large flaming red eye in the middle of his forehead, and long teeth protruding from his mouth, with which he* tore to pieces and devoured naughty little girls, especially those who did not know their lessons."[147]

It was not unusual during this time period for European children to be frightened of Napoleon, particularly English children. Like Betsy, they were raised and taught to fear him. Many children had been tormented with threats such as "*Be good or Boney will get you*" and "*Go to sleep or Boney will come.*"[148] Novelist William Thackeray discussed his own childhood fear of Napoleon when writing in *The Roundabout Papers*. He talked about his "*impression when at six years of age he visited the island [St. Helena]*. "*My black servant took me for a long walk over the rocks and hills until we reached a garden where we saw a man talking. 'That is he,' said the black man. 'That's Bonaparte. He eats three sheep a day and all the little children he can lay his hands on.'*"[149] The fear in the young of Europe towards Napoleon was real in many of their minds and hearts. To be a child and hear that the 'Corsican Ogre' was coming to stay at your home had to be something beyond frightful. Betsy possessed a sincere fear of this new visitor before his arrival. Years later, Betsy recalled her first meeting with the new prisoner of St. Helena.

> *How vividly I recollect my feelings of dread mingled with admiration, as I now first looked upon him whom I had learned to fear so much...He alighted at our house, and we all moved to the entrance to receive him. He was deadly pale, and I thought his features, though cold and immovable, and somewhat stern, were exceedingly beautiful. He seated himself on one of our cottage chairs, and after scanning our little apartment with his eagle glance, he complimented mamma on the pretty situation of the Briars. When once he began to speak, his fascinating smile and kind manner removed every vestige of the fear with which I had hitherto regarded him...The portraits of him, give a good general idea of his general features; but his smile, and the expression of his eye, could not be transmitted to canvas, and these constitute Napoleon's chief charm. His hair was dark brown, and as fine and silky as a child's, ra-*

ther too much so indeed for a man, as its very softness caused it to look thin. His teeth were even, but rather dark, and I afterwards found that this arose from his constant habit of eating liquorice, of which he always kept a supply in his waistcoat pocket.[150]

Once Napoleon took his seat in one of the cottage chairs, he turned his focus right to Betsy, who was caught quite off guard by his directness. He instructed Betsy to sit in one of the chairs next to him:

...which I did with a beating heart. He then said, "You speak French:" I replied that I did, and he asked me who had taught me. I informed him, and he put several questions to me about my studies, and more particularly concerning geography. He inquired the capitals of the different countries of Europe. "What is the capital of France?" "Paris." "Of Italy?" "Rome." "Of Russia?" "Petersburg now," I replied; "Moscow formerly." On my saying this, he turned abruptly round, and, fixing his piercing eyes full in my face, he demanded sternly, "Qui l'a brule?" [Who burned it?] When I saw the expression of his eye, and heard his changed voice, all my former terror of him returned, and I was unable to utter a syllable. I had often heard the burning of Moscow talked of, and had been present at discussions, as to whether the French or Russians were the authors of that dreadful conflagration, I therefore feared to offend him by alluding to it. He repeated the question, and I stammered, "I do not know, sir." "Oui, oui," [yes, yes] he replied, laughing violently: "Vous savez tres bien, cest moi qui l'a brule." [You know very well, It was I who burned it.] On seeing him laugh, I gained a little

> *courage, and said, "I believe, sir, the Russians burnt it to get rid of the French."[151]*

One could only guess at the facial expressions of Mr. and Mrs. Balcombe upon hearing these words that came from their daughter's mouth. The Emperor, on the other hand, burst into a laughter that was as loud as it was violent. He pinched Betsy's nose in approval and asked her to show him the garden.[152] Thus, began the sincere, innocent, childish, youthful, and playful relationship between the Emperor Napoleon Bonaparte and Miss Betsy Balcombe.

Before diving into these numerous warm, caring, and humorous events of Betsy and Napoleon, it seems best to first read the words of the middle-aged 'Betsy Balcombe' herself, which she placed in the Preface of her memoirs. It portrays the seriousness of her respect for the memory of a man who is esteemed and revered by history, and her desire not to tarnish that image with what some historians might characterize as 'childish' and 'demeaning tales' of Emperor Napoleon. Her goal was to tell of her own experiences with Napoleon through her interactions with him and to display this human side of him to the world.

> *The writer of the following pages trusts she will not be thought presumptuous in presenting them to the public. Thrown at a very early age into the society of Napoleon, and of those who composed his suite, she considers it an almost imperative duty to communicate any fact or impression, which, though uninteresting in itself, may still be worth recording as relating to him, and serving to elucidate his character. Could these recollections of the emperor have been published with out having her name appending to them, they would long ago have appeared, but feeling that the sole merit to which they could lay claim consisted in their being faithful records of him, and that if produced anonymously, there would be no guarantee for their truth; being moreover desirous to shun publicity, and unequal to the task of authorship,*

the undertaking has been postponed from time to time, and, perhaps would have been delayed still longer, but for the pressure of calamitous circumstances, which compels her to hesitate no more, but with all their imperfections on their head, to send these pages at once into the world. The authoress may compare her feelings, as she launches her little vessel on the waters, to those of Shelley, when, having exhausted his whole stock, he twisted a bank-note into the shape of a little boat, and then committing it to the stream, waited on the other side for its arrival with intense anxiety. Her ship-building powers, she fears, are as feeble, her materials as frail; but she has seen the little Paper Nautilus floating with impunity and confidence on the bosom of that mighty ocean, which has engulfed many a noble vessel: accepting the augury, she entrusts her tiny bark to the waves of public opinion, not with confidence, however, but with the timidity and hesitation, - yet is her solicitude not altogether unenlivened by the hope that it may reach its haven, if wafted by friendly breezes and favoured by propitious skies. The writer must crave indulgences for the frequent mention of herself during the narrative. The nature of the subject renders this unavoidable.

Lucia Elizabeth Abell[153]

There is no doubt that the adult Betsy worried that her recollections of Napoleon would not be viewed with credibility. Even more still, she did not feel confident in her ability to describe the events effectively for the reader and, more importantly, for history itself. Betsy kept a written journal of some of her and Napoleon's antics, but her record of all their playful times was not complete.

> *I shall never cease regretting that I did not keep a journal of all that occurred, but I was too young and too thoughtless to see the advantages of doing so; besides, I trusted to a memory naturally most retentive, thinking it would enable me at any time to recall the minutest incident concerning Napoleon. In this I deceived myself...Many of the circumstances I am about to relate, however, I did write down shortly after they occurred, and the others have been kept fresh in my memory by being repeated to friends; so that the reader of my little volume may depend on the absolute truth and fidelity of my narrative, a consideration, indeed, to which I have thought it right to sacrifice many others. I do not, then, profess to give a journal of what Napoleon daily said and did at the Briar; but the occurrences related I have inserted as nearly as possible in the order in which they took place.[154]*

As valet to Napoleon, Marchand was witness to many of the interactions that the Emperor had with the Balcombe family. He described in his journal how the two Balcombe daughters were sweet young ladies and that "*the younger, Miss Betsy, promised to become pretty. Both of them were pleasant and gracious...The Emperor sometimes went to their house to be amused by the naiveté of these young people, and to partake in a game of whist[155] that they offered him. He was moved by the great care this family took in offering their services and would have gone there more often, had he not noticed that curiosity brought to this house a few people desiring to see him.*"[156]

General Montholon also witnessed the Emperor's joy at spending time with the Balcombe family. He too saw the 'uniqueness' of Betsy. "*The Emperor frequently finished his evening in the drawing-room of Mr. Balcombe's cottage, either taking part in a game of whist, or listening to Creole anecdotes from the two sisters, who emulated each other in their efforts to be agreeable to their host...The younger of the two, who was very pretty, and even more mischievous than beautiful, felt that she could do anything and say anything with impunity, and had all the boldness of a spoiled child.*"[157] There was no doubt that Betsy was more bold and open with her approach to the Emperor than anyone else on the island. All could see this. But it was the openness and honesty of a child that intrigued the Emperor. The candid and uninhibited thoughts and words of a child both amazed and amused him.

*   *   *

The growing number of residents and visitors to St. Helena who wanted desperately to view Napoleon was a concern for Admiral Cockburn. Even though the Admiral was as accommodating to the Emperor as possible, the need to secure the prisoner and prevent any chances of rescue or escape were paramount to military courtesy to a former adversary. Therefore, restrictions had to be put into place while the Emperor was residing in the pavilion at The Briars.

The Admiral mainly placed restrictions on those who came to the island from various vessels anchored in Jamestown. Foremost, was the restriction that if Napoleon wanted to go riding, a British soldier must accompany him.[158] Though liberal with the distance surrounding The Briars that Napoleon could ride, the Emperor was angered by the impression that he was a prisoner who had to be watched. His anger at this notion would never cease.

The other restrictions stated that no one was allowed to disembark and visit either The Briars or Longwood except with Admiral Cockburn's permission. No letter, package, or any other object sent to the French suite was to reach them without strict permission from the Admiral. No one from any vessel was allowed to take possession of any package or communication from a member of the French suite.[159] Admiral Cockburn had to control what and who came near any member of the Emperor's entourage. He could not allow any possibility of escape or rescue. The Admiral was also wise enough to know that permitting Napoleon or any other member of his suite to communicate with Europe would be a public opinion war that the Emperor wanted to wage and one that the English would face difficulty in winning. For Cockburn, preventing the war of words in the public arena meant ensuring that the first battle not take place.

The restrictions imposed by the Admiral also made it difficult for members of Napoleon's entourage who remained lodged in Jamestown from seeing the Emperor when needed. For example, those Frenchmen and ladies who wished to visit Napoleon at The Briars "*were henceforth to be back in town before 9 p.m., lest they be arrested by sentries who had orders to prevent any traffic at that hour between Jamestown and The Briars.*"[160]

Napoleon's anger at the restrictions caused him to dictate his complaints to Admiral Cockburn. Even though the Emperor ordered Grand Marshal Bertrand to deliver the message to the Admiral, Bertrand did not do so out of concern for what was written. Napoleon relented and expressed his frustration with the British government.

> *You are perhaps right, Bertrand, they have condemned us – this is the anguish of death! They increasingly join outrage to injustice – what useless vexations! If I were so annoying to them, why did they not kill me? A ball through my heart or head would have sufficed, and there would at least be some courage in this crime...How is it that they do not see that they are preparing at St. Helena, with their own hands, the fate which awaits them, sooner or later, if they urge too far the patience of nations. I entered their capitals as a conqueror; what would have become of them, if I had brought thither the sentiments which they now express?...You are right, Bertrand, let these gentlemen make their complaint; mine are below by dignity and my character; I command or I am silent.*[161]

Napoleon's resentment toward his treatment as a prisoner mounted as the days continued. In one letter to Admiral Cockburn, the Emperor demanded "*news of his wife and his son – of knowing whether the latter is still alive – and protests anew against the extraordinary measures which have been adopted against him by the British government.*"[162] That same day, Napoleon dictated a formal grievance against the British government to be given to the Admiral:

> *The Emperor is not a prisoner of war. His letter, written to the Prince Regent, and communicated to Captain Maitland, before going on board the Bellerophon, sufficiently proves to the whole world the nature of his feelings, and his confidence in the treatment which he would receive under the protection of the English flag...He could have placed himself at the disposal of his father-in-law, the Emperor Francis; but from the confidence which he has always felt in the English nation, he wished for no other protection than that of Great Britain; and having renounced all public affairs, he wished to settle in no other country than one governed by fixed laws, independent of individual will...*
>
> *This policy (putting prisoners to death) would have been more humane and more confoundable to justice, than that of transporting him to a dreadful and barren rock. He could have been put to death on board the Bellerophon in Plymouth roads, which would have been by comparison, an act of benevolence... but should the British government persist in the present course of injustice toward him, he would regard it as a blessing to be put to death.*[163]

This was the war over public opinion that the Admiral knew was coming. For the most part, he would not engage. Admiral Cockburn was acting on experience with prisoners of war. With such a high valued prisoner as Napoleon Bonaparte, more thought and care had to be made in setting the restrictions. But he was also liberal in his 'freedoms' that he gave to Napoleon, particularly the circumference around The Briars that the Emperor was allowed to ride while accompanied by a British soldier. The future Governor of St. Helena who was soon to arrive to replace Admiral Cockburn would not be as kind.

The restrictions that caused the Emperor to be separated from the rest of his entourage also began the rift of jealousy that emerged amongst the officials sharing the Emperor's exile. Those in town were quite jealous of the intimacy that Las Cases shared with Napoleon by residing in the pavilion with him. Not as much animosity was directed at Marchand, for as the valet, it was expected that he would be with the Emperor during every moment. Gourgaud was especially enraged that Las Cases was chosen to be at the pavilion instead of him. But Gourgaud constantly felt that the Emperor was slighting him and it was a jealous feeling that the General would never overcome. Marchand believed that Las Cases was in a sense being favored by Napoleon at this point with good reason; *"an intimacy based on witty conversation and a very courteous nature was forming between the Emperor and himself, further strengthened by their similarity in ages. Those whose devotion had been demonstrated on the battlefield, and whose love for him was no less great, feared they would lose a part of this affection that was becoming their sole consolation on this miserable rock. Here they sought neither titles nor greatness, but a friendship whose worth everyone felt in this land of exile."*[164] As he witnessed this struggle amongst exiles, Marchand was entirely aware of his advantageous position as a valet; *"Certainly I would not have exchanged my shipboard mattress – although I felt the floor through it – for the most comfortable bed in the Porteous household."*[165]

Fighting the English for their maltreatment of their Emperor was the battle that the Frenchmen were willing to wage. The civil war amongst themselves for the attention of their Emperor had just begun.

*   *   *

During the evening on the day that Napoleon moved into the pavilion at The Briars, he joined the family in their drawing room. Due to the difficulty that Mr. and Mrs. Balcombe had with speaking French, Betsy served as the family translator, and also Napoleon's personal translator when Las Cases was unavailable.

While the family and other members of the Emperor's suite were conversing, Napoleon approached Betsy and asked if she liked music, which she answered in the affirmative. Teasing her, Napoleon said she was too young to play herself. 'Piqued' at his remark,

Betsy proclaimed that she could, and she sang and played a Scottish song to which the Emperor remarked "*was the prettiest English air he had ever heard.*"[166] Betsy replied that it was Scottish, to which Napoleon added, "*their music is vile – the worst in the world.*"[167]

> *He then inquired if I knew any French songs, and among others, "Vive Henri Quatre." I said I did not. He began to hum the air, became abstracted, and leaving his seat, marched round the room, keeping time to the song he was singing. When he [was] done, he asked me what I thought of it; and I told him I did not like it at all, for I could not make out the air. In fact, Napoleon's voice was most unmusical, nor do I think he had any ear for music; for neither on this occasion, nor in any of his subsequent attempts at singing, could I ever discover what tune it was he was executing.*[168]

Betsy had discovered Napoleon's 'poor' singing voice. It would not be the last time she would hear it. Once the Emperor knew that it amused her and made her laugh, he would sing a hundred times more throughout their friendship, just to make her laugh again. Napoleon would also imitate ladies who sang even worse than him to amuse Betsy. The Emperor would even purposely tease her by making these bad singers demonstrate their poor ability even more as he did on this same occasion.

> *A lady, friend of ours, who frequently visited us at the Briars, was extremely fond of Italian singing, which "she loved, indeed, not wisely, but too well," for her own attempts in the bravura style were the most absurd burlesque imaginable. Napoleon, however, constantly asked her to sing, and even listened with great politeness; but when she was gone, he often desired me to imitate her singing, which I did nearly as I could, and it seemed to amuse him. He used to shut his eyes and pretend he thought it was Mrs. -----, "our de-*

> *parted friend," and then pay me gravely the same compliments he would have done to her. They retired for the night shortly after my little attempt to amuse him, and thus terminated his first day at the Briars.*[169]

When the Emperor returned to the pavilion, he saw that everything had been put into place right where he had instructed Marchand to place them. Standing in the silence of the room, Napoleon gazed upon the portraits of his wife and his son, the King of Rome. This was his home, for now.

The humdrum had begun.

*   *   *

During the first couple of days that Napoleon stayed in the pavilion, the Balcombe children would come over and visit. Usually, the girls would converse with the Emperor while the two boys would sit on the floor and play with the toys they brought or with whatever Napoleon gave them. Their presence helped to break the boredom that the Emperor experienced from day to day. The little boys were around the same age as his own son and the children were much more enjoyable to be around than the stiff French officers who constantly fought amongst themselves to get close to the Emperor.

But Betsy began to warm up to Napoleon a lot more than the other children. The Emperor found her to be the most amusing as well. As the older daughter eligible for suitors, Jane was no longer the adolescent and therefore was focused on other things and did not have as much time to spend visiting the Emperor. The boys were much too young to realize the importance of this famous person who was giving them gifts and playfully pinching their ears.

For Betsy, after seeing the playful and childlike side to the Emperor, she became practically uninhibited with regards to her family's new guest, her new playmate. She was no longer afraid of Napoleon and would spend much of her time at the pavilion talking and playing games with him. Their time together would become the happiest times the Emperor would experience during his exile on St. Helena.

Not all were pleased with Napoleon spending so much playful time with the young teenager. The Emperor's officers were still competing for their master's attention and this little girl was invading their space. Whenever Gourgaud or Las Cases wanted to meet with the Emperor, they would often find him busy with Betsy engaged in some mischievous activity, teaching her French, or even playing Blind Man's Bluff with her and the rest of the Balcombe children. This irritated all of them immensely, Las Cases in particular. If Napoleon was dictating to Las Cases and his son and Betsy came in to see him, the Emperor would immediately turn his attention to the young visitor and go off and play with her. Las Cases would sit completely flabbergasted. The young Las Cases soon began to take quite a liking to her, something that Napoleon also noticed with great delight.

As it turned out, Betsy was not the only child on the island who had a fear of the 'Corsican Ogre.' Betsy's little friend, whom she referred to as Miss Legg, was also terrified of him. Being as mischievous as she was, Betsy decided to put that stated fear to the test.

> *Shortly after his arrival, a little girl, Miss Legg, the daughter of a friend, came to visit us at the Briars. The poor child had heard such terrific stories of Bonaparte, that when I told her he was coming up the lawn, she clung to me in agony of terror. Forgetting my own former fears, I was cruel enough to run out and tell Napoleon of the child's fright, begging him to come into the house. He walked up to her, and, brushing up his hair with his hand, shook his head, making horrible faces, and giving a sort of savage howl. The little girl screamed so violently, that mamma was afraid she would go into hysterics, and took her out of the room. Napoleon laughed a good deal at the idea of his being such a bugbear, and would hardly believe me when I told him that I had stood in the same dismay of him. When I made this confession, he tried to frighten me as he had poor little Miss Legg, by brushing up his*

> *hair, and distorting his features; but he looked more grotesque than horrible, and I only laughed at him. He then (as a last resource) tried the howl, but was equally unsuccessful, and seemed, I thought, a little provoked that he could not frighten me. He said the howl was Cossack,[170] and it certainly was barbarous enough for any thing.[171]*

During the evening hours, the Emperor often enjoyed taking exploring walks around the valley and hills surrounding The Briars.[172] Betsy and her other siblings would accompany Napoleon and one or more members of his entourage, though these members were often annoyed by the constant presence of Betsy. The Emperor's suite would become annoyed because the children infringed on the attention the individual member would receive from the Emperor.

On one occasion, the group decided to cut across a meadow where some cows were grazing. Spotting the intruders, one particular cow took a dislike of the Emperor.

> *...she saw our party, put her head down and (I believe) her tail up, and advanced a pas de charge against the emperor. He made a skillful and rapid retreat, and leaping nimbly over a wall, placed this rampart between himself and the enemy. But General Gourgaud valiantly stood his ground, and, drawing his sword, threw himself between his sovereign and the cow, exclaiming, "This is the second time I have saved the emperor's life." Napoleon laughed heartily when he heard the General's boast, and said, "He ought to have put himself in the position to repel cavalry." I told the cow appeared tranquillized, and stopped the moment he disappeared, and he continued to laugh and said, "She wished to save the English government the expense and trouble of keeping him.[173]*

Following a few days in the presence of the Emperor, Betsy noticed that Napoleon developed a pattern in his daily habits and mannerisms. To her own amazement, Betsy began to feel genuinely comfortable around the Emperor.

> *The emperor's habits, during the time he stayed with us, were very simple and regular. His usual hour for getting up was eight, and he seldom took any thing but a cup of coffee until one; he dined at nine, and retired about eleven to his own rooms. His manner was so unaffectedly kind and amiable, that in a few days I felt perfectly at ease in his society, and looked upon him more as a companion of my own age, than as the mighty warrior at whose name "the world grew pale." His spirits were very good, and he was at time almost boyish in his love of mirth and glee, not unmixed sometimes with a tinge of malice...Napoleon seemed to have no penchant for the pleasures of the table...When he was finished, he would abruptly push away his chair from the table, and quit the diningroom, apparently glad it was over...A few days after his arrival, he invited my sister and myself to dine with him, and began quizzing the English for their fondness for rosbif and plum pudding. I accused the French, in return, of living on frogs; and, running into the house, I brought him a caricature of a long, lean Frenchman, with his mouth open, his tongue out, and a frog on the tip of it, ready to jump down his throat: underneath was written, "A Frenchman's dinner!" He laughed at my impertinence, and pinched my ear, as he often did when he was amused, and sometimes when a little provoked at my "espieglerie."*[174]

This comfort and ease that Betsy felt around the Emperor was something that he wanted. When it came to children, Napoleon was at ease himself. His playful and childlike ways flowed directly from his heart and he wanted children to be just as open with him. This was Napoleon as the 'Italian grandfather.' He was always amused by them. Napoleon would often comment about how the heart, mind, and stomach of a child were always pure and honest.

These aspects of Napoleon's character are what led him to encourage Betsy to return the playfulness and mischief. Teasing her and purposely annoying her in a jovial manner led Betsy to throw aside her strict British manners and engage in 'play' as well. Age, rank, stature, rumors, and past history had no meaning when it came to the innocent, kind, humorous, and grandfatherly relationship between Betsy and Napoleon. He gave her permission to interrupt him whenever she wanted regardless of what he was doing, which she gladly put into practice immediately.

While staying in the pavilion, Napoleon "*had complete privacy; a key locked the little gate across the path, and not even the children dared enter without his permission. By his direction, she was exempt and he welcomed her at all times, even though awakened from sleep by her calling him to unlock the gate.*"[175]

Betsy would often times walk into the room during his dictation sessions and either sit and listen until he was finished, or, more usually, he would instantly cease what he was doing and go act in some innocent 'mischief' with Betsy. During the times when Betsy would sit and listen to him dictate, the Emperor would be in one of two positions: pacing the room, or leaning up against the mantle of the fireplace. When at the mantle, Betsy noticed that the Emperor had the habit of shrugging his right shoulder, as he would dictate. A couple of times she would quietly walk up to him and gently place her hand upon his arm, which would instantly cause the movement to end. The Emperor would then give her a warm smile and a pinch on the nose or ear.[176]

*   *   *

Count Las Cases' son Emmanuel began to acquire quite a fondness for Betsy, although she found him rather 'repulsive.' This was a fact that the Emperor knew all too well. Napoleon would tease Betsy constantly about Emmanuel until she would become extremely annoyed and lash out at the Emperor, which would cause him to laugh even more. On one occasion, Betsy got even with the Emperor for putting young Las Cases up to playing a trick on her.

> "Le petit Las Cases," as he called Count Las Cases' son, formed one of the party that day. He was then a lad of fourteen, and the emperor was fond of quizzing me about him, and telling me I should be his wife. Nothing enraged me so much; I could not bear to be considered such a child, and particularly at that moment, for there was a ball in prospect, to which I had hopes papa would allow me to go, and I knew that his objection would be founded on my being too young. Napoleon, seeing my annoyance, desired young Las Cases to kiss me, and he held both my hands whilst the little page saluted me. I did all in my power to escape, but in vain. The moment, however, that my hands were at liberty, I boxed le petit Las Cases' ears most thoroughly. But I determined to be revenged on Napoleon, and in descending to the cottage to play whist, an opportunity presented itself which I did not allow to escape. There was no internal communication between the part occupied by the emperor and the rest of the house, and the path leading down was very steep and very narrow. There being barely room for one person to pass at a time, Napoleon walked first, Las Cases next, then his son, and lastly, my sister Jane. I allowed the party to proceed very quietly until I was left about ten yards behind; and then I ran with all my force on my sister Jane, - she fell with extended hands on the little page, he was thrown upon his father, and the grand chamberlain, to his dismay, was pushed against the emperor, who, although the shock was somewhat diminished by the time it

> reached him, had still some difficulty, from the steepness of the path, in preserving his footing. I was in ecstasies at the confusion I had created, and exulted in the revenge I had taken for the kiss, but I was soon obliged to change my note of triumph. Las Cases was thunderstruck at the insult offered to the emperor, and became perfectly furious at my uncontrollable laughter. He seized me by the shoulders, and pushed me violently on the rocky bank. It was now my turn to be enraged. I burst into tears of passion, and, turning to Napoleon, cried out, "Oh! sir, he has hurt me." "Never mind," replied the emperor, "ne pleurs pas[177] - I will hold him while you punish him." And a good punishing he got; I boxed the little man's ears until he begged for mercy; but I would show him none; and at length Napoleon let him go, telling him to run, and that if he could not run faster than I, he deserved to be beaten again. He immediately started off as fast as he could, and I after him, Napoleon clapped his hands and laughing immoderately at our race round the lawn. Las Cases never liked me after this adventure, and used to call me a rude hoyden.[178]

This was the human side of Napoleon. No military protocol, imperial march or salutes, not when it came to children, particularly Betsy. This was Napoleon as the man, the father, and the playful grandfather as seen through the eyes of a child. The more time she spent with him, the more comfortable she became. Betsy increasingly began to view Napoleon not as the Majestic Emperor, but as someone of her own age: a playful and humorous companion.

> I never met with any one who bore childish liberties so well as Napoleon. He seemed to enter into every sort of mirth of fun with glee of a child, and though I have often tried his patience severely, I

> *never knew him to lose his temper or fall back upon his rank or age, to shield himself from the consequences of his own familiarity, or of his indulgence to me. I looked upon him, indeed, when with him, almost as a brother or companion of my own age, and all the cautions I received, and my own resolutions to treat him with more respect and formality, were put to flight the moment I came within the influence of his arch smile and laugh. If I approached him more gravely than usual, and with a more sedate step and subdued tone, he would, perhaps, begin by saying, "Eh bien, qu'as tu, Mademoiselle Betsee? Has le petit Las Cases proved inconstant? If he have, - bring him to me;" or some other playful speech, which either pleased or teased me, and made me at once forget all my previous determinations to behave prettily.*[179]

Out of this informal nature that their relationship began to take, Betsy used a nickname for the Emperor that was used by many English children, but one that Napoleon had never heard. When young Alexander Balcombe was playing on the Emperor's lap with a deck of cards, he took one of them that pictured a king and placed it directly in front of the Emperor's face and said, "*See, Bony, this is you.*" Betsy explained that this was an abbreviation for 'Bonaparte.' But Las Cases interpreted the word literally and Napoleon laughed and exclaimed that he was far from being 'bony.' Nevertheless, 'Bony' would be the name that Betsy would call him from then on, and the Emperor loved it.[180]

In her memoirs, Betsy described how gentle the Emperor's hands appeared. She described his hand as "*the fattest and prettiest in the world; his knuckles dimpled like those of a baby, his fingers taper and beautifully formed, and his nails perfect. I have often admired its symmetry, and once told him it did not look large and strong enough to wield a sword.*"[181] As the discussion turned to swords, one of the members of Napoleon's suite removed his sword to show the 'blood of Englishmen' to the young girl. This earned the man a stern reprimand from the Emperor who *"desired him to sheath it, telling him it was bad taste to boast, particularly before ladies."*[182]

In exchange for teaching Napoleon English, the Emperor would help Betsy with her French, particularly the pronunciations and writing of the language. Mr. Balcombe was very strict with his daughters when it came to their studies and always made sure that their work was completed on time and without mistakes. Here again, was a perfect opportunity for Napoleon to tease Betsy.

> *My father was very strict in enforcing our doing a French translation every day, and Napoleon would often look over them and correct their faults. One morning I felt more than usually averse to performing this task, and when Napoleon arrived at the cottage, and asked whether the translation was ready for him, I had not even begun it. When he saw this, he took up the paper and walked down the lawn with it to my father, who was preparing to mount his horse to ride to the valley, exclaiming as he approached, "Balcombe, voila le theme de Mademoiselle Betsee. Qu'elle a bien travaille;"[183] holding up at the same time the blank sheet of paper, and my name being mentioned by the laughing emperor, that he wished me to be scolded, and entering into the plot, he pretended to be very angry, and threatened if I did not finish my translation before he returned to dinner, I should be severely punished. He then rode off, and Napoleon left me, laughing at my sullen and mortified air.*[184]

Later on, yet again, Betsy would seek her revenge on the Emperor, and be successful. She waited until the perfect moment and caught him off-guard. As they sat out on the lawn, Napoleon showed his sword and case to Betsy and explained to her what it was made of and all the places he had worn it in battle. Betsy found the sword to be one of the most costly and elegant weapons she had ever seen.

I requested Napoleon to allow me to examine it more closely; and then a circumstance which I had been much piqued at the emperor's conduct (French lesson), flashed across me. The temptation was irresistible, and I determined to punish him for what he had done. I drew the blade out quickly from the scabbard, and began to flourish it over his head, making passes at him, the emperor retreating, until at last I fairly pinned him up in the corner; I kept telling him all the time that he had better say his prayers, for I was going to kill him. My exulting cries at last brought my sister to Napoleon's assistance. She scolded me violently, and she said she would inform my father if I did not instantly desist; but I only laughed at her, and maintained by post, keeping the emperor at bay until my arm dropped from sheer exhaustion. I can fancy I see the figure of the grand chamberlain (Las Cases) now, with his spare form and parchment visage, glowing with fear for the emperor's safety, and indignation at the insult I was offering him. He looked as if he could have annihilated me on the spot, but he had felt the weight of my hand before on his ears, and prudence dictated to him to let me alone. When I resigned my sword, Napoleon took hold of my ear, which had been bored only the day before, and pinched it, giving me great pain. I called out, and he then took hold of my nose, which he pulled heartily, but quite in fun; his good humour never left him during the whole scene.[185]

Some of the most humorous times between the Emperor and Betsy would occur when they would play card games, particularly one called 'whist.' Napoleon would often place bets with her as to who would win, which Betsy took rather seriously. To intentionally tease and annoy her, the Emperor would constantly cheat so that she would catch him. Each time Betsy would get enraged and yell at him to stop. But Napoleon would never admit to what he was doing, which angered her even more.

During one of these card games, the topic arose concerning the ball that was to be held by Admiral Cockburn at Plantation House, his residence.[186] All of the high-ranking British officers and their wives would be invited, along with the entire French suite, including the Emperor. But Napoleon outright refused, desiring not to be a spectacle. But Betsy, on the other hand, wanted desperately to attend the event. She wanted so much to be grown up and dress in elegant clothing like the other Frenchwomen at Longwood that she had come to admire over the past few weeks.

But, Betsy's father would not hear of such a thing. Mr. Balcombe believed that she was too young to attend such a formal event. When she learned of his decision, Betsy went to the Emperor to see if he would talk to her father to allow her to go, to which Napoleon gladly agreed. With his usual wit and charm, the Emperor had succeeded in winning Mr. Balcombe's approval.[187]

After Napoleon won Mr. Balcombe's permission, Betsy asked the Emperor to play cards. Once they sat at the table, Napoleon began dealing the hand. Betsy told him that she wanted to show him her new dress that she was going to wear to the ball. She ran up to her room and brought it down for him to see. When she returned with the dress, Napoleon said that it was "*very pretty.*"[188] Betsy laid the dress upon the sofa and sat to play cards.

Being that the game required four players, Betsy's sister, Jane, was a partner with the Emperor, and *le petit* Las Cases "*fell to Betsy's lot.*"[189] During the beginning of the game, the group had been playing for sugarplums, but typical of Napoleon, he raised the stakes. The Emperor said, "*Mademoiselle Betsee, I will bet you a Napoleon*[190] *on the game.*"[191] Betsy only had a pagoda that had been presented to her, which as she explained it, "*made up the sum of all my worldly riches,*" and was the only thing she possessed that would equal a gold Napoleon.[192] She agreed to place the bet.

The emperor agreed to this, and we commenced playing. He seemed determined to terminate this day of espieglerie[193] as he had begun it. Peeping under his cards as they were dealt to him, he endeavoured whenever he got an important one, to draw off my attention, and then slily held it up for my sister to see. I soon discovered this, and calling him to order, told him he was cheating, and if he continued to do so, I would not play. At last he revoked intentionally, and at the end of the game tried to mix the cards together to prevent his being discovered, but I started up, and seizing hold of his hands, I pointed out to him and the others what he had done. He laughed until the tears ran out of his eyes, and he declared he had played fair, but that I had cheated, and I should pay him the pagoda; and when I persisted that he had revoked, he said I was mechante[194] and a cheat; and catching up my ball dress from off the sofa, he ran out of the room with it, and up the pavilion, leaving me in terror lest he should crush and spoil all my pretty roses. I instantly set off in chase of him, but he was too quick, and darting through the marques, he reached the inner room and locked himself in. I then commenced a series of the most pathetic remonstrances and entreaties, both in English and French, to persuade him to restore my frock, but in vain; he was inexorable, and I had the mortification of hearing him laugh at what I thought the most touching of my appeals. I was obliged to return without it.[195]

Betsy was completely devastated. She waited out front of the pavilion for a long time, but the Emperor refused to answer her tearful calls or to come out at all. As it grew late, Betsy returned to the house. During the evening, the Emperor sent word to her through a message that he intended to keep the dress and that she might make up her mind not to go to the ball at all. At hearing this news Betsy explained that she "*lay awake half the night, and at last cried myself to sleep, hoping he would relent in the morning.*"[196]

But Betsy's hopes were again dashed the following day, for the messages that she sent to the Emperor the entire day were answered with statements that he either was sleeping or ill. She knew he was just doing this to tease her, though it did very little to comfort her disappointment at not being able to wear the new dress to the ball. Betsy had lost all hope of the Emperor returning her dress.[197]

When the time had come for the group to depart for Plantation House for the ball, and since the Emperor had not returned the dress, Betsy dressed herself in an older one and situated herself on top of her horse.

> *...to my great joy, I saw the emperor running down the lawn to the gate with my dress. "Here, Miss Betsee, I have brought your dress; I hope you are a good girl now, and that you will like the ball; and mind that you dance with Gourgaud." General Gourgaud was not very handsome, and I had some childish feud with him. I was all delight at getting back my dress, and still more pleased to find my roses were not spoiled. He had ordered them to be arranged and pulled out, in case any might have been crushed the night before. Napoleon walked by the side of our horses until he came to the end of the bridle-road which led to the Briars.*[198]

To Betsy, the Emperor would not go unpunished for this little trick. Earlier during his time at The Briars, Betsy discovered Napoleon's sincere distaste for ugly women. She would constantly beg him to meet a particular woman or group of women, knowing full well that he would find them ugly. Betsy would relish in observing his annoyance.

During one occasion, Betsy came to the gate and called for the Emperor. "*He came up to the door, and asked me what I wanted. I said, "Let me in, and you shall know." He replied, "No, tell me first what it is, and then you shall come in."*[199]

Betsy was then forced to reveal that she had a beautiful woman waiting in the house who wished to be introduced to him. After stating that he was unwell, Betsy told him that she would be very disappointed. Fearing she was another ugly woman, Napoleon asked if she was like the one he had met before, to which Betsy assured him that she was not. Agreeing to Betsy's proposition, the Emperor opened the door and was about to exit as Betsy raced into the pavilion and snatched up some of his papers that he had just dictated.

> *"Now," I said, "for your ill nature in keeping me so long at the door I shall keep these, and then I shall find out all your secrets." He looked a little alarmed when he saw the papers in my hand, and told me to put them down instantly; but I refused, and set off round the garden, flourishing my trophies. At last he told me, if I did not give them up he would not be my friend, and I relinquished them. I then took hold of the emperor's hand, for fear he should escape, and led him to the house...*[200]

To the Emperor's amazement and delight, the woman that Betsy introduced to him was very attractive and they conversed for quite a while.

Betsy and her siblings would often take walks with the Emperor in the garden of The Briars and also the immediate surrounding area. Though a guest in their home, Napoleon was still a prisoner of the English and could not venture far. At the same time, it was well known down in Jamestown that the Emperor was temporarily residing in the pavilion of the home. Often times, people from town and visitors to the island would make their way up to The Briars to catch a glimpse of the famous figure. This irritated the Emperor immensely and he did everything in his power to prevent from being viewed as a caged animal. In her memoirs, Betsy recounted a time when Napoleon literally ran from a crowd of strangers looking to see him.

> *One day...we were walking with him down the Pomergranate Walk which led to the garden, when suddenly the voices of strangers were heard, and he began running away as fast as he could towards the garden gate, but found it locked from within. The strangers' steps approached nearer and nearer, and Napoleon had nothing left for it, but to jump over the garden fence, which, unfortunately, was defended on the top by the prickly pear, a plant covered with thorns. When he found himself on the top, there he stuck, the thorny bush preventing his extricating himself. At length, after a considerable struggle, torn clothes, and with his legs much scratched, the discomfited emperor descended on the garden side of the hedge, before the advancing company surprised him. The wounds he received that day were of no trifling nature, and it required a little of Dr. O'Meara's skill to extract the thorns which the prickly pears had deposited in his imperial person.*[201]

*   *   *

Though most of the episodes that occurred between Betsy and the Emperor were playful and humorous, there were others that took on a more serious and emotional tone. During these times, Betsy would uncover the emotions that hid behind the imperial façade.

Beneath the alabaster exterior was not only the mind and heart of a human being but a heart that was emotionally wounded as well.

There was an old slave of the Balcombe's by the name of Toby to whom the Emperor took a great liking. Betsy explained to Napoleon that he had "*a girl just my age, who is very like me!*"[202] She sought to have the Emperor restore Toby to his children by hoping he would intervene and win the poor slave his freedom. Napoleon decided to do just that and approached Mr. Balcombe about purchasing Toby's freedom in the hopes of returning him to Africa. The Admiral agreed to petition the English government for permission but did not receive a response from his superiors in London on the subject.[203] Due to the lack of permission, Napoleon was denied the request.

Out of Napoleon's sincere interest in the slave, Toby took quite a liking to Napoleon and referred to him as the "*Good Gentleman.*"[204] Betsy recorded that Toby "*retained afterwards the most grateful sense of Napoleon's kindness, and was never more highly gratified than when employed in gathering the choicest fruit, and arranging the most beautiful bouquets, to be sent to Longwood, to "that good man, Bony" as he called the emperor.*"[205] Wherever Napoleon went on St. Helena, he was known for giving money to any slave that come in contact with him.[206]

While staying at The Briars, Betsy began to notice that whenever the Emperor was in the presence of her mother, he would often gaze upon her at great length and appear as though sadness and grief had overcome him. The emotion just painfully hung from his face. After witnessing this once again, Betsy asked him one day why he would look at her mother in such a way. Napoleon explained that Mrs. Balcombe held such a striking likeness to Josephine that it was one in the likes that he had never seen before. The Emperor said, "*she was the most truly feminine woman that he had ever known.*"[207] He often referred to her as being the most amiable, elegant, charming, and affable woman in the world.[208]

Upon hearing these words, Madame Bertrand produced a miniature of Josephine and presented it to the Emperor. "*He gazed at it with the greatest emotion for a considerable amount of time without speaking. At last, he exclaimed it was the most perfect likeness he had ever seen of her...*"[209] Napoleon asked Madame Bertrand if he could keep the painting to which she gladly agreed. He kept it with him until his death. Betsy explained in her memoirs that in terms of Josephine, "*her memory appeared to be idolized by him, and he was never weary of dwelling on her sweetness of disposition and the grace of her movements.*"[210] That evening, Betsy recorded that the Emperor appeared in mournful reflection, and was still more melancholy and dejected for the rest of the evening.[211]

One incident stood out among the others when it came to eliciting emotion in the Emperor. It was also an incident that caused the innocently playful Betsy to be severely punished by her father.

Betsy received a toy from some family in England and presented it to the Emperor. It was a caricature of Napoleon "*in the act of climbing a ladder, each step he ascended represented some vanquished country; at length he was seated astride upon the world. It was a famous toy, and by a dexterous trick Napoleon appeared on the contrary side tumbling down head over heels, and after a perilous descent, alighting on St. Helena.*"[212]

Napoleon became very silent and did nothing but stare at the toy. Not only did all of Europe mock him, but so did her children as well. Betsy, realizing what she had mistakenly done, pleaded for him to forgive her. The Emperor quietly excused himself and took refuge in the pavilion. Betsy was truly upset over what she had done and "*was guilty of every description of mad action, though without any intention of being unkind.*"[213]

But when Mr. Balcombe discovered what had occurred, he was not at all forgiving of the disrespect committed by his daughter. As was his usual punishment for his children, one in which Betsy had experienced before, Mr. Balcombe placed her in the dark cellar of The Briars to remain there for one week, only to emerge to be provided with sanitary means and for sleep. As Betsy explained, it was not an easy punishment to bear.

> *I did not soon forget that punishment, for the excavation swarmed with rats, that leaped about me on all sides. I was half dead with horror, and should most certainly have been devoured alive by the vermin, had I not in despair seized a bottle of wine, and dashed it amongst my assailants; finding that I succeeded in occasioning a momentary panic, I continued to diminish the pile of claret near me, and kept my enemies at bay.*[214]

The Emperor was mortified at learning of Betsy's punishment and went to Mr. Balcombe in an attempt to win her freedom. But for once, the Imperial endorsement failed to produce the intended result.[215] After leaving her father, Napoleon went round the house to the window of the cellar in which Betsy was housed. Seeing that she had been crying, Napoleon tried to make her smile. Betsy explained that he "*was much amused by my relation of the battle with the rats; he said, he had been startled by observing a huge one jumping out of his hat, as he was in the act of putting it on...and he generally succeeded in making me laugh, by mimicking my dolorous countenance.*"[216] The Emperor returned every day and kept Betsy company to pass the time of her punishment.

The tables had now been turned: Napoleon was comforting the new prisoner on St. Helena.

*   *   *

It did not take long after Betsy's 'release' for the pair to return to their regular antics. Not soon after this incident, an older gentleman nicknamed 'Old Huff'[217] had committed suicide. He had been the tutor of Betsy's younger brother, Alexander. Only days following his suicide, Betsy made the grave mistake of informing the Emperor that she was terrified of ghosts. That was all Napoleon needed to know.

> *I had amongst many other follies a terror of ghosts, and this weakness was well known to the emperor, who, for a considerable time after the suicide of poor Huff, used to frighten me nearly into fits. Every night, just before my hour of retiring to my room, he would call out, "Miss Betsee, ole Huff, ole Huff." The misery of those nights I shall never forget...One evening, when my mother, my sister and myself were quietly sitting on the porch of the cottage, enjoying the coolness of the night breeze, suddenly we heard a noise, and turning round beheld a figure in white – how I screamed. We were then greeted with a low gruff laugh, which my mother instantly knew*

> to be the emperor's. She turned the white covering, and underneath appeared the black visage of a little servant of ours, whom Napoleon had instigated to frighten Miss Betsee, while he was himself a spectator of the effect of his trick.[218]

Napoleon took great enjoyment in playing with Betsy and the rest of her siblings. He loved to make her two little brothers laugh. Betsy described how one of Napoleon's servants was quite the odd character, but he was always creative at making little toys that would amuse the children.

> Napoleon would often send for the scaramouch to amuse my brothers, who were infinitely delighted with his tricks and buffooneries. Sometimes he constructed balloons, which were inflated and sent up amidst the acclamations of the whole party. One day he contrived to harness four mice to a small carriage, but the poor little animals were so terrified that he could not get them to move, and after many ineffectual attempts, my brothers entreated the emperor to interfere. Napoleon told them to pinch the tails of the two leaders, and when they started the others would follow. This he did, and immediately the whole four scampered off, to our great amusement, Napoleon enjoying the fun as much as any of us, and delighted with the extravagant glee of my two brothers.[219]

One of the most enjoyable pastimes for the Emperor and Betsy was playing 'Blind Man's Bluff.'[220] They would play until the Emperor was out of breath and sweating profusely. To the irritation of his valets, the Emperor would return to the pavilion covered in dirt and grass in some of his best clothes. But as in all of their other mischievous games, Napoleon was known to cheat constantly.

During one particular game, Napoleon took a handkerchief out of his pocket, tied it around Betsy's eyes, and asked if she could see him.

"I cannot see you," I replied; but a faint gleam of light did certainly escape through one corner, making my darkness a little less visible. Napoleon then taking his hat, waved it suddenly before my eyes, and the shadow and the wind it made, startled me, and I drew back my head: "Ah, leetle monkee," he exclaimed in English, "you can see pretty well." He then proceeded to tie another handkerchief over the first, which completely excluded every ray of light. I was then placed in the middle...and the game began. The emperor commenced by creeping stealthily up to me, and giving my nose a very sharp twinge; I knew it was he both from the act itself and from his footstep. I darted forward, and very nearly succeeded in catching him, but bounding actively away, he eluded my grasp. I then groped about, and, advancing again, he this time took hold of my ear and pulled it. I stretched out my hands instantly, and in the exultation of the moment screamed out, "I have got you – I have got you now, you shall be blind-folded!" but to my mortification it proved to be my sister, under the cover of whom Napoleon had advanced, stretching his hand over her head. We then recommenced, the emperor saying that I had named the wrong person, I must continue blindfolded. He teased me and quizzed me about my mistake, and bantered me in every possible way, eluding at the same time, with the greatest dexterity, all my endeavours to catch him. At last when the fun was growing "fast and furious," and the uproar was at its height, it was announced that some one desired an audience of the emperor, and to my great annoyance, as I had set my heart on catching him and insisting on his being blindfolded...[221]

How amazing to read the words and memories of a child; the Great Napoleon Bonaparte playing a game of Blind Man's Bluff. The man who sent terror into the minds of all the heads of Europe, who was banished to a castaway rock, took to laughter and enjoyment from the smiles and joy of children. To escape the sadness of exile, he was able to turn to the hearts of the young.

But the time had come. Napoleon was to leave The Briars.

*   *   *

Admiral Cockburn, along with some of his officers, made a visit to the Emperor at The Briars to give Napoleon a message; Longwood was complete.

The Emperor responded that he was unwilling to move on such short notice and especially if Longwood was still tainted with the smell of fresh paint. Even with the Admiral's assurance that it had been thoroughly aired out, Napoleon stated that he would send the Grand Marshal to inspect the completed residence. The Admiral vigorously insisted that Napoleon would be moving to Longwood on his orders, and no one else's. Not only was Admiral Cockburn asserting his authority, but he also did not want Napoleon still lodged at The Briars' pavilion when the new Governor arrived to St. Helena.[222] There was no choice left; the Emperor would go to Longwood.

Betsy, on the other hand, did not want to accept what she had just heard.

> *I was crying bitterly, and he came up and said, "You must not cry, Mademoiselle Betsee; you must come and see me next week, and very often." I told him that depended on my father. He turned to him and said, "Balcombe, you must bring Misses Jane and Betsee to see me next week, eh? When will you ride up to Longwood?" My father promised he would, and kept his word. He asked where mamma was, and I said she desired her kind regards to the emperor, and regretted not being able to see him before his departure, as she*

> *was ill in bed. "I will go and see her," and up stairs he darted before we had time to tell my mother of his approach. He seated himself on the bed, and expressed his regret at hearing she was unwell. He was warm in his acknowledgements of her attention to him, and said, he would have preferred staying altogether at the Briars, if they would have permitted him. He then presented my mother with a gold snuff-box, and begged she would give it to my father as a mark of his friendship. He gave me a beautiful little bon-bonniere, which I had often admired, and said you can give it as a gage d'amour to le petit Las Cases. I burst into tears and ran out of the room.*[223]

On December 10th, 1815, almost two months after his arrival at St. Helena, when the dreaded moment finally came for the Emperor to depart, Betsy could not stand to see him go. Her friend, her playmate was leaving. Betsy did not care that he was an Emperor, a Frenchman, or even a prisoner. To her, he was a loving friend who cast aside his majestic ways and enjoyed the same mischievous moments that she did. She loved knowing that she could merely walk to the pavilion and he was there dictating, napping, conversing, and most importantly, waiting to play. The humorous grandfather figure was now leaving and her heart was breaking. She remained in her bedroom while the rest of the family was outside to bid farewell. But there still remained that small tugging in her heart that made her take one more look.

> *I stationed myself at the window from which I could see his departure, but my heart was too full to look on him as he left us, and throwing myself on the bed, I cried bitterly for a long time.*[224]

Napoleon was now traveling to where he would die; Longwood.

I am an Emperor in my own circle, and will be so as long as I live... Europe will hereafter judge of my treatment, and the shame of it will fall on the English nation.

Napoleon

Remember, you must always meet your enemies with a bold face, otherwise they think they are feared, and that gives them confidence.

Napoleon

Chapter 4

"This Is My Sure Test"

With all the goodbyes having been said at The Briars, the Emperor, his entourage, Admiral Cockburn, and his officers made their way down the road for Longwood. The house was situated on a higher point than the pavilion where Napoleon lived these past two months. The area was quite rocky with little vegetation and "*pockets of soil spread by time gave birth to a few, stunted trees and patches of greenery*" which provided a little shade for the weary.[225] The wind dominated the countryside. The house was constructed on a hill, which consisted of layers upon layers of cooled lava. This prohibited a cellar from being constructed, thus creating an atmosphere inside of Longwood that was either cool and damp, or extremely humid.[226]

As they continued on, the group passed Alarm House, which housed the military secretary to the Governor and was located three kilometers from Longwood on the road into Jamestown. For security purposes, "*a guard post was established nearby, as well as the cannon that sounded at sunrise, at sunset, and whenever a ship approached. A signaling system with flags allowed the soldiers to communicate with the governor through relays at Rupert's Hill and Ladder Hill.*"[227] If a blue flag was raised, it was to mean that the Emperor had escaped. In the fields on both sides of the road were the encampments of the 53rd Regiment numbering over five companies and close to 1000 soldiers all settled into an area which became known as Deadwood Camp. It is interesting to contemplate the need for 1000 troops to prevent the escape of one man.

When the group came closer to Longwood, a drumbeat sounded, and the British soldiers lined the road under arms. Ironically, as Napoleon first approached the drive to the house, his horse reared as if sensing danger and wanting to turn around and go no further.[228] The Emperor was entering the final door to his last 'prison cell.'

After dismounting, the Admiral presented Longwood to the Emperor and gave him a tour of the residence. Napoleon remained silent throughout the whole ordeal and retired to his room upon the moment Admiral Cockburn departed. The Emperor could see that the prison walls were slowing closing around him and his movements were going to become more limited. Marchand felt that "*with the way things were going, it was easy to perceive the cooling taking place between them, and it was to be feared that surveillance at Longwood would become more stringent.*"[229]

The only thing that appeared to breathe some life into the Emperor that fateful day was the hot bath that Marchand had drawn for him. The Emperor, known for always taking hot baths, had not been able to take one at The Briars because there had been no tub for him to do so. But upon seeing the one that had been prepared for him by his beloved valet filled him with happiness and he jumped into the bath "*with childish joy.*"[230]

In regards to Longwood itself, the Emperor had the home to himself and his servants. Another building was being constructed attached to Longwood that would house Gourgaud, Las Cases and his son, Montholon and his family, Dr. O'Meara, and a duty officer. Grand Marshal Bertrand and his family lived in a home called Hutt's Gate, which was situated close to Longwood. This provided for Bertrand's larger family and also served as a requirement of the Emperor's Imperial etiquette. To have an audience with Napoleon, a request had to go through the Grand Marshal. Therefore, his location at Hutt's Gate served as a "buffer" between the Emperor and the English. But the absence of Grand Marshal Bertrand from Napoleon's inner circle at Longwood annoyed the Emperor. When Bertrand told the Emperor of his intentions of residing at Hutt's Gate, Napoleon responded, "*Do whatever you wish…Montholon will lodge with me.*"[231] This certainly did not help in calming the growing jealousy and animosity that existed among the Emperor's officers.

In his memoirs, Marchand provided a detailed description of Longwood. In Longwood proper, the Emperor's bedroom consisted of two small rooms,

> *each ten feet square; one of them was to serve as his study. In each of them, a small field bed was set up; the walls of both were decorated with nankeen bordered with a paper rose edging, and they were lit by two small windows known in France as the "guillotine"*

> *type. The view from these two rooms looked out upon the camp about a mile away. The window curtains were of white calico; a carpet in both rooms concealed the severely rough flooring. In the room fashioned into the bedroom, there was a small fireplace made entirely of wood painted grey; a small iron grate inside indicated that coal was to be burnt in it. The fireplace was decorated with a small wooden frame with gilt columns, and a small mirror about eighteen inches tall and fifteen inches wide was attached above it. The two rooms were nine feet high, and were furnished with a few chairs and armchairs with caned backs painted green, a dresser, a settee, and a table covered with green cloth, to be used as a desk. I decorated the mantelpiece with torches taken from the Emperor's travel kit, a gilt cup and its saucer, and in incense burner made of the same metal. On either side of the mirror I hung two small portraits of the King of Rome; above them hung Frederick the Great's alarm clock on one side and the Emperor's watch on the other. To the left of the fire-place, I placed the Emperor's travel kit on a small table, opened it in order to decorate the room a little more, and hung over it a third portrait of the King of Rome..."*[232]

Marchand and the other servants did their best to make the rooms most comfortable for the Emperor. Though it was not the Tuileries

Palace or that of St. Cloud, Longwood would have to suffice as the 'royal court.'

In terms of the French suite that accompanied Napoleon to Longwood and were in charge of the residence, their names and positions in the household were as follows:

Servants of the Chamber

Marchand	1st Valet de Chambre
St. Denis (Called Ali)	Valet de Chambre
Noverraz	Valet de Chambre
Santini	Usher

Servants of Livery

Archambault, Senior	Groom
Archambault, Junior	Groom
Gentilini	Footman

Servants for the Table

Cipriani	Maitre d'hotel
Pierron	Butler
Lepage	Cook
Rousseau	Steward[233]

These men were entirely dedicated to the Emperor and were with him at every moment of the day in every capacity needed of them. He, in turn, relied heavily upon them and was quite grateful to them for their sincerity and loyalty. Las Cases recorded that Napoleon "*never forgets services performed for him...The Emperor is sincere in his attachments, without making a show of what he feels.*"[234]

Valet St. Denis felt the same strong attachments to the Emperor explaining that he had a really kind heart. "*In his household at St. Helena he was an excellent father of a family in the midst of his* children. His bad humor never lasted long; it disappeared a short time after it had shown itself. If he was in the wrong, he would soon come and pull the ear of the one on whom his anger had fallen, or give him a slap on the back. After saying a few words relating to his irritation he would lavish the most agreeable expressions on him – "My son – My boy – My child." What would not one do for such a man, for such a master?"[235]

Napoleon also cared about their well-being, particularly if they were sick. St. Denis described that once when Marchand was ill Napoleon

> had his bed moved into the middle of the dining room so that he would be cooling instead of the damp and hot loft that he slept in. "Every morning the Emperor did not fail to ask how he was as well as during the day. When he went to walk in the gardens, if he happened to pass through the dining room, he would come up to the sick man's bed and say to him, "Well, Mam'zelle Marchand, is the princess coming to see you? Has she sent to know how you are? Look out, she may be unfaithful to you." (Marchand had a mistress named Esther who lived in Jamestown. She came to Longwood habitually every week with her little boy, who was called Jimmy.)[236]

The servants of Napoleon saw him as a father and longed for his attention and approval. Seeing him falter as a prisoner in exile rather than the sovereign of a proud nation pained them immensely.

*   *   *

Once at Longwood, Napoleon at first wore a shooting coat, but soon began to wear civilian clothes while in the house. His famous tri-cornered hat was never far away. If the Emperor ventured into the garden just outside the home *"he wore a hunting waistcoat, nankeen pantaloons with feet, a broad-brimmed straw hat with a narrow black ribbon, and red or green slippers on his feet. He usually* had in his hand a little rosewood billiard cue which served him both for a stick and a measure...when casually in doors working, wore a madras handkerchief on his head."²³⁷

Now that the Emperor was lodged at Longwood, Admiral Cockburn still had to ensure that the Emperor did not attempt an escape from the island or that a rescue mission could be made from the waters below. To ensure this

> *A subaltern's guard was posted at the entrance of Longwood, about six hundred paces from the house, and a cordon of sentinels and picquets, were placed round the limits. At nine o'clock the sentinels were drawn in and stationed in communication with each other; surrounding the house in such positions, that no person could come in or out without being seen and scrutinized by them. At the entrance of the house, double sentinels were placed, and patroles were continually passing backward and forward. After nine, Napoleon was not at liberty to leave the house, unless in company with a field officer; and no person whatever was allowed to pass without the counter-sign. This state of affairs continued until daylight in the morning. Every landing-place in the island, and indeed, every place which presented the semblance of one, was furnished with a picquet, and sentinels were even placed upon every goat-path leading to the sea, though in truth, the obstacles presented by nature in almost all the paths in that direction, would, of themselves, have proved insurmountable to so unwieldy a person as Napoleon.²³⁸*

To ensure prevention of Napoleon's escape or rescue, the Admiral made it mandatory that a British officer actually see the Emperor in person twice a day. Admiral Cockburn instructed the Grand Marshal that Napoleon must comply with this restriction. This rule, in particular, enraged the Emperor and he did everything possible to avoid complying with the measure. According to Napoleon's English doctor, Barry O'Meara, the Admiral instituted *"every human precaution to prevent escape, short of actually incarcerating, or enchaining him."*[239] The Admiral did allow Napoleon to ride on horseback unaccompanied twelve miles in circumference around Longwood. But again, with the soldiers of the Deadwood camp close by, he was still being watched.

If not on horseback, Napoleon was allowed to walk in a marked area. According to Marchand, the area was not much more than four miles. In this area, Napoleon could go for a stroll with members of his entourage. Often times, the Emperor would walk to Hutt's Gate which was located just on the outskirts of his restricted area and then come back to Longwood, having walked the entire reserve for Napoleon. His inability to walk beyond that point angered Napoleon considerably. *"The Emperor could not accept that, sent 2,000 leagues away from Europe, on a rock 600 leagues from both the continents of Africa and America, he would not be allowed to roam the entire island, which was so narrow and unhealthy as a prison and impossible to be entered without authorization from the admiral..."*[240] For the Emperor, being a prisoner was bad enough, being commanded by another was unbearable.

During one particular stroll, the Emperor walked through what he thought was a mere mud puddle and instead found himself practically waist high in mud. Both General Gourgaud and Las Cases had to pull him out. On his return to Longwood, he told Marchand, *"It was the marsh of Arcole! What would they have said in Europe?"* he added laughing, *"had I disappeared in it? That it was a just punishment for all my crimes!"*[241]

But the Emperor was greatly angered at the restriction that required a British officer follow him whenever he desired to ride on horseback outside of the boundaries established by Admiral Cockburn. Napoleon saw this restriction as proof that Admiral Cockburn saw him as a prisoner, which he denied unconditionally until the day he died. Permitting British Captain Poppleton to ride along side for surveillance of his person would be seen as the Emperor acknowledging his acceptance as a prisoner. Napoleon would do whatever was still in his power to avoid giving into this notion. In many instances, the Emperor was fighting a mind war against reality.

But Napoleon could also battle realities with humor when possible. Even though Captain Poppleton would attempt to get as close to Napoleon as possible when riding, early on, the Emperor would demonstrate his superior riding abilities by putting the British officer to the test. On these rides, Captain Poppleton was ordered "*that he was not to lose sight of Napoleon.*" Betsy recorded the incident.

> *The latter was one day riding with Generals Bertrand, Montholon, Gourgaud, and the rest of his suite, along one of the mountainous bridle-paths at St. Helena, with the orderly officer in attendance. Suddenly the emperor turned short round to his left, and spurring his horse violently, urged him up the face of the precipice, making the large stones fly from under him down the mountain, and leaving the orderly officer aghast, gazing at him in terror for his safety, and doubt as to his intentions. Although equally well mounted, none of his Generals dared to follow him. Either Captain Poppleton could not depend on his horse, or his horse was unequal to the task of following Napoleon, and giving it up at once, he rode instantly off to Sir George Cockburn, who happened at the time to be dining with my father at the Briars. He arrived breathless at our house, and, setting all ceremony aside, demanded to see Sir George, on business of the utmost importance. He was ushered at once into the dining-room. The Admiral was in the act of discussing his soup, and listened with an imperturbable countenance to the agitated detail of the occurrence, with Captain Poppleton's startling exclamation of "Oh! sir, I have lost the emperor." He very quietly advised him to return to Longwood, where he would most probably find General Bonaparte. This, as he prognosticated, was the case, and Napoleon often afterwards laughed at the consternation he had created. On Captain Poppleton's arriving at Longwood he found the emperor seated at dinner, and was unmercifully quizzed by him for the*

want of nerve he displayed in not daring to ride after him.[242]

General Gourgaud recorded in his memoirs that the Admiral responded to Captain Poppleton by stating, "*That's nothing. There's no danger. Just a lesson for you.*"[243] Even though the Admiral wanted to ensure that the Emperor would not escape the island, he was also quite familiar with Napoleon's sense of humor and knew all too well that he would ride back to Longwood to trick the Captain.

There was another occasion where Napoleon's anger at the British escort almost caused him to be fired upon. Gourgaud explained how on one ride the Emperor, Las Cases, and he were riding and were approached by a British sentry who shouted commands that they stop immediately. Gourgaud went back to confront the sentry while the Emperor and his secretary galloped off at a quick pace. Seeing the Emperor escape, the sentry dismounted and proceeded to load and aim his rifle. Gourgaud described the incident:

> *He uses threats, and refuses to listen to my reasoning. He cocks his rifle, and would given chase to His Majesty, but I stop him. I tell him that those are not his orders. I have something of a struggle with him, and I wonder whether I ought to use my sabre. I request the brute to fire on me rather than the others. His Majesty is well away. The sentry accompanies me to within 150 yards of the Guard House, but Hut's Gate. There, he realizes his mistake. He thought we were outside the limits....I go to the camp to complain to Bingham, or to Ferzen, but neither of them is to be found. I inform His Majesty of what I have done. He expresses satisfaction, and says: "Poor Las Cases thought he would get a bullet in his back!"*[244]

The Admiral spent many evenings for dinner with his prisoner at Longwood. Often times it was when a visitor to St. Helena wished to see the Emperor. Montholon explained "*when passengers, on their way from India or China, requested the Grand Marshal to* *present them to the Emperor, or any of the inhabitants of the island came on a visit, they were received from two till four o'clock. Very often the Emperor kept them to dinner. Admiral Cockburn had many times the honor, as well as Sir George Bingham, Colonel of the 53rd, and the Captain of the Grenadiers, whose wife was a descendent of Cromwell."*[245]

When it was just the French suite sharing a meal with Napoleon, the Emperor would often *"follow the practice of finishing the evening at table...He said to us: "To what play should we go this evening? Shall we hear Talma or Fleury?" The reading continued till 10 or 11 o'clock, and when our family day was come to a close, he always took some one of us into his chamber, undressed, and worked or conversed, till he became disposed to sleep."*[246]

In terms of Napoleon's sleeping habits, he struggled in getting his mind to rest. If he was unable to achieve enough rest the night before, the following night's attempt at sleep would be even more difficult.

> *Generally he slept poorly, there were few nights when he did not go from one bed to another. If he asked me for his covered lamp, then he worked or read and went back to bed, waiting for daylight to arrive so he could get dressed and go riding. He had lunch when he came back, went back to bed if he was tired enough to do so, took his bath at two o'clock, using the hours he spent there to chat or to dictate to one or the other of these gentlemen, then got out, dressed...These were the Emperor's habits during the first years of our stay at Longwood; they changed later due to his health. If he went to bed during the day, then the darkness had to be absolute; in the evening when he went back to his apartment, which occurred regularly at 10 p.m., either he went to bed or wanted to chat with the person who had accompanied him. He would have his covered lamp taken into the adjourning room, and chat with that person until he fell asleep or dismissed him,*

never exceeding a half hour or forty-five minutes.[247]

The mind of Napoleon was constantly in motion. Not only was he continuously contemplating information and decisions, he could switch topics in a moment's notice to discuss another topic, then come back to the original one without missing a beat. Napoleon often said "*he was equal to killing six secretaries. Those who wrote from his dictation, although they wrote in the most abbreviated way, were always one or two, or even three, sentences behind. Only stenographers were able to keep up with him.*"[248] He would often have two or more secretaries in the room ready to take down his dictations. Napoleon would have each one take down a particular topic and he would pace the room or stand at the mantle and dictate from memory constantly shifting between the subjects of his past.

St. Denis said that the Emperor "*could dictate for several hours together without stopping. His memory furnished him with everything that he needed. He compared it to a piece of furniture composed of a great number of drawers; he could pull out that one which he needed in order to take from it the materials which belonged to his subject.*"[249] It was this ability that enabled him to have the perfect command of a battlefield. To see all aspects of the fighting, to predict the moves of the enemy and then know how to counter it before it happens; it was this mind of Napoleon that made him the envy of military commanders across Europe, but also their worst nightmare as well.

Napoleon was a master at dictating, but when it came to writing, all that knew him were quite aware that his writing was practically unreadable. Josephine knew how horrible it was even going to the lengths of stating, "*I cannot make out his letters; he writes like a cat.*"[250] St. Denis once mentioned to the Emperor that he could not read his handwriting. Napoleon would not admit such a thing.

"*What, imbecile, don't you know how to read?*"
"No, Sire." St. Denis said.
"Yet it is written as clearly as though it were printed. Look!"
"Sire, I have looked with all my eyes. I can't make out the word which Your Majesty has written."

> *The Emperor would look, too, but he would not prove more skillful than I. After trying in vain for a minute or two he would say to me, "Sit down there and write," and he would go to work to dictate to me a few phrases of a paragraph to take the place of the part where there were illegible words.*[251]

When Napoleon would review his writing, he would always read it with his thumb.[252]

Napoleon's moods would often shift back and forth from contentment to depression. Being in exile, so different from where Napoleon was just months before, it is easy to see how the mind could face difficulty in remaining 'joyful.' On November 29, 1815, Napoleon described to Las Cases how perhaps their situation might even have had its benefits.

> *The eyes of the universe are fixed upon us! We are martyrs in an immortal cause! Millions of human beings are weeping for us; our country sighs, and glory mourns our fate! We here struggle against the oppression of the gods, and the prayers of nations are for us!...Besides, this is not the source of my real sufferings! If I considered only myself, perhaps I should have reason to rejoice! Misfortunes, are not without their heroism and their glory! Adversity was wanting to my career! Had I died on the throne, enveloped in the dense atmosphere of my power, I should to many have remained a problem; but now misfortune will enable all to judge of me without disguise.*[253]

Napoleon would often lapse into these deep, emotional thoughts. Many of the members of his entourage had been with him for some time and knew his personality quite well. The mere look on his face could tell those close to him if something weighed on his mind. Often he would share his feelings and contemplations with them.

Las Cases remembered one particular incident when Napoleon shared these reflections.

> *During the last three days, in our rides about the park, he several times alluded to this circumstance with considerable warmth, desiring me [Las Cases] to keep close by his side, and ordering my son to ride on before. On one of these occasions the following observation escaped him; - "I know I am fallen. But to feel this among you!"...These words, the gesture, the tone that accompanied them, pierced my very heart. I was ready to throw myself at his feet and embrace his knees. "I know," continued he, "that man is frequently unreasonable and susceptible. Thus, when I am mistrustful of myself, I asked should I have been treated so at the Tuileries? This is my sure test."...His reflections on these subjects were numerous, powerful and just.*[254]

Las Cases was able to observe Napoleon seizing upon his misfortunes as a way to influence not only his situation at present but his overall history as well. Napoleon was a master at politics and influencing those around him. There was no secret to the fact that Napoleon would use all means necessary to mold how the world would judge his reign along with his exile at the hands of the British.

But over those first few months at Longwood, Las Cases also saw the Emperor in his more human moments. Napoleon was very fond of young Emmanuel Las Cases and took every opportunity to jest with him. The Emperor knew that an adult sharing in his exile was difficult enough, but seeing a teenage boy share it was another thing to witness. Las Cases explained that in December of 1815, "*the Emperor summoned me and my son to our accustomed task. He said that I had been idle, and called my attention to my son, who was laughing behind my back. He asked why he laughed; and I replied that it was probably because his Majesty was taking revenge for him. "Ah!" said he, smiling, "I see I am acting the part of the grandfather here.*"[255]

A few weeks later, on the day before Christmas, Napoleon was playing cards and began to get tired. All of a sudden he looked as if deep in thought and turned to Las Cases and said, *"'Where do you suppose Madame Las Cases is at this moment?" – "Alas, Sire," I replied, "Heaven knows!" – "She is in Paris," continued he; "to-day is Tuesday; it is nine o'clock; she is now at the Opera." – "No, Sire, she is too good a wife to go to the theatre while I am here." – "Spoken like a true husband," said the Emperor laughing, "ever confident and credulous!" Then turning to General Gourgaud, he rallied him in the same style with respect to his mother and sister. Gourgaud seemed very much downcast, and his eyes were suffered with tears, which the Emperor perceiving, cast a side-glance towards him, and said, in the most interesting manner, "How wicked, barbarous, and tyrannical I must be thus to trifle with feelings so tender!"*[256] Napoleon realized that his need for conversation and inquiry quickly was causing more harm than good for the members of his entourage. Las Cases knew that he felt sincere remorse for his inquisitive questioning.

As secretary to the Emperor, Las Cases was often in charge of reading and translating documents and newspapers to Napoleon. Las Cases recorded an incident when his eyes became weary and tired and it was becoming difficult for him to continue reading. Upon seeing this, Napoleon told him to stop and rest and that it could wait until tomorrow. This caring, fatherly side of the Emperor touched the heart of his secretary: *"How humane and kind he seemed! How just and true was every observation that escaped him! These were a few of the precious moments when Nature, taken by surprise, exposes the inmost recesses of the human heart and character. I left him, saying within myself, how little has the character of the Emperor been known to the world."*[257]

The vacillating through emotions and temperaments would become a repeated occurrence for the Emperor. Anger, sadness, boredom, humor, contentment, and rage would race through the mind and veins of the fallen Emperor as he labored to make sense of his reality. In one moment of contemplation, Napoleon turned to Gourgaud and commented how he felt that *"it would be nice to fall asleep and not wake up for a year or two! We would then find big changes."*[258] The gamble for the Emperor would lie in what changes would await him upon awaking from his desired slumber. Changes were coming for Napoleon, but not the ones he hoped would arrive.

As New Year's Day, 1816 arrived, Napoleon *"tried to make this day less gloomy, by bringing an air of gaiety to the heartfelt wishes of each* of them. Children had their turn, and he gave them some New Year's gifts and spent part of the morning being amused by their childish pleasure."²⁵⁹ But as the day went on, Napoleon became more melancholy. When this state of emotion would occur, the Emperor would retreat to his bedroom. There, his worst enemy would come back to haunt him; time.

> *No matter how much care the Emperor took to distract himself with work; and no matter how many horseback rides he took within the boundaries or around the island with the grand marshal or General Gourgaud, there were still many moments where painful thoughts haunted him. He would then say his enemies would have been less barbaric had they had him shot rather than bringing him to Saint Helena. His mental sufferings must have been great. The restrictions imposed on him were also a source of aggravation; one would have thought that a conversation between the Emperor and the admiral, following a luncheon where the latter expressed a desire to please him and to improve the state of affairs, would have brought the admiral to get rid of the boundaries, but this never happened. The only change he made was to order Captain Poppleton to follow the Emperor dressed in civilian clothes instead of in uniform. It was not the uniform that displeased the Emperor, but the constant surveillance made of his speech or his actions by the person wearing it.*²⁶⁰

But the Emperor's troubles had only just begun. Just a few months after arriving at St. Helena, the Admiral's replacement arrived at St. Helena. If Napoleon was angered at the restrictions placed upon him by Admiral Cockburn, the restrictions yet to come from the new Governor would be intolerable for the Emperor. This man who was setting foot on St. Helena at that very moment was looking to follow his orders from London, not make a new friend in the form of a fallen Emperor.

*   *   *

On April 14th, 1816, the sounding of the cannon at Alarm House signaled the arrival of the new Governor. The Emperor and the French suite were looking upon this moment with some optimism. But to their horror, they would encounter something entirely worse.

The British Government had selected Lieutenant General Sir Hudson Lowe as the new Governor of St. Helena, replacing the temporary Governor, Admiral Cockburn. Lowe was a tall, thin man about the same age as the Emperor. He was very moody and the complete opposite of Admiral Cockburn. The selection of Lowe would later prove to be both damaging to the Emperor and to the reputation of the British Ministry. For Napoleon, it would prove to be a fatal decision.

To fully grasp the hatred that the Emperor had for this man, one would only have to read a brief description of Lowe's military experience and record and it would instantly become apparent as to why. During his early military career, Sir Hudson Lowe commanded an army of Corsican rebels in an attempt to rid the island of Corsica of its 'French oppressors.' This fact angered and insulted the Emperor for two distinct reasons.

The first is quite obvious in that Corsica was the birthplace of Napoleon. It was this French influence and control that provided him with the opportunity to attend military school and eventually rise to become Emperor of the French. The second reason is one that is typical of Napoleon. The Emperor was someone who excelled through merit and believed that it was the only true way to achieve success and reward. Much of the foundation in how he organized his military and government were based on this principle, the Legion of Honor being a prime example. To be guarded by someone who led 'Corsican deserters,' as Napoleon referred to them, was an insult and a slap in the face. If he had to be held here against his will, it at least should be by someone who had achieved success on the battlefield in an honorable manner. Admiral Cockburn had earned this right in the eyes of the Emperor. To have this person of such low-level military rank was disrespectful. It is also very possibly exactly how the British Ministry wanted this action to be viewed.

Either way, one could easily predict that their relationship would not be a friendly one.

The mind game was about to begin.

*　　　　　*　　　　　*

Upon setting foot in Jamestown, the new Governor made it known that he would visit the prisoner the next morning at nine o'clock. The Emperor outright refused due to the fact that Lowe did not follow his protocol of going through the Grand Marshal. *"He can come whenever he wants, but I will only receive him when he asks properly...he knows very well that I never receive at nine o'clock...it is lacking in generosity to add insult to misfortune."*[261] Barry O'Meara, Napoleon's English doctor, explained to the Emperor that Lowe did not want to follow Admiral Cockburn's advice. Napoleon was still annoyed and said, *"If you say so. I am willing to admit his strong and loyal character, but nevertheless he is a real shark. I have sought refuge among you, and I have found nothing here but poor treatment and insults. If the governor wishes to be presented to me, let him put in his request through Bertrand."*[262]

On April 15th, 1816, Governor Lowe kept to his word and arrived at Longwood at exactly nine o'clock. St. Denis informed the Governor that the Emperor was *"ill and had not yet risen. Lowe retreated and walked with long strides under the windows of the Emperor, who saw him without being seen."*[263] As his frustrations quickly mounted, Governor Lowe went to the Grand Marshal who informed him that Napoleon was sleeping and could not see him today. Grand Marshal Bertrand told him to come back tomorrow at two o'clock.[264] The new Governor was furious. Marchand captured the moment with perfect sarcasm when he recorded in his diary that *"Sir Hudson Lowe's debut in his new government was not a fortunate one."*[265]

Later that evening, Napoleon discussed the events of the day with his entourage. Many expressed their anticipation at what this new Governor had ready for them. Some were nervous and others were already angry. General Gourgaud expressed his feeling that he would almost rather be shot than be in the hands of the English under such conditions. The Emperor responded saying, *"You see...it requires more courage to suffer than to die."*[266] The men surrounding their Emperor were silent. The last entry for that day by Gourgaud merely said, *"The dinner is a very sad one."*[267]

Governor Lowe returned the next day at the fixed time, accompanied by Admiral Cockburn. Due to Napoleon's protocol and the Englishmen's lack of understanding, quite an incident occurred upon Governor Lowe's entrance. Montholon described "*the eagerness of Sir Hudson Lowe deranged everything, and gave rise to a scene which was equally painful to the Admiral and to us.*"[268] The Grand Marshal was in the practice of only allowing the person who requested to meet with the Emperor an audience and not those who may wish to enter. Thus being the practice, Noverraz allowed Governor Lowe to enter the drawing room at Longwood and when Admiral Cockburn followed to enter as well, the servant inadvertently slammed the door in the officer's face. Completely offended, the Admiral marched to his horse and returned to town.[269]

When Napoleon was told of the mishap that occurred, he "*expressed his regrets for this, and asked Dr. O'Meara to convey this to Sir George Cockburn. In addition, he sent one of his officers to clear up, if possible, the unpleasantness of such an involuntary lack of courtesy. Although he had cause to complain about the admiral, he used to say of him: "Under his uniform beats the heart of a soldier.""*[270]

During this first meeting between the Emperor and Governor Lowe, the two men were very cold to each other and talked only of the present conditions and regulations. Being that both men spoke Italian fluently, the Emperor chose that language to converse with the Governor. General Gourgaud instantly took issue with the fact that Governor Lowe referred to Napoleon as 'General' and not 'Emperor.'[271] Napoleon also was quite displeased with this disrespectfulness. During their conversation, the Emperor "*asked the Governor how many years' service he had done. "Twenty-eight years," was the answer. "Well, then," said the Emperor, "I am an older soldier than you. I have done nearly forty." Lowe replied: "Your years are so many centuries."*"[272] Napoleon merely smiled. The tension between the two men was incredible.

Little was revealed as to what the new Governor would decide to do in regards to his newly acquired prisoner. But the anticipation by the French of Lowe's actions would be short.

His regulations would come within days, and with it, the prison walls would begin to close around Napoleon.

*   *   *

The members of Napoleon's entourage who were present during this first meeting with Lowe all recorded in their memoirs the Emperor's reaction to Governor Lowe. Marchand said that Napoleon remarked:

> "This man has a repulsive appearance and does not have an honest gaze. We must not rush to judge him, but I need to have his behavior reassure me about his physical appearance. His looks," said the Emperor laughing, "remind me of a Sicilian thug; what do you think, Bertrand?"[273]

Montholon remembered a similar response by the Emperor when he recorded that Napoleon said:

> "That man is malevolent; whilst looking at me, his eye was like that of a hyena taken into a trap; put no confidence in him; we complain of the Admiral – we shall perhaps regret him...His [Lowe] appearance and expression recall to my mind those of the Sbirri of Venice. Who knows! perhaps he will be my executioner. Let us not, however, be hasty in forming our judgments; his disposition may, after all, atone for his sinister appearance."[274]

The Emperor's wish to remain impartial about the new Governor would soon end with Lowe's first demand. Governor Lowe instructed the Emperor's entourage that they were to sign a declaration of their intent, which was ordered from the British Ministry in Europe. The following is the order Lowe brought with him from London:

Downing Street, 10 January 1816

I must now inform you of the wishes of his Royal Highness the Prince Regent, which is that on your arrival in Saint Helena you will inform all the persons in Napoleon Bonaparte's following, in-

> *cluding domestic servants, that they are free to leave the island immediately to return to Europe, adding that no one will be allowed to remain in Saint Helena except those who declare, in a written statement to be deposited in your hands, that it is their desire to remain on the island and submit to all the restrictions necessary to impose on Napoleon Bonaparte personally. Those among them who decide to return to Europe must be sent at the first favorable opportunity to the Cape of Good Hope. The governor of that colony shall be charged with providing them the means of returning to Europe.*
>
> *Signed: Bathurst*[275]

Napoleon was furious at the audacity of the British Ministry to order his officers and servants to do anything. After Grand Marshal Bertrand failed to persuade Lowe to change the wording of the declaration, the Emperor dictated his own declaration to Montholon to have the members of his entourage sign it. It read

> *We the undersigned, wishing to remain in the service of the Emperor Napoleon, agree to remain here, no matter how horrible the stay in Saint Helena, and to submit to the restrictions, no matter how unjust and arbitrary, that have been imposed on His Majesty and the personnel in his service.*[276]

Napoleon instructed Montholon to "*let those of my servants who wish to sign, sign, but don't try to influence anyone.*"[277] All of the members joyfully signed the Emperor's declaration. But Governor Lowe was insistent that no imperial title be used in reference to Napoleon. He also wanted the French to understand that by signing the declaration meant that no one would be allowed to leave the island until the Emperor's death. Lowe sent his officer, Sir Thomas Reade, to inform them of his instructions. Marchand responded on everyone's behalf, "*"Colonel," I said to him, "we all came here to share in the Emperor's misfortune, to serve him, and to lighten his chains as much as possible. What could these restrictions possibly mean to us? We are all here to live and die with him.'"*[278]

There is no doubt that the British Ministry had two aims in this declaration. One was to ensure that the group of exiles did not disobey any restrictions set by the government without threat of penalty. The second, and probably main goal was to quickly reduce the number of people surrounding the Emperor as another form of punishment. There is no doubt that most 'prisoners' would never be allowed to have such a 'following' in prison as Napoleon did, and thus the Emperor was extremely fortunate to have so many people with him. But this regulation would inflict more of a mental wound by peeling away those who he trusted, those who served him, and those that could help to ease the suffering of time and boredom. One thing was quickly becoming apparent to the French exiles: Lowe would follow his orders from London to the final letter.

Marchand witnessed firsthand how these first few days under Governor Lowe was affecting Napoleon.

> *During all this time the Emperor was deeply saddened; his great soul seemed to hesitate between the sacrifice he would have to make in letting these gentle-men leave, and the complete isolation he would find himself in after their departure. So religious a devotion on the part of all, when he learned of it, eased the pain that filled him. Such was the first act of Sir Hudson Lowe on his arrival in St. Helena: it was the prelude to the arsenal of restrictions to be established out of hatred for the Emperor, and which he intended to put into practice no matter how valueless they were.*[279]

The valet was very aware of the feelings and emotions of Napoleon. Marchand was with him literally every second of the day. As the days went on since moving to Longwood, he could see a change occurring in the Emperor. Napoleon's passivity to most issues regarding his person now developed into anger and combativeness towards the British Ministry's treatment of him.

Until he moved to Longwood, the Emperor had remained more or less indifferent to everything going on around him; he let matters run their course, and seemed to notice very little the deprivations surrounding him. At The Briars however he had strongly resented the harassment inflicted on his officers, and he had suffered from not being able to remedy the situation. But once he was at Longwood, faced with the restrictions imposed on him, he rejected the outrages and the persecutions, his soul so full of indignation, and behind his moral barrier he had imposed on himself, he demonstrated what a great man is like in adversity. From that moment on, it can be said that Napoleon's martyrdom began, and that Saint Helena was to become his calvary. The hatred on the part of the ministry shall be a stain on British honor forever.[280]

The Emperor's anger at Governor Lowe was a constant. When the Governor attempted a few days later to come and see Napoleon, a servant replied that he was too ill for the visitation. But not fifteen minutes later the Emperor "*climbed into his carriage with the ladies, so that Lowe would clearly understand he had not wanted to see him. Another time, as he was about to get in his carriage, he spotted Hudson Lowe arriving at Longwood; he went back inside and did not come out again.*"[281] Lowe would not take this insult lightly.

Napoleon's English doctor was summoned numerous times for conversations with Governor Lowe. The Governor would pose countless questions to the doctor in attempts to gain some insight into what occurred inside the walls of Longwood. To his surprise, the Governor was met with defiance from O'Meara. At one point, Governor Lowe said to O'Meara, "*General Bonaparte is not satisfied, it appears, to have created for himself an imaginary France and an imaginary Poland...but he now wants to create an imaginary Saint Helena here.*"[282] When Napoleon was told of this comment by the Governor "*he could not refrain from laughing.*"[283]

When Napoleon discovered that O'Meara had met with Lowe on these occasions, he summoned the doctor to his room immediately. The Emperor was very direct with O'Meara about his concerns that he may be a spy for the British.

> *Napoleon, after a few questions of no importance, asked me in both French and Italian, in the presence of Count Las Cases, the following questions: - "You know that it was in consequence of my application that you were appointed to attend upon me. Now I want to know from you precisely and truly, as a man of honor, in what situation you conceive yourself to be, whether as my surgeon...or the surgeon of a prison ship and prisoners? Whether you have orders to report every trifling occurrence, or illness, or what I say to you, to the governor? Answer me candidly. What situation do you conceive yourself to be in?" I replied, "As your surgeon, and to attend upon you and your suit. I have received no other orders than to make an immediate report in case of your being taken seriously ill, in order to have promptly the advice and assistance of other physicians." "First obtaining my consent to call in others," demanded he, "is it not so?" I answered that I would certainly obtain his previous consent. He then said, "If you were appointed as surgeon to a prison, and to report my conversations to the governor... I would never see you again."*[284]

Since the arrival of Governor Lowe, Napoleon was increasingly concerned over spies around Longwood who would report to Lowe over the doings of the French suite. But convinced of O'Meara's loyalty, he sought to reassure the doctor when he stated, "*Do not...suppose that I take you for a spy; on the contrary, I have never had the least occasion to find fault with you, and I have a friendship for you and an esteem for your character, a greater proof of which I could not give you than asking you candidly your own opinion of your situation."*[285] The Emperor had won the admiration of the Englishman and he remained dedicated to Napoleon the entire time he served as his doctor on St. Helena.

On May 6, 1816, Napoleon agreed to a visit by Governor Lowe. Once he arrived, the Governor explained that the components for a new house to be built for Napoleon were en route to the island as they spoke and he wished to know what the Emperor's preference was for its location. It appears word had reached England that Longwood and its condition would not be suitable for the Emperor by even England's standards. In fact, many in England believed that Plantation House should have been used to house Napoleon and his entourage.[286] Along with the materials for the new house, the English had shipped new furnishings and a billiard table. Montholon recorded Napoleon's terse response to Governor Lowe:

> *In short, sir, I wish for nothing from you; I have no request to make but one – leave me in peace...you tell me, your instructions are more rigid than those given to the Admiral. Be it so – take courage, and execute them boldly; I am prepared to expect anything from your government; here I am, execute your orders. Are they to put me to death by sword or by poison? I know not to what means you may resort to poison me, but as to putting me to the sword, you have proved that you have the means, by threatening the officer to have the door of my chamber broken open by violence, if he refused to open it to you. The brave 53rd know that they can only enter by passing over my dead body. Dare to order them to exchange the glorious recollections inscribed upon their colours, for the words 'Assassination of Napoleon!"...I shall never acknowledge, by any act of my life, that I am your prisoner.*[287]

Marchand also was present during this interview and recorded a very similar response from the Emperor. The valet added that Napoleon's anger increased when he added, "*You know very well that the only surveillance needed to keep me here is that provided by your cruisers, and that to place an officer galloping behind me is absurd. But what you do not appear to know is that you are covering your name with shame and that your children will be ashamed to carry it.*"[288] Governor Lowe remained calm with a stoic look on his face. It is almost as if Napoleon's anger may have amused him.

In terms of the new house, Napoleon later said to Montholon, "*This palace which they send me, according to reports, is just so much money thrown into the sea. I would rather they sent me 400 volumes of books, than the whole of this house and its furniture. First it will require several years to build this pretended palace, and before it is finished, I shall be dead.*"[289] Napoleon would steadfastly reject the new house, but he did relent and took the new furniture to Longwood and also the billiard table. Though he didn't play, he enjoyed rolling the balls around and using the cue as a walking stick.[290]

The Emperor was so infuriated with the mere presence of Governor Lowe that he worried that the man could poison him with his eyes. "*I never saw such a horrid countenance. He sat on a chair opposite to my sofa, and on the little table between us there was a cup of coffee. His physiognomy made such an unfavorable impression upon me, that I thought his looks had poisoned it, and I ordered Marchand to throw it out of the window; I could not have swallowed it for the world.*"[291]

When the Emperor was alone with Las Cases later in the day, he again reflected on the meeting with Lowe. He explained that the two of them "*had a violent scene.*"

> *I have been thrown quite out of temper! They have now sent me worse than a gaoler! Sir Hudson Lowe is a downright executioner! I received him to-day with my stormy countence, my head inclined, and my ears pricked up. We looked most furiously at each other. My anger must have been powerfully excited, for I felt a vibration in the calf of my left leg. This is always a sure sign with me; and I have not felt it for a long time before.*[292]

Las Cases later explained to Governor Lowe why the Emperor was so angered by his presence and approach to dealing with the French suite. Napoleon's secretary explained to Lowe:

> *the method he was pursuing was quite hostile to our habits. I assured him that the Emperor was desirous of being as accommodating as possible, in the new situation in which he was placed: that he wished to retire within himself asking for nothing but to be left unannoyed: that fortune had indeed robbed him of his power, but that nothing could deprive him of his self-respect; and finally, that the consciousness and the delicacy of his dignity were the only things that remained to him of which he could call himself the master.*[293]

But the Governor had his orders from England and was also left to his own discretion in some matters. He would not be dictated to or receive orders from his prisoner. Napoleon and his suite were to obey the restrictions. If they chose not to, the members of the Emperor's suite would be removed from the island. The Emperor could not understand this man. Ironically, Napoleon admired men of character who obeyed orders and executed them to the fullest. Why was Lowe different? Simply put, this man held the keys to the Emperor's cell.

*   *   *

Throughout his time at Longwood, Napoleon often received British officials who were making the stopover at St. Helena or other British citizens who were stationed on the island. They desperately wanted to see the famous prisoner with their own eyes, hear his words, and be able to tell their friends and family that they had seen 'him.' None were allowed to enter Longwood without the permission of the Governor. He did grant most requests. At the commencement of every visit, Napoleon was the perfect gentleman and would inquire to learn more about the person who had come to converse with him.

During these conversations, the Emperor took every opportunity to work in his grievances against Lowe and the British government for their daily harassments to his person and the other members of his suite. Napoleon's hopes were that they would take his complaints with them to Europe and proclaim them to whomever they encountered. He often succeeded. Much of Napoleon's grievances made it to the pages of newspapers in Europe and the United States.

One person in particular that Napoleon would invest much of his complaints was British Admiral Sir Pulteney Malcolm and his wife, who resided at Plantation House from June of 1816 through July of 1817. Admiral Malcolm was the commander of the Cape Station, which covered a span from St. Helena to Cape Town on the southern tip of Africa. He made visits to Longwood to converse with the Emperor on many occasions and Napoleon enjoyed their time together. Lady Malcolm was at first frightened by the notion of meeting Napoleon, but was instantly set at ease after talking with him in those early moments during their first visit. She took particular interest and enjoyment in his "*great good humour*" and his incredibly loud and hearty laugh.[294]

When it came to Admiral Malcolm, the two military men got right to discussing military affairs. In jest, Admiral Malcolm remarked that Napoleon was "*fond of war*," to which the Emperor smiled.[295] There was no denial. But this would not be the focal point of their discussions.

> *Bonaparte then began on his grievances. He expressed his dislike of Sir Hudson's manners...The following were some of his expressions: "He's not the character of an Englishman. He is a Prussian soldier.*[296] *He is clever and cunning..." He added that he felt more angry in being placed under the charge of such a man, than in having been sent to such a vile place as St. Helena. "His manners are so displeasing to me, that if he were to come to tell me that a frigate was ready to take me to France, and I was at liberty to go where I pleased, he could not give me pleasure." The Admiral endeavoured to persuade him that it was only*

manner, and that he knew Sir Hudson was very desirous of doing everything in his power to render him comfortable. Bonaparte allowed that it was manner more than matter, that so frequently vexed him. He instanced some things that had been done by way of civility, but the manner prevented them being received as such. "In short, he cannot please me. Call it enfantillage, or what you will, so it is!"[297]

The conversations between Admiral Malcolm and Napoleon covered a variety of topics with which both men were perfectly at ease and conversed as if they had known each other for years. Napoleon asked pointed questions, and Admiral Malcolm gave truthful responses. The Emperor directly asked the British officer if he believed the English government would keep him at St. Helena forever. Malcolm replied in the affirmative and "*recommended to him to endeavor to be content with his situation.*"[298] Napoleon considered the response before he replied, "*men had escaped from dungeons, where they had been tied hand and foot…It is only a bird that can escape from hence. Why all the guards on the tops of hills? – if the coast was guarded, it would be enough. I can see that he is no general; indeed he never commanded anything but Corsican deserters.*"[299] The resentment of Napoleon at being guarded by a man such as Lowe would never end.

Whether in fact infantile or not, the relationship between the Emperor and Governor Lowe would become so filled with anger and hatred that the two men would only meet again three more times before Napoleon's death. The Emperor could just not stomach the sight of the man.

But Napoleon had some specific reasons for despising Lowe. It would not take the new governor long to overturn many of the regulations and restrictions that had been put into place by Admiral Cockburn and had become tolerated by the exiles of Longwood. Lowe would not only do away with many of them, he would impose new ones that would ignite the temper of Napoleon and his entourage and cause the relationship between the two men to become more destructive. Lowe was constantly obsessed with ensuring that his prisoner would never escape St. Helena.

In May of 1816, Napoleon received the official declaration signed by the Allies at the Congress of Vienna. The words of the men who crafted the document made the Emperor's blood boil. The document referenced *"Napoleon Bonaparte being in the power of the Allied sovereigns...Napoleon Bonaparte is considered...to be their prisoner...His guard is specifically entrusted to the British government...The imperial courts of Austria and Russia and the royal court of Prussia shall name commissioners to proceed to and live in the place the British government assigns as Napoleon Bonaparte's residence...and will ensure that he remains there.*[300]

Napoleon reiterated his denial at being the prisoner of anyone. He added:

> *If the people, whose interests have been conquered at Waterloo, submit to the iron yoke imposed upon them by the congress of Vienna, we shall not be worth the money which it will cost England to keep us here, and English interests will require them to get rid of us. The expenses of my captivity will certainly exceed 10,000,000 francs per annum. But, after all, what signify ten millions to England?*
>
> *...we have another chance of escape: perhaps, by a course of adverse advents, the sovereigns may be forced to acknowledge the error which they have committed in dethroning me, and may call me to their aid in the immense struggle of the past against the French revolution. I should be a natural mediator..."*[301]

In Napoleon's mind, he could still be needed and useful to Europe. To the sovereigns of Europe, he needed to remain on St. Helena until his death.

* * *

Often times in the evenings, the Emperor would become more reflective. As night conquered the day, his mind would replay moments of his glory, his victories, or to the things he missed most. Napoleon's armies had conquered countries, but his mind struggled to conquer time and boredom. He contemplated happier times, which would lead to more somber moods. Silence was an enemy proven to be a formidable force against a mind that sought for answers and victories and was left with neither. St. Helena became Napoleon's purgatory. He was trapped between the heavenly memories of his past glory and the hell of his present reality. Many times his words expressed hope for a swift end by means of execution but at other times he reveled in the joy of a new task or goal as simple as they were in or around the grounds of Longwood. The human mind can be a person's greatest asset then in the blink of an eye becomes the means of one's utter self-destruction. It is often difficult to conquer and control one's own thoughts, even for the greatest of generals.

During these times, Napoleon displayed some of his most human moments. Montholon recalled that during one night in May of 1816, the Emperor "*spoke to us of nothing, during the evening, but the Empress Josephine.*"[302] He loved her immensely and thought of her much more than his second wife, the Empress Marie Louise. During this moment in particular, Napoleon imagined what his life would have been like if Josephine was able to have another child.

> *A son by Josephine, would have rendered me happy, and have secured the reign of my dynasty...The French would have loved him very much better than the King of Rome, and I never would have put my foot on the abyss covered with flowers which was my ruin...My poor Josephine had the instinct of the future, when she became terrified at her sterility; she knew well that a marriage is only real when there is an offspring; and in proportion as fortune smiled, her anxiety increased she built her hopes on my adoption of Eugene,[303] and this was the cause of all the disagreements with my brothers...I was the object of her deepest attachment, and I am so convinced of*

> it," he added, smiling, "that I believe she would have left the rendezvous of love to come and find me. If I went into my carriage at midnight for a long journey, there, to my surprise, I found her seated before me and awaiting my arrival. If I attempted to dissuade her from accompanying me, she had so many good and affectionate reasons where-with to oppose me, that it was almost always necessary to yield. In a word, she always proved to me a happy and affectionate wife, and I have therefore presented the tenderest recollections of her.[304]

Once again when Napoleon finished talking of Josephine, he remained in quiet reflection for the rest of the evening.

A few days later, the Emperor shifted topics to an issue that most fascinated him about the English: their tendency to get drunk. Napoleon was absolutely convinced that most Englishmen desired to consume as much drink as possible. Whenever he was in the presence of an Englishman with whom he felt comfortable, the Emperor would pose the question to them. Both Marchand and O'Meara recorded how Napoleon questioned the English doctor concerning a dinner the doctor had the night before. Marchand explained the event.

> One day the Emperor was ailing and kept to his bed. He summoned the doctor:
> "Yesterday you had company for dinner. How many of the men were drunk?"
>
> "Not one of them," the doctor replied laughing.
>
> "You are not telling the truth. There must have been a few of them under the table. Was not our friend Captain Ross not slightly inebriated?"

> "Feeling good, yes, but inebriated, no; the only one exceeding mere happiness was Captain Piontkowski, whom I had invited to dinner."
>
> "Piontkowski, who sometimes dines at the camp with the officers of the 53rd, says that once the tablecloth has been removed, they pay so much an hour to drink, and this lasts late into the night."
>
> "I can assure you," replied the doctor, "that is utterly untrue, and that there are officers in the camp who drink wine twice a week."[305]

Napoleon responded with his usual hearty laugh. This would not be the last time he would question someone about his theory concerning the drinking habits of the English.

Betsy also recalled an episode that occurred in her presence in which the Emperor jested her father about his drinking. What made the incident so humorous was the fact that Napoleon was trying to speak in English.

> The emperor's English, of which he sometimes spoke a few words, was the oddest in the world. He had formed an exaggerated idea of the quantity of wine drunk by English gentlemen, and used always to ask me, after we had had a party, how many bottles of wine my father drank, and then laughing, and counting on his fingers, generally made the number of five. One day, to annoy me, he said that my country-women drank gin and brandy; and then added, in English, "You laike veree mosh dreenk, Meess, sometimes brandee, geen." Though I could not help laughing at his way of saying this, I felt most indignant at the accusation, and assured him that the ladies of England had the utmost horror of drinking spirits, and that they were even fastidious in the

refinement of their ideas and in their general habits. He seemed amused at my earnestness, and quoted the instance of a Mrs. B-----y, who had, in fact, paid him a visit once in a state of intoxication. It was singular, indeed, that one of the few English ladies he had ever been presented to should have been addicted to this habit. At last he confessed, laughing, that he had made the accusation only to tease me. When I was going away, he repeated, "You like dreenk, Meess Betsee; dreenk! dreenk!"[306]

Napoleon's laugh would fill the room. It would be a laugh that would slowly be replaced with anger and depression.

The battle between Napoleon and Governor Lowe had only just begun.

1. Napoleon Bonaparte, Emperor of France

2. Count de Las Cases, Secretary to Napoleon

3. Grand Marshal Henri Bertrand

4. General Charles-Tristan de Montholon

5. *General Baron Gourgaud*

6. *Dr. Barry O'Meara, Napoleon's English Doctor*

7. Lt. General Sir Hudson Lowe, Governor of St. Helena

8. Napoleon dictating to General Gourgaud, from a lithograph after Steuben. From Norwood Young's "Napoleon in Exile at St. Helena," 1915.

9. Betsy Balcombe Abell's dedication to Lady Malcolm's son inscribed on the front page of her memoir in 1866. At the top of the page, Betsy wrote "From the author to the son of dear Lady Malcolm"

10. Longwood, Napoleon's residence on St. Helena. Napoleon's bedroom is located in the right wing of the building where the three windows can be seen facing the garden area. Photo courtesy of Margaret Rodenberg

11. Front view of Longwood, Napoleon's residence on St. Helena. Photo courtesy of Margaret Rodenberg.

12. Room used as Napoleon's bedroom towards the end of his life. His campbed was moved to this room to make him more comfortable. Photo courtesy of Margaret Rodenberg.

13. Napoleon's campbed featuring his death mask. This is the location where Napoleon died on May 5, 1821. Photo courtesy of Margaret Rodenberg.

14. Bust of the King of Rome, Napoleon's son. Napoleon deeply missed his son and would often gaze lovingly upon this bust. Photo courtesy of Margaret Rodenberg.

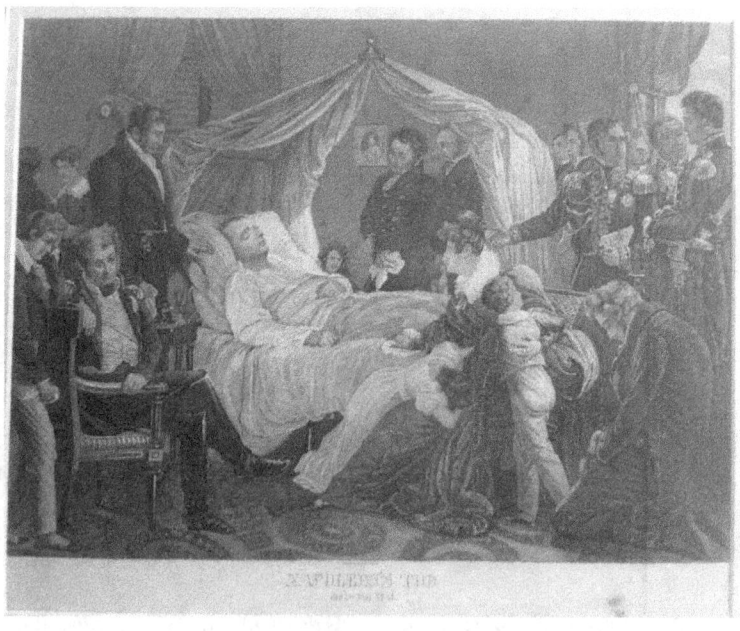

15. Napoleon on his deathbed. With all surrounding the Emperor in deep grief, this illustration appropriately captures the devastation felt by the children at the loss of their beloved Emperor.

I am prepared for everything. They will kill me here, it is certain.

Napoleon

Chapter 5

Torment By Vexation

The noose was slowing closing around Longwood. Lowe began to institute more restrictions upon the French suite out of fear of Napoleon's potential escape. The mental chess match between the Governor and Napoleon was going into a dangerous stage. As Lowe restricted what the Emperor could do, where he could go, and who he could see, Napoleon reacted by refusing to leave the Longwood grounds. When the game became worse, Napoleon would retreat and hunker down behind the façade of Longwood's walls.

One of the first new regulations was that any items sent to the Emperor from people on the island or from Europe had to first be inspected by Lowe himself. He next forbade any business in Jamestown from selling goods to the French without his prior approval. Following this, he ordered that the residents of Jamestown and the rest of the island were not to converse with any of the French exiles without Lowe's permission. By May 1816, Lowe topped off this barrage of regulations by forbidding any British soldier from the 53rd Regiment from talking with Napoleon unless they then reported the conversation directly to Lowe after. One British officer said to Montholon, "..this man wishes us, after having visited you, to go to him and give an account of everything you say."[307] Napoleon would not have it.

One object did make it through to Napoleon without Lowe getting a hold of it first. Hidden in a letter written to Marchand was a folded piece of paper labeled 'King of Rome's hair.' When the valet handed the folded paper to the Emperor, he opened it to reveal the "*beautiful blond hair of his son, he told me to place it in his travel kit. I placed it next to a lock of hair of Empress Josephine's sent to him on the island of Elba.*"[308] Protected inside this travel kit of the Emperor's were objects that brought him closest to the two people he loved most. If he could not hold them in his arms, he could still hold and gaze upon something that was 'them.'

A few days later, Las Cases described how Napoleon received the first letter from his family. Its contents moved him immensely.

> *I handed it to him. He read it over once and sighed; and then, having read it a second time, he tore it, and threw the fragments beneath the table. This letter was delivered open! The Emperor then resumed his perusal of the Journal [from Europe], and suddenly stopping, he said, after a few moments' silence: --"That letter was from poor Madame [Napoleon's mother]: she is well and wishes to come to reside with me at St. Helena!" After this he continued reading. This, which was the first letter that the Emperor had received from any individual of his family, was in the handwriting of Cardinal Fesch [Napoleon's uncle]. The Emperor was evidently much hurt by its having been delivered to him open.*[309]

What made it emotionally painful for the Emperor were the words of his mother. She wrote to her son, "*I am very old,*" she says in her letter to the Emperor, "*to undertake a voyage of 2,000 leagues. I shall probably die on the way, but what does it matter? I shall die near you.*"[310]

This issue of the Governor opening and reading letters addressed to the Emperor and members of his entourage greatly angered Napoleon. In his mind, they were personal letters from family that had no bearing on their exile nor did they possess anything that would compromise his detention. Lowe feared that any correspondence could either aid in an escape or else influence public opinion in Europe.

Shortly after the incident of the letter from Napoleon's mother, another batch of letters was held by the Governor simply because they were not properly addressed to him as the Governor of the Island. Lowe's orders were that any correspondence to Longwood must be addressed to him and only after his review would the Governor have them delivered to the French. Since the letters were not properly addressed, he held them back. According to Las Cases, the letters were sent back to England without the French being told from whom the letters had come. Napoleon said that if this was true, "*there was something peculiarly cruel in the conduct of the Governor.*"[311]

To Napoleon, the Governor's conduct seemed to be an overall plan by the English to drive the Emperor to suicide. But he would not have it. Instead of driving the Emperor to suicide, it created a new battle for him to win.

> *I have always regarded it as a maxim, that a man exhibits more real courage by supporting calamities and resisting misfortunes when they occur, than by putting an end to his life. Self-destruction is the act of a gambler who has lost all, or that of a ruined spend-thrift, and proves nothing but a want of courage. [The English] deceives itself, if it supposes that by having recourse to all possible means of overwhelming me, such as sending me into exile on this rock, depriving me all communication with my nearest relations, to such an extent as to leave me in absolute ignorance at this moment whether any of my blood are alive, isolating me from the world, and imposing vexations and useless restrictions, which become more and more rigorous every day, it thinks to exhaust my power of endurance, and to drive me to commit suicide.*[312]

Napoleon would battle on.

During the middle of May 1816, Lowe made a surprise visit when Napoleon was in the garden. Napoleon was absolutely furious, not only that Lowe wanted to see the Emperor, but that he did not follow the protocol of requesting the visit first with the Grand Marshal. Montholon recorded that "*this circumstance led to deplorable results, and as it was the first cause of the Emperor's determination not to leave the house – a determination which contributed more than anything else to the development of the malady which killed him.*"[313] Napoleon would leave the grounds of Longwood less and less.

Bertrand informed Governor Lowe of Napoleon's annoyance with his unannounced visit and especially with the fact that the Emperor was required to have an English soldier escort him when he went out riding. The Governor brushed aside the complaint and said that he himself would accompany the Emperor if he wished. Lowe even hinted at requiring an English escort if Napoleon wanted to sit in the garden of Longwood. Grand Marshal Bertrand became enraged at the notion. *"Well!"* cried Bertrand, *"that is a way of polishing the Emperor off more quickly."* Whereupon, Lowe replied: *"No one wishes to kill him. It is he himself who is doing that."*[314]

Once his temper eased over this surprise visit by the Governor, Napoleon reflected upon the anger that Lowe could induce in him. In conversation with Las Cases, the Emperor discussed the first meeting the two men had.

> *I behaved very ill to him, no doubt,"* said he, *"and nothing but my present situation could excuse me; but I was out of humour, and could not help it; I should blush for it in any other situation. Had such a scene taken place at the Tuileries, I have felt myself bound in conscience to make atonement. Never, during the period of my power, did I speak harshly to any one without afterwards saying something to make amends for it. But here I uttered not a syllable of conciliation, and I had no wish to do so. However, the Governor proved himself very insensible to my severity; his delicacy did not seem wounded by it. I should have liked, for his sake, to have seen him shew a anger, or bang the door after him when he went away. This would at least have shown that there was some spring and elasticity about him; but I found nothing of the kind.*[315]

Montholon could easily see how the Emperor could flash this moment of anger when in the presence of Governor Lowe. Napoleon was not at the Tuileries, nor Versailles, nor on the battlefield listening to the begging of the sovereign he had just defeated. He was instead in a renovated barn on an island in the middle of the Atlantic attempting to keep whatever reminisces of his Imperial Court while at the same time hoping for some word from his loved ones in Europe. Montholon described the difficulty Napoleon faced when he recorded that *"in captivity, the smallest circumstances often furnish a pretext for an explosion of bad temper. A man must have worn a prisoner's chain in order to comprehend how much moral courage it requires to restrain the sufferings of the mind, and not to suffer oneself to be ruled by spirit of acrimony, which is always ready to see an insult in a smile, a bitter word, or a difference of opinion.*"[316]

Unfortunately for the Emperor, it was not just Governor Lowe that frustrated him. Even his own entourage began to battle one another. General Gourgaud was very jealous if any other member of the French suite seemed to garner more favor with the Emperor than he. Gourgaud particularly disliked the attention that Montholon received from Napoleon. The arguments between the two men reached such a peak that a duel was going to take place. Upon hearing of the proposed duel, Napoleon "*intervened and summoned them: he preached conciliation, and disarmed them both with his paternal words. A few words uttered by General Gourgaud annoyed the Emperor.*"[317] Napoleon rebuked Gourgaud.

> "*Much as I like to have you near me if you live together in peace, you disturb me if you cannot share with me the few joys that are left to us; I would prefer to see you both go. It would be quieter if I were alone with Marchand.*"[318]

Though flattered by Napoleon's confidence in the valet's company, Marchand knew that losing these men would cast the Emperor further into the humdrum abyss of boredom and silence. "*The Emperor, if left alone, would have quickly realized the deep solitude in which he would have found himself with only me near him when everything that surrounded him barely sufficed to occupy the prodigious activity of his mind.*"[319]

Montholon also recorded this incident in his memoirs. He too remembered the event leading to a potential duel and the Emperor intervening.

> *Paris to Longwood, what an immense transition! I accuse no one. At first, it was too much for us all. A duel was about to take place; the Emperor heard of it, and disarmed us by saying with the emotion of a father: "Do you wish to fight under*

> *my very eyes? Am I then no longer the object of your care? Are not the eyes of our enemies fixed upon Longwood? You have quitted your families, you have sacrificed everything from love to me, and in order to share my misfortunes, and you are now about voluntarily to aggravate them, and to render them insupportable. Be brothers! otherwise you will be only an additional punishment to me! Be brothers, I command you – I entreat you as a father!*[320]

But on this issue, the Emperor's generals would not obey. Their constant squabbling would make life for Napoleon even more difficult at Longwood.

On the night of June 5, 1816, Las Cases found the Emperor to be somewhat withdrawn and depressed. "*Towards evening, the Emperor sent for me in his own room. I found him alone, near a small fire, but almost in the dark, the light being placed in the next apartment. This obscurity, he said, was in harmony with his melancholy. He was silent and dejected.*"[321]

But Napoleon's life was about to get more difficult. Another ship had landed in Jamestown and on board were the Allied Commissioners.

*   *   *

The Allied Commissioners were now on St. Helena. These were the men who represented the nations of France, Russia, and Austria on the island of St. Helena. They were as follows: Count Balmain of Russia, Baron Sturmer of Austria, and Marquis de Montchenu of France. They were commissioned, on behalf of their countries, to ensure that Napoleon remained on the island and did not escape. They were expected to view the prisoner with their own eyes. Napoleon would never let this happen.

The Emperor let it be known that he would not meet these men in their official capacity as Allied Commissioners. To do so, would be to accept his position as a prisoner. This, Napoleon would not do. The Emperor said he would only see them as private citizens. While visiting with Admiral Malcolm, Napoleon explained his reasoning. *"If I saw them as Commissioners, it would be acknowledging that I was a prisoner to their masters, which I am not."*[322] Napoleon then turned his anger towards the leaders of the Allied nations.

> *What could I say to the Austrian Commissioner, who comes from my father-in-law without a kind word, or even to say my son, his grandson, is alive, from a man who pressed me to marry his daughter, and to whom I twice restored his kingdom? And how am I to address the Russian, whose Emperor has been at my feet, and who called me his best friend? I am less embarrassed with the Frenchman. Louis owes me nothing. But it does not signify seeing them; why were they sent?*[323]

Admiral Malcolm explained to him that England would probably rather they never came to the island. He believed the English Ministry found them more of a nuisance than a benefit. But Napoleon would have none of it and continued his complaints against the British Crown. As Lady Malcolm recorded, Napoleon *"always returned to his grievances."*[324]

Napoleon did question his doctor, Barry O'Meara, as to whether or not he had seen the men yet. When the doctor answered in the affirmative, Napoleon asked about the French minister in particular. O'Meara explained how he saw the men in town and how French Commissioner Montchenu complained that his role would be difficult because he did not speak any English. *"Napoleon laughed very heartily at this, and repeated, bevard, imbecile, several times. "What folly it is," said he, "to send those commissioners out here. Without charge or responsibility, they will have nothing to do but to walk about the streets and creep up the rocks. The Prussian government has displayed more judgment and saved their money.'"*[325] To Marchand, Napoleon said that he knew of Montchenu and mocked him when Marchand reported that the Frenchman wore a uniform and a sword around the island. The Emperor said, *"I know the man...he's an old dotard, a 'carriage general' who has never heard a shot in his entire life."*[326]

The Commissioners came directly to Longwood as soon as they could to execute their orders to see the prisoner with their own eyes so that they could report back to their respective countries. When Napoleon was told they were coming towards Longwood, he asked for his spyglass so that he could view them. The Emperor had cut a slit in the shutter so that he could view people outside of Longwood without them being able to view him.[327] Bertrand, Gourgaud, Montholon, and Las Cases went out to meet the men to explain that Napoleon would not see them. The Russian Commissioner complained that they "*would be the laughingstock of Europe when people heard that, having come to Saint Helena, they had departed without seeing the Emperor.*"[328] All the Commissioners complained of the poor weather of the island and the fact that boredom had already set in.

With the continuous vexations by Lowe in the form of new regulations, his insistence that the Emperor be seen daily by a British officer, and threatening deportation to members of Napoleon's entourage for disobeying his restrictions, the Emperor retreated to the seclusion of his bedroom. He would remain there for days, without leaving the room for fresh air. The combination of the Governor's paranoia and the Emperor's stubbornness led to a gradual decline in his health. The lack of exercise and the dampness of the climate took its toll on his stomach and legs. His stomach would cause him immense pain and his legs began to wobble when he walked. As idleness chipped away at his strength and stamina, time began to chip away at his hopes of ever seeing Paris, his family, and his son again. The heart reminds the brain of what the brain cannot forget, while the brain reminds the heart of what the heart cannot heal. The mental strain rises from the struggle of coping with the two as they battle one another. The battle for Napoleon was no longer on a distant field glistening with the morning dew; it was now within him against the humdrum of his present existence. The new reality was that he could not change what went on around him. He could only command what happened within the walls of Longwood. But this did not prevent him from trying even as the battle was taking its toll on him.

Only one person could calm the turmoil that plagued this lonely man's mind: Betsy.

*   *   *

Holding good to his promise, Mr. Balcombe brought his daughters to visit the Emperor as often as possible. When Betsy first went to visit Napoleon at Longwood after he moved out of The Briars, she found him to be more lonely and depressed. But she knew that once they got back to their usual antics, she could cheer him right up.

One of the first things they did consisted of Napoleon teaching Betsy how to shoot pistols at a target. Contrary to the logic of a prison guard, Lowe permitted Napoleon and his entourage to keep their pistols and rifles. Probably the security of over a thousand British soldiers nearby allowed the Governor the peace of mind to rest comfortably knowing that the French exiles would be hard pressed to begin an armed rebellion against his authority. Betsy recorded the lesson with Napoleon in her memoirs.

He put one [pistol] into my hand, loaded, I believe, with powder, and, in great trepidation, I fired it off; he often called me afterwards "La petite tirailleure," and said he would form a corp of sharpshooters, of which I should be the captain. He then went into the house, and he took me into the billiard-room, a table having been just set up at Longwood. I remember thinking it too childish for men, and very like marbles on a larger scale. The emperor condescended to teach me how to play, but I made very little progress, and amused myself with trying to hit his imperial fingers with the ball instead of making cannons and hazards.[329]

The playfulness of the Emperor's heart was there at a moment's notice to enjoy in some mischievous adventures with Betsy. But at the same time, she could see "*he was more subject to depression of spirits than when at the Briars, but still gleams of his former playfulness shone out at times.*"[330] There was no doubt in the mind of this young adolescent that "*Napoleon's health and activity began to decline soon after his arrival at Longwood. In consequence of the unfortunate disputes with the governor, Sir Hudson Lowe, his health became visibly impaired. He was unable, consequently, to enjoy that buoyancy of spirit which had probably been the chief cause of his allowing me to be so often in his society, and of his distinguishing me with so much regard. But he never failed to treat me with the greatest tenderness and kindness.*"[331] Though the mental battle with Lowe was taking its toll physically on the Emperor, the caring and gentleness of his heart was still there.

The humorous episodes, the mischievous tricks, and the playful relationship that occurred between the Emperor and Betsy became the talk of the island of St. Helena. But that was not the only place. Europe was beginning to hear about the stories of their 'relationship' to which rumor and sensationalism took their hideous form, due to the French Commissioner, the Marquis de Montchenu. Along with numerous other writings, the Marquis had written a letter in which "*he described all the romping games that had taken place between Napoleon and our family, such as blindman's bluff, the sword scenes, and ending his communication by observing, that "Miss Betsee" was the wildest little girl he had ever met; and expressing his belief, that the young lady was folle* [madwoman]."[332]

Against the angry protests of Mr. Balcombe, and with the overriding approval of Governor Lowe, Montchenu was given permission to interview Betsy. During the interview, the French Commissioner asked Betsy all about the playful acts that had occurred between them, specifically the sword incident. When Montchenu asked if she had wanted to kill the Emperor with the sword, it was reported that Betsy answered, "*Not really, just puncture him slightly for fun.*"[333]

But her innocent answers and descriptions were purposely taken out of context by the Frenchman, and published in the papers of Europe. The articles depicted the Emperor as courting the young girl and that a secret relationship was occurring between them. When copies of these papers arrived at St. Helena, Mr. Balcombe became enraged and Betsy explained that he "*wished to call the marquess to an account for his ill nature; but my mother's intercessions prevailed, and she obtained an ample apology from the marquess.*"[334]

The Emperor was also thoroughly disgusted with the treatment of Betsy and the publication of the lies in the articles.

> *On hearing of the affront that "Miss Betsee" had received from the vieux imbecile, [Montchenu] as Napoleon generally denominated him, he re-*

quested Dr. O'Meara would call at the Briars on his way to St. James's Valley, with a message to me, which was to let me know how I might revenge myself. It so happened, that the marquess prided himself on the peculiar fashion of the wig, to which was attached a long cue. This embellishment to his head Napoleon desired me to burn off with caustic. I was always ready for mischief, and in this instance had a double inducement, on the emperor's promise to reward me, on the receipt of the pigtail, with the prettiest fan Mr. Solomon's shop contained. Fortunately I was prevented indulging in this most hoydenish trick, but the remonstrances of my mother. The next time I saw the emperor, his first exclamation was, "Eh, bien, Mademoiselle Betsee, a tu obei mes orders et gagne l'eventail?" (did you obey my orders and earn the fan?) In reply, I made a great merit of being too dutiful a daughter to disobey my mother, however much my inclinations prompted me to revenge the insult. He pinched my ear, in token of approval, and said, "Ah, Miss Betsee, tu commences a etre sage." (you are becoming wise). He then called Dr. O'Meara, and asked him if he had procured the fan? The doctor replied, that there were none pretty enough. I believe I looked disappointed; on perceiving which, Napoleon, with his usual good nature, consoled me with the promise of something prettier – and kept his word. In a few days I received a ring of brilliants, forming the letter N, surmounted by a small eagle.[335]

Napoleon always did things for Betsy, and the children in his entourage, out of the kindness of his heart and loved to see the excitement that filled their eyes, made them smile, and induced laughter, which left him with joy and happiness. For Betsy, in particular, Mr. and Mrs. Balcombe met his kind gestures with thanks and appreciation.

But the Governor was a completely different story. Lowe was keeping a watchful eye on how close Mr. Balcombe and the prisoner were becoming. The growing friendship between Mr. Balcombe and the Emperor was becoming a problem for Governor Lowe. Unfortunately, on a couple of occasions, Betsy was placed in the middle.

> *One of the many instances of Napoleon's great good nature, and his kindness in promoting my amusement, was on the occasion of the races at Deadwood, which had been instituted by the Honourable Henry John Rous, the present member for Westminster, and which were at that time anticipated by the inhabitants of the island is a kind of jubilee. From having been, as was often the case, in arrears with my lessons, my father, by way of punishing me, declined that I should not go to the races; and fearing that he might be induced to break his determination, lent my pony Tom, to a friend of his for that day. My vexation was very great, at not knowing where to get a horse, and I happened to mention my difficulty to Dr. O'Meara, who told Napoleon; and my delight may be conceived when, a short time after our party had left the Briars for Deadwood, I perceived the doctor winding down the mountain path which led to our house, Followed by a slave leading a superb grey horse called "Mameluke" with a lady's sidesaddle and housings of crimson velvet embroidered with gold. Dr. O'Meara said that on telling the emperor of my distress, he desired the quietest horse in his stable to be immediately prepared for my use. This simply good-natured act of the emperor occasioned no small disturbance on the island, and sufficiently pu-*

> *nished me for acting contrary to my father's wishes, by the pain it gave me to hear that he was considered to have committed a breach of discipline in permitting one of his family to ride a horse belonging to Longwood establishment, and for which he was reprimanded by the governor.*[336]

Governor Lowe would not forget this incident. His eye was squarely on Mr. Balcombe.

*   *   *

Even at a young age, Betsy was quite aware of the boredom that ruled Napoleon's world on St. Helena. She recorded that "*there was so very little to vary the monotony of Napoleon's life, that he took an interest in the most trifling attempts at gaiety in the island, and he generally consented to our entreaties to be present at some of the many entertainments which my father delighted in promoting.*"[337] When Betsy's birthday approached, Mr. Balcombe planned a large outdoor party for her in which many of the most prominent people of the island were invited. Excited as she was about the event, Betsy begged the Emperor to come to her party. He promised that he would. As she was enjoying the party and playing with her friends, Betsy witnessed "*the emperor riding along the hill's side towards the house.*"

> *But on seeing such an assembly, he sent to say he would content himself with looking at us from the heights above. I did not consider this was fulfilling his promise of coming to the party, and not liking to be so disappointed, I scampered off to where he had taken up his position, and begged he would be present at our festivity, telling him he must not refuse, since it was my birthday. But all my entreaties were unavailing; he said he could not make up his mind to descend the hill to be exposed to the gaze of the multitude, who wished to gratify their curiosity with*

the sight of him. I insisted, however, on his tasting a piece of birthday cake, which had been sent for that occasion by a friend from England, and who little knowing the strict surveillance exercised over all those in any way connected with the fallen chief and his adherents, had the cake ornamented with a large eagle; this, unluckily for us, was the subject of much animadversion. I named it to Napoleon as an inducement for him to eat the cake, saying, "It is the least you can do for getting us into such disgrace." Having thus induced him to eat a thick slice, he pinched my ear, calling me a saucy simpleton, and galloped away humming, or rather attempting to sing, with his most unmusical voice, "Vive Henri Quatre."[338]

Napoleon was quite interested in trying to learn the English language. Las Cases tried to teach the Emperor the language but found success to be quite difficult. Betsy also made the same attempt and became increasingly frustrated with the lack of progress by her student. *"For my part, I seldom had patience to render him much assistance, my sister being generally obliged to finish what I had begun, for in the middle of his lesson I would walk away attracted by some frivolous pursuit; on returning I was always saluted with a tap on the cheek or a pinch of the ear, with the exclamation of "Ah! Mademoiselle Betsee, petite etourdie que vous etes, vous ne devenez jamais sage (small that you are, you will never become wise).""*[339]

It is remarkable how Betsy was allowed into the most intimate moments of Napoleon's exile. On one occasion, the young girl observed the Emperor during an instance where he was attempting to relive and almost correct the past. Betsy explained how she and her sister *"found him in the billiard-room, employed looking over some very large maps, and moving about a number of pins, some with red heads, others with black. I asked him what he was doing. He replied that he was fighting over again some of his battles, and that the red-headed pins were meant to represent the English, and the black to indicate the French. One of his chief amusements was going through the evolutions of a lost battle, to see if it were possible by any better maneuvering to have won it.*"[340]

Even in exile, Napoleon's military mind was still churning out strategies to outwit his opponents, to correct previous mistakes in battle, and to replay military situations to exploit whatever weakness he could find in his enemies. The sadness in this situation is that Napoleon's mind would never rest. As General, Legislator, and Emperor, this was an invaluable asset that made him successful. In exile on St. Helena, it became an adversary that would not rest or surrender. But he still made every attempt to battle the past.

*   *   *

Word was sent to Longwood that a ball was going to be given by the officers of the 66th Regiment. This provided some enjoyment to the French ladies at Longwood and "*afforded some variety to the dreariness of Madame Bertrand's changed existence.*"[341] Betsy explained that she, her sister, and mother were also invited to attend the event and that the Emperor decided that the Balcombes would travel to the ball with the French ladies together in Napoleon's carriage. To Betsy's delight, the Emperor invited the family to dine with him before they left for the affair.

Before the meal, Madame Montholon had her maid arrange Betsy's hair to which she described that she was made to "*look like a Chinese.*"[342] It was not only her appearance that made her uncomfortable but the fact that she knew all too well that Napoleon would have some sarcastic comment about her appearance. To her amazement, he complimented her by saying "*it was the only time he had ever seen it wear the appearance of any thing like neatness.*"[343] A typical Napoleon response to Betsy; compliment laced with a playful jest. But the Emperor was a little put out with the shortness of her frock. "*He declared it frightful...and desired me to have it lengthened.*"[344]

As they sat for dinner, the Emperor took great interest in the drinking habits of Mr. Balcombe, though he was not even present at the meal. He explained how he found it odd that Englishmen enjoyed sitting so long at the dinner table after the meal to consume continuous glasses of alcohol.

I recollect his remarking upon the want of gallantry displayed by Englishmen, in sitting so long after dinner. He said, "If Balcombe had been here, he would want to drink one, two, three, ah! cinq bouteilles, eh? (five bottles) Balcombe go to Briars to get droonk?" It was one of his early attempts at expressing himself in English. I think I can see him now, holding up one of his exquisitely taper fingers, and counting how many bottles my father usually drank before he joined the ladies. "If I were you, Mrs. Balcombe," he said, addressing my mother, "I should be very angry at being turned out to wait for two or three hours, whilst your husband and his friends were making themselves drunk. How different are Frenchmen, who think society cannot be agreeable without the presence of ladies!"[345]

But Betsy knew Napoleon all too well and was quite aware of his own dinner routine and antics. She described his way of letting those know at the dinner table that he was done with his meal. Betsy wrote that *"the emperor's signal of rising from table, his manner of performing that ceremony being brusque and startling. He would push his chair suddenly away, and rise as if he had received an electric shock."*[346]

A short time later, Betsy made another visit to Longwood to find the Emperor in severe pain from a tooth that had to be extracted by Dr. O'Meara. Napoleon's mouth was very swollen and he explained to his young visitor of the immense pain he was experiencing. Betsy would have none of Napoleon's complaining. She exclaimed, *"What! – you complained of the pain so trifling an operation can give? You, who have passed through battles innumerable, amid storms of bullets whizzing around you, and by some of which you must occasionally have been hit! I am ashamed of you. But, nevertheless, give me the tooth, and I will get it set by Mr. Solomons as an ear-ring, and wear it for your sake."*[347]

Napoleon roared his usually hearty laugh at her mocking words and remarked that he hoped she should never cut her wisdom teeth. Betsy enjoyed kidding the Emperor and explained that "*he was always in extra good humour with himself whenever he was guilty of any thing approaching to the nature of a witticism.*"[348]

There was one thing that Betsy loved to purposely annoy the Emperor with and that was his incredible issue with ugly women. He emphatically became aggravated with their presence. Betsy thoroughly enjoyed bringing women who were less than attractive to Longwood and to observe the reaction of Napoleon.

> *...knowing this weakness, I one day begged he would allow me to introduce to him a Mrs. S., the wife of a gentleman holding a high official appointment in India. I must confess feeling rather nervous at the time, knowing her to be one of the very plainest persons ever seen. She had, nevertheless, all the airs and graces of a beauty, and believed herself to be as lovely as Chinerey had pourtrayed her on ivory. She thought she might make an impression on the great man, and for that purpose loaded herself with all the finery an Indian wardrobe could afford...When introduced to Napoleon, and after he had put the usual questions to her, as to whether she were married, how many children she had, and so on; he scrutinized her over and over again, trying, but in vain, to discover some point whereon to compliment her; at last he perceived that she had an immense quantity of coarse, fuzzy, black hair, which he remarked, by saying to her, "Madame, you have the most luxuriant hair." The lady was so much pleased with this speech of the emperor's, that on her arrival in England she published in the newspapers an account of her interview with him, and said "Napoleon had lost his heart to her beauty." I really did incur the emperor's displeasure for a few days by the trick I had played him, having led him to suppose he was about to see a*

perfect Venus; and he prohibited me from ever introducing any more ladies to him.[349]

Through all the vexations that the Emperor experienced at the hands Governor Lowe and the island of St. Helena, Betsy was always there to lighten his mood and bring some amusement to his captivity. But when she went back to The Briars at the end of the day, reality would soon rear its ugly head.

*   *   *

In June of 1816, Governor Lowe paid another visit to Longwood. The purpose of his visit was to explain to the Emperor that the expenses of the French suite were becoming more than London was willing to bear. According to Las Cases, Lowe stated to Grand Marshal Bertrand that *"his government…had never intended to allow the Emperor more than a table of four persons daily at most, and company to dine once-a-week."*[350] The Governor even requested that if Napoleon had funds in France, he should send for those funds to help supplement the cost of his table at Longwood.[351] Bertrand instructed the Governor to tell the Emperor himself.

With that, Governor Lowe, accompanied by Admiral Malcolm entered the garden outside Longwood, and Napoleon came out to meet them. The Emperor greeted the Admiral *"graciously and the governor with a cool politeness."*[352] When the Governor proceeded to dive right into the topic, the Emperor completely lost his temper and unleashed it on the man. Marchand recorded Napoleon telling Lowe to *"settle this matter with my butler: don't send anything if you like, I'll go and sit at the table of the officers of the 53rd regiment: I'm sure there is not one of them who would refuse to share his dinner with an old soldier like myself. You have…full control over my body, but my soul shall always elude you. Know well that I am as proud on this rock as when I commanded all of Europe. Had you any honor, you would request your transfer."*[353] Dr. O'Meara described Napoleon as someone *"who appeared at times considerably animated, frequently stopping and again hurried in his walk, and accompanying his words with a good deal of action."*[354]

Montholon recorded that Napoleon continued his rampage at the Governor by exclaiming,

> *How should I know you in any other relation than that of my jailor? You never suffer a day to pass without torturing me by your insults. Where have you ever commanded anything but bandits or deserters, the refuse of every country? I am well acquainted with the names of all the English generals of distinction, I have never heard your name mentioned except as a brigand chief. You have never commanded men of honour... Moreover, I do not believe your government to be so blinded by their hatred towards me, as to disgraced themselves by prescribing the infamous course of conduct which you preserve. In short, do not weary me any more with the disgusting details of your regulations respecting my table; send nothing to Longwood.*[355]

It was Admiral Malcolm himself that distinctly added to the recollection of the moment. His memoirs record a very detailed exchanged between the three men. Admiral Malcolm explained how Napoleon would only address him; the Emperor would not address the Governor directly. The Emperor did this as a way to delegitimize the authority of Governor Lowe. The Admiral recollected Napoleon stating indirectly to Governor Lowe,

> *You are a Lieut.-General, but you do your duty like un consigne (an order); you never commanded any men but Corsican deserters; you vex us hourly, by your little ways; you do not know how to conduct yourself towards men of honour, your soul is too low. Why do you not treat us like prisoners of war? You treat us like Botany Bay convicts." Here he stopped. Sir Hudson with much coolness replied: "I have every desire to render your situation as agreeable as it is in my power, but you prevent me. General Bertrand has written to me that I render your situation dread-*

ful; he accuses me, as you do now, of abuse of power and injustice. I am the subject of a free government; I hold every species of tyranny and despotism in execration, and I will repel every attack upon my character on this point, as a calumny against a man who cannot be attacked with the arms of truth."[356]

Admiral Malcolm tried to calm the situation by explaining that the two men of honor may not be understanding one another and that much of the information the two received may have been misrepresented or exaggerated to create tension. The Emperor would have none of this. He turned to the Admiral again and raged at Governor Lowe.

"Do you know he has had the meanness to keep from me a book, because on its cover I was designated Emperor, and he has boasted of having done so." "I boast?" said Sir Hudson. "Yes," added Bonaparte..."Permit me," said the Admiral, "to explain to you the story of the book..."[357]

Admiral Malcolm proceeded to explain to the Emperor that the Governor was not permitted to let things reach Napoleon if they were addressed to him with the Imperial title of 'Emperor.' Napoleon reminded him that other letters had reached Longwood with that very title. The Admiral replied that they had gone through the Governor's office first and had been written by Frenchmen, not Englishmen.[358] Napoleon would not back down.

"He has also had the meanness to speak of the contents of our letters that came open to him. My old mother, although I forbade her to write to me, wrote to say that she would come to St. Helena and die with me. This was told round the island." "Not by me," said Sir Hudson. "Yes, by you," rejoined Bonaparte;

"Mr. Balcombe mentioned it."[359]

The Emperor then dove into another list of grievances against the Governor building himself into a rage. Governor Lowe stood there stone-faced. The Admiral was also calm for the purposes of trying to mediate the situation that would be agreeable to both men. Napoleon continued his attack upon Lowe.

> *"If you were ordered to assassinate me, would you do so?" "No," answered Sir Hudson, "I would not. My countrymen do not assassinate." Bonaparte went on: "I see by your arrangements that you are afraid I should escape; you take useless precautions. Why do you not tie me hand and foot? And then you will be tranquil. You are not a general, you are only a scribe of office. To-morrow you will receive a letter from me, which I hope may be known in all Europe." Sir Hudson answered, that he should not have any objections, if all his proceedings were published in England and in every other country.*[360]

The volley of insults seemed to have no end. Napoleon continued with his attacks and the Governor continued to respond with an alabaster glare. The Admiral just could not seem to defuse the situation. Napoleon went on the counter attack again.

> *"It has insulted me in sending a man like you to guard me; you are no Englishman." Sir Hudson replied, "That makes me laugh." "What, laugh, sir!" said Bonaparte, turning to Sir Hudson with a look of surprise. "Yes, sir," answered Sir Hudson; "I say what I think; I say it not only makes me laugh, but it excites my pity, to see how misinformed you are with respect to my character, and for the rudeness of your manners. I wish you good morning." Sir Hudson then quitted him abruptly without further ceremony.*[361]

Governor Lowe was disgusted at the tone of the Emperor and the words he expressed to him and was seen to "*abruptly turn about and withdraw, without saluting Napoleon.*"[362] He went to voice his anger with Bertrand, but the Grand Marshal refused to meet with him. So the Governor then expressed his rage to Dr. O'Meara stating, "*Let General Bonaparte know that it depends on me to make his situation easier, but if he continues to show me no respect, I will make him experience my power. He is my prisoner, I have the right to treat him in accordance with his conduct, and if needed, I have the power to lock him up.*"[363] Upon hearing this account, Napoleon referred to Governor Lowe as a *sbirro Siciliano* (Sicilian spy.)[364]

Unable to find an outlet for his anger, Governor Lowe had dinner with the officers of the 53rd that night and explained to them that Napoleon "*no longer wanted to see them, because a red uniform made him sick.*"[365] The Emperor would not permit this false claim to go unchallenged. He sent for Marchand and had him immediately bring Captain Poppleton to the drawing room. Once he arrived, Napoleon said, "*Sir...you are, I believe, the oldest captain in the 53rd; please tell your comrades that they have been lied to, when it was insinuated that I no longer wanted to see them and that the sight of a red uniform made me sick. Tell them that I shall always see them with pleasure: I have great esteem for the 53rd, it is a regiment of brave men who have fought against me valiantly; I like brave soldiers who have received the baptism of fire, no matter what flag they fight under.*"[366] The Captain thanked the Emperor for his kindness and promised that he would.

*   *   *

On August 14, 1816, the Emperor enjoyed a few moments peace under a tent outside in the garden conversing with Las Cases about a number of topics. As he was listening, Napoleon caught sight of little Tristan Montholon and called him over. "*The Emperor placed little Tristan, whom he saw crossing the meadow, at table, and was much amused with him during the whole of the repast.*"[367] The playfulness of a child always amused the Emperor and comforted any anguish that may have plagued his mind.

Later that evening, it was remarked that the Emperor's birthday was the following morning. Napoleon responded by saying, "*Many healths will be drunk to-morrow, in Europe, to St. Helena. There are certainly some sentiments, some wishes, that will traverse the ocean.*"[368] The Emperor was enough of a realist to know that there were many in Europe who were not drinking to his health and good fortunes.

August 15, 1816, came to find the Emperor experiencing his 47th birthday in the land of exile, surrounded by the last followers of his reign. As he did on other birthdays, the Emperor took great joy in playing with the children and made sure to give each one a gift as had been his tradition. To them, Napoleon was their beloved grandfather who spoiled them with not just gifts, but with love and affection. They, in turn, were all too willing to return the same emotion and fondness to him. *"In the evening, the second class of domestics, including the English, had a grand supper, and a dance afterwards. To the astonishment of the French, not an Englishman got drunk."*[369] There is no question that Napoleon would have taken great interest in the lack of inebriation on behalf of the English.

The stress of the visit on Napoleon agitated an already growing pain in the lower part of the Emperor's side. He had complained about it before on a number of occasions, but would use his usual remedy of rubbing *"it briskly with a soft brush, then with his hand put cologne on it."*[370] But the pain continued to increase. Napoleon asked Dr. O'Meara what he believed caused liver disease and the doctor replied drunkenness to which the Emperor reacted with laughter and replied that this cause could never be the case with him. Napoleon responded that it was the recent encounter with Lowe that agitated his side. He complained to the doctor about the Governor withholding a book that was sent to Longwood entitled "To Napoleon the Great." The Emperor mocked Lowe saying *"What a pity! A printed book! It is with the same spirit that the newspapers are censored before I receive them; he fears I might find something in those he holds back to comfort my misfortune. I never want to lay eyes on that man again."*[371]

The issue of Governor Lowe reducing the expenditures of the French Suite and asking the Emperor to send for funds from Europe to make up the difference also led to Napoleon's growing anger. On September, 9, 1816, Napoleon dictated a lengthy letter to Montholon that was to be delivered to Governor Lowe listing his grievances against the newest restriction by the British jailor. In one paragraph of the letter, the Emperor takes direct aim at Lowe's reputation. *"Instead of endeavouring to reconcile your various duties, you seem, Sir, resolved to persist in a system of continual vexations. Will this do honor to your character? Will it deserve the approbation of your government, and of your nation? Allow me to doubt it."*[372]

In response to Governor Lowe's request that Napoleon send for money for his table at Longwood, the Emperor ordered that his trusted servant, Cipriani, break up his silver plates and sell them in town for British pounds. The money was to be brought to the Governor at Plantation House to be used to fund the food for the French Suite. Napoleon would play the game. He knew quite well that the sight of one of the Emperor's men selling his possessions in town to 'feed' them would find its way not only back to Lowe, but to Europe as well. The servant had 65 pounds, 6 ounces of silverware broken up. The action had its desired effect and the Governor quickly galloped to Longwood to confront Montholon. He angrily expressed his angst at Cipriani selling the plate to "*the Jews in James Town; and that if I insisted on the sale taking place, I must send and sell the plate to certain persons whom he [Governor] would point out to me.*"[373]

Montholon found it difficult seeing the Emperor's silver being destroyed just to provide food at Longwood. On this one occasion, the General disobeyed an order from his Emperor and instead sold Bertrand's silver in town. Napoleon "*laughed very heartily at the fraud which my solicitude for his comfort had suggested to me, and said, "Upon my faith, you have done well! and so much the better, that you have succeeded with this bandit, Lowe, as well as if I had not a silver dish left. As to Bertrand, so much the worse for him, if he has nothing but china! It was his advice which I followed.*"[374]

There is no doubt that Governor Lowe was fearful of how this incident would make its way back to Europe. In the eyes of Montholon, "*the English ministry feared the impression which would be made on public opinion, should the true state of affairs at St. Helena become known.*"[375]

Whether it was the provisions for Longwood or the communications the French had with the locals, Governor Lowe's paranoia was growing. The Governor's concern over 'misinformation' reaching London regarding his conduct and detention of Napoleon consumed every moment of Lowe's day and night. If information reached the British Ministry that Lowe was not doing his job effectively or to the extent that the King wanted, his reputation would be tarnished beyond repair. This was not some bureaucratic assignment of managing military supplies as a Quarter Master; this was protecting the world from the number one prisoner of the British

Empire. If reports were to reach Europe of his failure at securing Napoleon, Sir Hudson Lowe would be publically humiliated. The Governor would never let this happen.

Like other members of the Emperor's retinue, the effects of Lowe's restrictions on Napoleon infuriated Las Cases.

> *The vexations by which Napoleon was assailed were incessant; they pursued him at every moment of his existence. Not a day passed without the infliction of a fresh wound; and one of the torments recorded in fabulous history may be said to have been thus realized...to see him...chained like Prometheus to a rock, and, like him, under the claws of a vulture, which delights in tearing him to pieces...*[376]

It was these vexations by the Governor that plagued Longwood and would continue to do so. But little did Napoleon know that the French entourage and his new English friends that helped to fill his exile with some sort of enjoyment and content would quickly decline in number within the next few months. Lowe would make the prison walls of St. Helena rapidly close in on the Emperor by removing the very people that Napoleon relied on the most.

*It is at the moment we are going to part with
existence that we cling to it with all our might*

Napoleon

Chapter 6

"The Soul Is Beyond Their Reach"

As September 1816 approached, the Emperor reflected on his situation saying, *"We have now,"* said he, *"been at St. Helena more than a year, and with regard to certain points we remain just as we were on the first day of our arrival."*[377] This was going to change and there was little he could do about it.

If the Emperor believed for a moment that the vexations created at the hands of Governor Lowe would subside, he would be proven wrong. But this was Napoleon Bonaparte, and he never expected the British Governor to change his tone, and he did not. The battle between the two men would rage on.

Napoleon could always distract himself from the constant irritations of Lowe by immersing himself in the dictations of his history. The occupying force of work provided the Emperor with a temporary refuge from the relentless contemplating of ways to outwit the Governor. These dictations *"were a certain means of calming the mind of the Emperor, by raising him above his present situation and making him hover above the world like that eagle which he had taken for his arms, and which will one day again be the arms of France."*[378] Montholon was very hopeful in his words that he recorded in his memoirs. But the hope of Napoleon returning to his beloved country, or to any country outside of St. Helena, was rapidly fading. Though the Emperor might not return to Europe, many members of his entourage would, very soon.

* * *

The Emperor enjoyed walking in the garden to gain some fresh air and to acquire a bit of exercise. Many members of his suite were quick to observe the difference in his appearance and especially in his lack of mobility. If he became too weak to walk, he would often go for a ride in the calash with Madame Montholon or others from his entourage.

During one walk in the garden on September 16, Madame Montholon scared away a dog that had wandered into the area. *"You do not like dogs, Madame?"* said the Emperor. – *"No, Sire."* – *"If you do not like dogs, you do not like fidelity; you do not like those who are attached to you; and, therefore, you are not faithful."* – *"But...but..."* said she – *"But...but..."* repeated the Emperor, *"where is the error of my logic? Refute my arguments if you can!"*[379] Madame Montholon was not amused with the Emperor.[380]

But his humor could not disguise the deteriorated feeling that would overcome him from his lack of exercise. Las Cases explained that Napoleon was *"very much altered in his looks, particularly since his last illness. He grows very weak, and feels fatigued after two turns round the garden...his step becomes heavy and lagging, and his features altered. His resemblance to his brother Joseph is now striking; so much so, that, on going to meet him the other day in the garden, I could have sworn it was Joseph* [Bonaparte]*."*[381] Fatigue, depression, and anger were rapidly aging the fallen Emperor.

During the latter part of September 1816, when Secretary Las Cases would meet with the Emperor to record his dictations, he found him reflecting more on his family and his emotions concerning their absence from his life. When discussing his mother, Napoleon would have tears in his eyes. Madame Mere was quite alive still at this time and in Europe longing to be with her exiled son. Napoleon explained his devotion to his mother saying, *"I certainly love my mother with all my heart; there is nothing that I would not do for her...I belong to my mother, but my wife and son belong to me."*[382]

This led Napoleon to talk of his son, the King of Rome, very affectionately to Las Cases. Over the years, Las Cases had many discussions with those who served in the interior of the Emperor's household, particularly Marchand, and all shared how *"fond he was of indulging his feelings of affection towards his family."*

> *[Napoleon] would sometimes take his son in his arms, and embrace him with the most ardent demonstrations of paternal love. But most frequently his affection would manifest itself by playing teasing or whimsical tricks. If he met his son in the gardens, for instance, he would throw him down or upset his toys. The child was brought to him every morning at breakfast time,*

and he then seldom failed to besmear him with every thing within his reach on the table.[383]

As Napoleon continued to discuss his family, the emotional contemplation would wear upon his heart. This always led him to remain sober the rest of the evening. These memories were successful in bringing him moments of joy, but they could also viciously inflict painful wounds.

* * *

The restrictions that Lowe had placed upon Longwood were about to go beyond just the food for the table; they were now going to reduce the number of people there as well. Through direct orders from Lord Bathurst in England, Governor Lowe was to remove some of the Emperor's entourage and place them on the next available vessel to transport them back to Europe. The added cost to support their stay at Longwood was weighing on the English Treasury. But Bathurst encouraged Lowe to mask the removal as being requested by the very persons themselves and not by the English.

The first to be removed from the Emperor's entourage were Rousseau, Archambault, Santini, and Captain Piontkowski.[384] The French were considerably outraged at Governor Lowe's removal of these individuals while it also sent fear through their own veins. Marchand explained, "*this departure was not only felt by all of us, but left those who remained fearing they might be removed by a similar order.*"[385] Santini was so enraged by this action that he offered to kill Lowe for Napoleon. The man was so devoted to Napoleon that he was just waiting for the order to carry out the act. "*It was with great difficulty that the Emperor had obtained from him a solemn promise to renounce a project which he had formed, one fine morning, of lying in wait for Sir Hudson Lowe, at the turn of a road, and killing him, as his countrymen were in the habit of doing with their enemies.*"[386]

The Emperor responded to Santini in Corsican and said, "*Come, you rascal, you want to kill the governor? Don't you realize that I would be accused of having ordered you to do so!...I forbid you to think about such a thing in the future...*"[387] Though Napoleon made his point clear, Marchand recorded that the Emperor still ordered Cipriani "*to frequently impress on Santini that such a crime must not be committed."*[388] They were to leave aboard the next available ship bound for Europe.

To add salt to the wound, the Governor was now requiring all remaining members of the Emperor's entourage to sign new declarations vowing to follow all the new restrictions or face removal from St. Helena. Lowe was so steadfast in his actions that he personally came to Longwood to demand that his declarations be signed within 24 hours or all would be removed immediately. Marchand and others felt that Las Cases was a particular target of Lowe, fearing he was trying to illegally communicate with Europe through the smuggling of letters.[389] Pettiness and paranoia were definite flaws of Governor Lowe's character, but his suspicions sometimes were correct. Las Cases had been successful in smuggling a number of communications from the island at the orders of the Emperor himself.

The declaration by the Governor referred to Napoleon as 'General' and not 'Emperor,' which incensed the entire French suite. Napoleon dictated his own version of the declaration substituting the word 'Emperor,' but Lowe threatened to remove anyone who did not sign his version. This incident had quite an affect on the Emperor and he "*remained in his room, sad and preoccupied, pretending a calm he did not feel. For everyone, there was no doubt that the governor's words would be carried out.*"[390]

On October 15, 1816, Las Cases found the Emperor still deep in contemplation about the declarations that the French were required to sign. Napoleon agonized intensely over what was being required of his trusted followers.

> *"The insults," said he, "which are daily heaped upon those who have devoted themselves to me, insults which, it is very probable, will be multiplied to a still greater extent, present a spectacle which I cannot and must not longer endure. Gentlemen, you must leave me; I cannot see you submit to the restrictions which are about to be imposed on you, and which will doubtless soon be augmented. I will remain here alone. Return to Europe, and make known the horrible treatment to which I am exposed; bear witness that you saw me sinking into a premature grave. I will not al-*

> *low any one of you to sign this declaration in the form that is required. I forbid it. It shall never be said that hands which I had the power to command were employed in recording my degradation. If obstacles are raised respecting a mere foolish formality, others will be started tomorrow for an equally trivial cause. It is determined to remove you in detail; but I would rather see you removed altogether and at once. Perhaps this sacrifice may produce a result."*[391]

Las Cases pledged to the Emperor his eternal devotion and wish to remain with Napoleon on St. Helena. The Emperor still paced the room in thought. *"Such, however, is my fate,"* replied the Emperor calmly, *"and I must prepare for the worst; my mind is strong enough to meet it. They will cut short my life; that is certain."*[392]

After continuing to focus on the Governor and his restrictions, Napoleon expressed a profound belief to his secretary; *"Be this as it may, their power extend only to my body; the soul is beyond their reach: it will soar to Heaven even from the dungeon."*[393]

There was no way that any of the Emperor's companions were going to willingly leave him in his hour of need. Against Napoleon's orders, but out of devotion to their beloved Emperor, the French exiles signed Governor Lowe's declaration. They would attempt to remain on St. Helena until the very end.

The following morning, Las Cases found the Emperor to be in better spirits. As he entered Napoleon's bedroom chamber, the secretary found him seated while Santini was cutting his hair. While conversing with the Emperor, Las Cases observed a large piece of his hair fall to the floor from the scissors. *"I stooped to pick it up, and the Emperor, observing me, asked what I was doing. I replied that I had dropped something, upon which he smiled and pinched my ear; he guessed what I had picked up."*[394]

But Las Cases' presence on the island was about to come to an end.

Earlier in 1816, Las Cases had told the Emperor about his plan to send secret communications through his mulatto servant who was returning to London. The servant had recently been removed by Governor Lowe and was waiting for the next ship back to England. But the man had found a way to sneak out and visit Las Cases to offer his services to the Emperor in the form of carrying secret letters. Las Cases' goal was to write to Napoleon's brother, Lucien, to describe the deplorable conditions that the Emperor was experiencing on St. Helena at the hands of Governor Lowe. By using the servant, Las Cases could bypass the eyes of Lowe.

Napoleon listened to the proposal but instructed his trusted secretary to not carry out the plan. The Emperor explained that Cipriani had already established a clandestine line of communication using a tradesman from the island. The information that Napoleon wanted to reach Europe had already done so. Therefore, he reiterated to Las Cases that the plan, though noble, was not needed. The Emperor expected that his secretary would obey his order, but Las Cases did not.

* * *

On November 25, 1816, Napoleon spent a relaxing afternoon in the garden conversing with Admiral Malcolm. The British officer had brought some oranges to the Emperor that had just arrived from Cape Town. Upon the Admiral's departure, Napoleon retired to the drawing room to work on his memoirs with Las Cases.

Later in the afternoon, Marchand noticed Governor Lowe "*surrounded by a large staff, approaching at a gallop and heading for the house.*" Marchand continued by explaining how he "*stepped aside to let them go by, saluting them, and they returned the salute. The governor was accompanied by Sir Thomas Reade, his ADCs Gorrequer and Prichard, two dragoons, and a gentleman in civilian clothes, whom I later learned was the police commissioner who had come from the Cape on the frigate Adamant.*"[395] Moments later, the valet witnessed Las Cases being led away by the same group.

Napoleon summoned Gourgaud, Montholon, and Grand Marshal Bertrand to discuss what had occurred. The Emperor naturally concluded that Las Cases and disobeyed his wishes to not use his mulatto servant to send secret letters to Europe. Montholon informed the Emperor that Governor Lowe had brought the Commissioner of Police to search Las Cases papers while the secretary was with Napoleon in the drawing room. Once the search was completed, Governor Lowe ordered Las Cases arrested, his papers seized, and that he and his young son be brought to town.[396] Apparently, Las Cases' servant had been caught with secret letters written upon the inner silk of his jacket to be smuggled to Europe. The servant had confessed that he had been ordered to carry these letters by Secretary Las Cases.

Gourgaud recollected how the Emperor was distraught at the decision that Las Cases had made. *"A man in whom I had placed implicit confidence – who had seen all my papers – to behave like this! To try and send letters, via a slave!"*[397] Later that night as the Emperor and the rest of the French suite sat in the drawing room, Napoleon looked at the group and said, *"It seems to me,"* says the Emperor, *"as if I saw savages from the South Seas dancing round a prisoner whom they are about to devour."*[398]

In talking with Doctor O'Meara on the same day, Napoleon reiterated that he did not order Las Cases to carry out his plan and especially disapproved *"of the bungling manner in which he attempted it."*

> *I can only account for it by supposing, that the weight of affliction which presses upon us, together with the melancholy situation of his son, condemned to die of an incurable malady, have impaired his judgment. All this I wish to be known. I am sorry for it, because people will accuse me of having been privy to the plan, and will have a poor opinion of my understanding – supposing me to have consented to so shallow a plot...*

> *Las Cases has with him my campaigns in Italy, and all the official correspondence between the admiral, governor, and Longwood; and I am told that he has made a journal, containing an account of what passes here, with many anecdotes of myself. I have desired Bertrand to go to Plantation House and ask for them. It is the least interesting part of my life, as it only relates the commencement of it; but I should not like this governor to have it.*[399]

A few days later, Napoleon expressed his concern over his papers again to O'Meara. The Emperor was concerned that if he wrote his entire history while on the island that Governor Lowe might wait until Napoleon was finished then would send his British staff to come and seize that as well. The Emperor even wondered aloud if he should destroy the rest of his manuscripts. *"I must burn the whole of what I have written. It served as an amusement to me in this dismal abode, and might perhaps have been interesting to the world, but with this sbirro Siciliano* (Sicilian spy) *there is no guarantee nor security. He violates every law, and tramples under foot decency, politeness, and the common forms of society. He came up with a savage joy beaming from his eyes, because he had an opportunity of insulting and tormenting us."*[400]

Upon their next meeting, O'Meara expressed to Governor Lowe Napoleon's desire to have his papers returned to him safely and unread. To Napoleon's relief and O'Meara's surprise, Lowe agreed to return the papers and manuscripts to Longwood. But the Emperor still expressed concern over what was written in Las Cases' journal just in case the Governor read it. Napoleon summoned St. Denis who the Emperor knew had made a copy of Las Cases' journal. Napoleon quizzed St. Denis as to what the journal contained.

> *St. Denis replied that it was a Journal of everything remarkable that had taken place since the embarkation on board of the Bellerophon; and contained divers anecdotes of different persons, of Sir George Cockburn, &c. "How is he treated?" says Napoleon, "Comme ca, Sire, (indifferently). Has he said that I called him a requin, (shark!") "Yes, Sire."..."Anything about Admiral Malcolm?" "Yes, Sire." "Does it say that I observed, Behold the countenance of a real Englishman?" "Yes, Sire, he is very well treated." "Anything about the governor?" "A great deal, Sire," replied St. Denis, who could not help smiling. "Does it say that I said, Ciest un home ignoble, (he is a vile man,) and that his face was the most ignoble I had ever seen?" St. Denis replied in the affirmative, but added, that his expressions were very frequently*

moderated. Napoleon asked if the anecdote of the coffee-cup was in it: St. Denis replied, he did not recollect it. "Does it say that I called him sbire Sicilien?" "Oui, Sire." (Yes, sir.) "C'est son nom," (that is his name) said the emperor.[401]

On one hand, Napoleon was concerned about what the Governor might learn from reading the manuscripts of his memoirs. But on the other hand, the Emperor was not willing to back down on his critical assessment of Governor Lowe's character.

There was no doubt that Napoleon was going to quickly feel Las Cases' absence. Marchand recounted "*the Emperor was about to be dealt a blow in his habits and affections that could not be replaced;*"

...it was about to reach one of his officers and reduce to three the number of those remaining near him. It was another privation in the resources of the mind that he found in each of them. In his daily habits, he was about to feel a great void. Count Las Cases always read the newspapers to him as soon as they arrived; speaking English better than these gentlemen, during the horseback rides the Emperor, General Gourgaud, and he himself would take, he acted as interpreter in conversations with the people they met. Along with these gentlemen he had his working hours, and his conversation with the Emperor dealt with a past these much younger gentlemen had not known.[402]

Out of all the devoted men in the Emperor's entourage, Secretary Las Cases was of similar age and could have conversations with Napoleon about issues and events that they both experienced. Men quite younger than himself now surrounded the Emperor.

Montholon also recognized how devoted Las Cases was to Napoleon. In his memoirs, Montholon explained how the secretary's "*devotion to the Emperor never flagged; and it may be said with truth, that his thoughts were the same in Europe as at St. Helena, entirely occupied in the service of the Emperor."*[403]

Before Las Cases was to leave for Europe, Napoleon addressed a letter to his secretary in December of 1816. In it, Napoleon expressed his gratitude to Las Cases for his years of service and dedication to his Emperor. He also absolved Las Cases of any intentional motive to deceive the British or to carry out some secret correspondence with his letter that the Governor confiscated.

> *They were looking for a pretext to seize your papers. A letter to your friend in London could not warrant a police visit to your home, for it contained no plot, no mystery, and was only the expression of a noble and frank heart. The illegal and precipitous conduct of this occasion bears the mark of a lowly and personal hatred...Your services were necessary to me; only you read, spoke, and understood English...Once you arrive in Europe, whether you go to England or return to the motherland, forget the evils you have suffered here. You may boast of the loyalty you have shown me and the affection I hold for you. If someday you see my wife and son, please embrace them; for two years I have had no news of them, directly or indirectly. For the last six months there has been a German botanist here who had seen both of them in the gardens of Schoenbrunn; a few days before his departure, the barbarians prevented him from coming to give me news of them.*[404]

But Napoleon did not end his letter with pleasantries to his secretary. He used the moment to make direct accusations at his British jailors. He was well aware that Las Cases would spread the words of this letter across Europe with the hopes of ruining the credibility of Governor Lowe. The Emperor continued the letter by instructing Las Cases to:

> *console yourself and console my friends. My body, it is true, is within the power of the hatred of my enemies; they forget nothing that can assuage their vengeance. They are killing me with pinpricks, but providence is too just to allow this to last much longer. The unhealthiness of this devouring climate, the lack of everything that can sustain life, will shortly, I feel, put an end to this existence whose last moments shall be the shame of British character. Europe will someday point with horror at this hypocritical, evil man, whom true Englishmen will disavow a Britisher.*[405]

For days following the removal of Las Cases and his son from Longwood, Napoleon continuously contemplated the event itself. Russian Commissioner Count Balmain was well aware of the impact that Las Cases' deportation had on the Emperor. In his memoirs, Count Balmain recorded that "*Bonaparte remains very melancholy. The loss of Las Cases is a blow to his pride. He affects an indifferent air, but in the depths of his soul there is real suffering.*"[406] In a conversation with Dr. O'Meara, the Emperor insisted that Las Cases would not be the last to be removed. "*The next,*" said he, "*to be removed under some pretext, will be Montholon, as they see that he is the most useful and consoling friend to me…After they (Napoleon's officers) have been taken away, you will be sent off…*"[407]

Napoleon was partially correct. Governor Lowe was not finished removing people from St. Helena.

*   *   *

As the days lingered on, Napoleon's health continued to decline. Dr. O'Meara often checked upon the Emperor out of concern over this decline and the doctor reiterated Napoleon's need for daily exercise. During one of these visits, the tables were actually turned. While the doctor was conversing with Napoleon, his vision became blurred and he fell to the floor.

> *When I recovered my senses and opened my eyes, the first object which presented itself to my view, I shall never forget: it was the countenance of Napoleon, bending over my face, and regarding me with an expression of great concern and anxiety. With one hand he was opening my shirt collar, and with the other, holding a bottle Of vinaigre de quatre voleurs (double distilled vinegar) to my nostrils...He told me that he had lifted me up, placed me in a chair, torn off my cravat dashed some eau de Cologne and water over my face, &c. and asked if he had done right. I informed him that he had...When I was leaving the room, I heard him tell Marchand in an undervoice, to follow me, for fear I should have another fit.*[408]

Dr. O'Meara was well aware of the physical exercise that Napoleon was used to enduring daily while in France. To now be reduced to walking through the house and an occasional stroll in the garden would render the Emperor's health in such a state that would surely put him in his grave sooner rather than later. When O'Meara instructed Napoleon to get more exercise, the Emperor blamed the restrictions placed upon him by the Governor as his reasoning for not resuming his daily horseback rides.

In early December 1816, O'Meara wrote an account of Napoleon's health and the doctor's recommendation for more exercise and sent it to the Governor. Lowe responded by paying a visit to the doctor. "*His excellency then made some remarks upon "General Bonaparte's constantly confining himself to his room," and asked what I supposed would induce him to go out? I replied an enlargement of his boundaries, taking off some of the restrictions, and giving him a house on the other side of the island.*"[409] Lowe responded to O'Meara by saying that "*the British government did not wish to render General Bonaparte's existence miserable, or to torture him.*"[410] Needless to say, Napoleon did not believe the Governor's words when O'Meara told him.

But to the Governor's credit, he did keep his word and sent for O'Meara to come to Plantation House. Once the doctor arrived,

Governor Lowe explained to O'Meara that he wished to have the doctor inform Napoleon *"that several of the restrictions should be removed, especially those relative to speaking; that the limits should be enlarged, and that liberty should be granted to people to visit him, nearly as in former times under the admiral."*[411] This still did not fully satisfy the Emperor.

Montholon reported to Napoleon that one of the Allied Commissioners came to Montholon to share a conversation that he had had with Governor Lowe. The Commissioner said that Lowe shared with him about loosening the restrictions that the Governor had placed on the prisoner. Governor Lowe also expressed concern regarding his fear that he would be blamed for Napoleon's death.

> *I am about to arrange matters in such a way, as to allow him to take horse exercise; I have no wish that he should die of an attack of apoplexy – that would be very embarrassing both to me and the government; I would much rather he should die of a tedious disease which our physicians could properly declared natural.*[412]

Governor Lowe's fear was that the lack of exercise by Napoleon could lead to some sort of stroke or other ailment that could lead to his death, thus laying the blame at the feet of Lowe and the British government. Napoleon knew of Lowe's fear and used it to antagonize the Governor. The Emperor explained to Gourgaud *"what terrifies Hudson Lowe is my staying indoors day after day."*[413] Napoleon was correct on this assessment, but it would come at a cost.

Napoleon's war with Governor Lowe was slowly and painfully serving as unintentional suicide.

Governor Lowe sent word to Napoleon through Montholon that he would be altering the restrictions so that the Emperor could obtain more exercise. But the letter was also laced with pointed statements for Napoleon.

> *General Bonaparte cannot be allowed to traverse the island freely. Had the only question been that of his safety, a mere commission of the East India Company would have been sufficient to guard*

him at St. Helena. He may consider himself fortunate that my government has sent a man so kind as myself to guard him, otherwise he would be put in chains, to teach him to conduct himself better.[414]

These aggressive words by Lowe could not go unanswered by the Emperor. Napoleon dictated a response to Montholon to be given directly to Governor Lowe.

In this case it is obvious that, if the instructions given to Sir Hudson Lowe by Lords Bathurst and Castlereagh do not contain an order to kill me, a verbal order must have been given; for whenever people wish mysteriously to destroy a man, the first thing they do is cut him off from all communication with society, and surround him with the shades of mystery, till having accustomed the world to hear nothing said of him, and to forget him, they can easily torture him, or make him disappear.[415]

The mental war between Governor Lowe and Napoleon would continue to be waged.

With Las Cases now gone, it left a void amongst those that remained at Longwood. Tensions began to mount between General Gourgaud and Montholon as to who would gain more access and time with the Emperor. General Gourgaud instigated much of the quarrel. He was remarkably insecure, almost borderline immature, about not having enough of the Emperor's attention. At the same time, Montholon took pride in flaunting his trusted relationship with Napoleon. This was more than Gourgaud could take. On December 19, Napoleon's servant, Cipriani, informed Gourgaud that the Emperor wished to dine alone and for the General to take his food in his own room. As Gourgaud expressed his outrage to the servant, Cipriani explained that it was Madame Montholon's suggestion. This sent Gourgaud into a rage and he confronted Montholon over the actions of his wife. Gourgaud explained to him that he deplored Montholon's conduct and "*warned him to tell his wife* that, if she attempts to harm me, I shall hold him responsible....Montholon assures me that his wife said nothing to the Emperor."[416] But Gourgaud did not believe him.

A few days later, Gourgaud felt that Napoleon was ignoring him and he instantly took his anger out on Montholon.

> I remind Montholon that, the day before yesterday, his wife went to His Majesty's room before he was even dressed. Madame Montholon must have had serious reasons for doing so. He replies that that is true, she did go to the Emperor's room, but the Emperor did not receive her. Yesterday the Emperor sent for Montholon, and, on hearing that I hadn't uttered a single word, His Majesty declared that we were all to dine in our own rooms. However, I repeat what I had previously said to Montholon, and demand an explanation; and I add: "To-morrow, if you will, with Pistols, in the corner of the ploughed field. I shall bring Bertrand as my second.[417]

Gourgaud was alluding to the rumor that was circulating around Longwood. The rumor was that Napoleon had taken Madame Montholon as his mistress. The General was using this as a way to agitate Montholon. In most cases, Montholon would not take the bait. Part of Gourgaud's jealousy came from his belief that he had saved the Emperor's life on many occasions and had aided Napoleon in many of his victories. He felt that Napoleon should be giving him more honor and respect for all that he had done for him in the past. In the eyes of Gourgaud, the Emperor did not recognize all that the General had done for him and France.

Bertrand warned Gourgaud about taking this argument to extremes. *"I don't ask you to esteem the Montholons...But imitate my behavior. Do you think that I do not suffer, and have not suffered by their scheming?"*[418] Grand Marshal Bertrand gave this advice as a warning that if the quarrel reached the ears of the English, it could be used to harm the Emperor.

Bertrand was absolutely correct in his assessment of not only the English officers hearing of the infighting amongst the French but the rest of the island was hearing about it as well. Commissioner Count Balmain had a keen sense of this tension in Longwood and gave his own assessment of the situation.

> *But the fact remains that all of his French people hate each other cordially. Each wishes to be favorite of the master; hence arise very ridiculous scenes. Montholon, charged with the interior of the palace, is jealous of Bertrand, who has charge of the exterior. Gourgaud, tired of parading his quality of aide-de-camp in an antechamber...It is in thus blinding themselves to the reality of their position that these unhappy exiles...are exciting the ridicule of everybody.[419]*

Napoleon had little patience for such juvenile pettiness. When Gourgaud complained to Napoleon about his lack of respect to the General, the Emperor unleashed a tirade upon him.

> *You thought that in coming here you were my friend. I am nobody's friend. No one can take ascendancy over me. You would like to be the centre of everything here, as the sun is the centre of the planets. You have been the cause of all our anxieties since we came here. If I had known, I would have brought no one but servants. I can live here alone well enough, and when one is tired of life, a dagger can do the rest quickly enough. If you're so maltreated here, rather than quarrel with Montholon, you had better leave us.[420]*

The Emperor had to deal with the vexations at the hands of the British Governor on a continual basis. The last thing he wanted to deal with was the childish squabbles of his Generals who were there to make his life better, not laden it with more burdens. Napoleon continued his rage at Gourgaud stating that the General was "*always inventing idle theories*" and "*full of pretensions*" and considered himself superior to even Bertrand.[421] The words of the Emperor did little to calm the insecurities of Gourgaud. The General began to feel like the very Emperor he so proudly served no longer wanted him on the island.

*   *   *

January 1, 1817, ushered in another year of exile for Napoleon Bonaparte and his diminished French suite. A few years earlier, the Emperor of the French was in Paris in command of people and armies. Now, he was barely in command over his own existence. Valet Marchand wrote about this comparison between the days of the Emperor's reign and the lingering hours on St. Helena that now was their reality. "*Today, forced to seek shade under a tent erected close to his house, there being none elsewhere, he received not the caresses of a charming wife he loved, nor those of a son who represented all his hopes, but only the wishes – sterile but full of heart and soul – of a few companions in captivity.*"[422]

Montholon echoed those sentiments of sadness on that first day of the New Year in his own memoirs writing that the day "*presented itself this time as a dreary gateway to a year still more dreary than that which had just passed.*"

> *Instead of the Tuileries, our miserable habitation; instead of France, so often regretted, St. Helena, so often lamented; instead of the caresses of family, the congratulations of courtiers, the shouts of a nation, and the homage of Europe – the good wishes, though without hope, of some companions in captivity, whose numbers might at any moment be diminished by the caprice of an odious gaoler.*[423]

But Napoleon did find joy in celebrating the New Year with the children of his companions. The Emperor insisted on having the children join him for dinner saying, "*Your children shall dine with me. I wish their joy to be complete.*"[424] Napoleon absolutely enjoyed the children and took immense happiness in seeing their excitement as he gave each a present. Montholon recorded that "*the *dinner was really a family dinner; all the expenses were borne by our children, and their childish happiness awakened in the Emperor the remembrance of his youth."*[425] Though exiled to a rock in the Atlantic, Napoleon Bonaparte found some happiness in the New Year of 1817.

With the arrival of 1817, the Emperor was finally persuaded to take a walk in the garden. This was quite an accomplishment on behalf of the Emperor's suite because he had refused to leave Longwood in the chance that he would either encounter Governor Lowe or inadvertently submit himself to being seen by a British officer. This walk in the garden was the first time Napoleon had been outside of Longwood in 43 days. But it had been so long since the Emperor had taken any extensive exercise that "*he complained of violent sickness and remained four hours in the bath."*[426]

Napoleon experienced severe dysentery for the entire first week in January. He was given calomel as a medicine and it appeared to help him. He felt well enough to venture out again into the garden. "*As soon, however, as he perceived Sir Hudson Lowe, accompanied by two or three officers, at full gallop towards our residence, he precipitately returned into his chamber."*[427] Napoleon was adamant about not wanting to have any interaction with the Governor.

The news of Napoleon's illness swept across the island and created a panic amongst the British. Even Allied Commissioners became worried about his condition. They insisted upon seeing the Emperor with their own eyes so that they could provide an accurate report to their respective countries regarding his truth health. But Governor Lowe refused and instead gave them each a copy of Dr. O'Meara's recent report.

Even though the Allied Commissioners were on St. Helena as part of the Peace Treaty in Europe, they were human enough to understand the situation that the Emperor was currently experiencing. While on the island of St. Helena, Russian Commissioner Count Balmain began to date the daughter of Governor Lowe, but this did not cloud his judgment on the manner in which Lowe treated his prisoner.

> *Sir Hudson Lowe is not successful in the same way [as Malcolm]. He [Malcolm] treats him [Napoleon] with respect and ceremony, does not complain of his brusque manner, tolerate his ca-*

> *prices, in short achieves the impossible. But he [Lowe] will never be anything except his scourge. There is too much incompatibility between the two men. The mind of one is still restless. He is a wandering genius who, in the circumstances where fate has reduced him, wishes to take his flight and seeks perhaps to make converts for himself. The other opposes to this strong will merely an inexhaustible fund of commonplace ideas and a cold suspicious nature, a repulsive exterior with, however, the best intensions in the world, and a tyrannical precision in fulfilling his duty. To sum up, he who knows only how to command is at the mercy of him who knows only how to obey. Hence, there is no manner of displeasing his jailer which the prisoner has not tried.*[428]

It was becoming quite evident that many were growing concerned over Napoleon's deteriorating health. For Napoleon, who was well known for his physical stamina on horseback, it perplexed many that he would be weakening so rapidly at only 47 years old. In the Emperor's mind, his determination at refusing to leave Longwood because of the Governor and the British sentries was his way of continuing to win the battle of the minds. At the same time, Napoleon's stubbornness only served to further damage his health.

But, there was no doubt; the Emperor was dying.

*   *   *

January 21, 1817, was a day that seemed to bring Napoleon some humor. A book by author Pillet entitled "Amours Secretes de Napoleon Buonaparte" had reached the Emperor at Longwood and he took great amusement in reading its pages. Napoleon shared some of the stories with General Gourgaud and the General wrote in his diary, "*He is laughing heartily, and says he knows none of the women mentioned. "They make a Hercules of me!" he exclaims.*"[429]

Dr. O'Meara also wrote in his memoirs that Napoleon thoroughly enjoyed the tales from the Pillet book. "*Napoleon sat up until late at night reading Pillet, and I was informed he was heard repeatedly to burst into loud fits of laughter.*"[430] The Emperor needed to laugh a little.

The following day, Madame Bertrand gave birth to a child; a boy named Arthur Bertrand. The Emperor believed that this birth was so important that he decided to pay a visit to her down at Hutt's Gate. This was the first time Napoleon ventured away from Longwood since November 20. The Emperor repeatedly complimented Madame Bertrand on the beauty of her child. The little infant touched his heart. Madame Bertrand replied saying, "*I have the honor to present to your majesty le premier Francais* (the first Frenchman) *who, since your arrival, has entered Longwood without Lord Bathurst's permission.*"[431] The sight of this child filled the Emperor with joy. He later told Gourgaud about his visit with Madame Bertrand and her new child. Napoleon said that he "*is of the opinion that the deepest feeling in Nature is that existing between mother and child.*"[432]

This visit with Madame Bertrand brought Napoleon emotional pain about being away from his own son. To see this bond between mother and child, and knowing that his own son was thousands of miles away, out of reach to hold and comfort, must have been painful for Napoleon. But at the same time, the Emperor was also truly close with his own mother. He knew that she shared in his misery and wanted to be with him. This joy of birth brought the Emperor happiness, but also stung agonizing wounds as well.

The next few months found the Emperor in a state where his legs swelled to the extent that he took to his bed. Being bedridden led to extensive pains in his stomach. Dr. O'Meara was called to examine Napoleon, and the doctor recommended medicine. The Emperor outright refused. O'Meara then suggested that Napoleon get some exercise in his legs. Marchand wrote that the Emperor responded to the doctor saying, "*where would you have me exercise, as my executioner has taken away from me all means of doing so?*"[433]

In his memoirs, Marchand was quite detailed in his recording of the Emperor's health. During this period from January to May 1817, the valet explained how "*from time to time he was taken with shivering, forcing him to go to bed...His stomach pains were quite frequent...The governor was aware of this, and although he knew the lack of exercise could bring about this disorder in the Emperor's* health, he changed nothing in the restrictions, continuing his system of sequestration which he found not even complete enough."[434]

*   *   *

Though these months contained days of pain and suffering for the Emperor's health, there is one person who could lift his spirits momentarily: Betsy.

When Betsy and her family came to see the Emperor during the winter months of 1817, the once mischievous adolescent girl had become a very beautiful young woman. Though her appearance now exemplified a more mature woman, her heart was still that of the playful child who shared those earlier months with the Emperor at The Briars. But when she saw Napoleon upon this visit, her heart sank at the shock of his deteriorating appearance.

> *When we saw Napoleon...his appearance was sad to look upon. His face was literally the color of yellow wax, and his cheeks had fallen in pouches on either side of his face. His ankles were so swollen that the flesh literally hung over his shoes; he was so weak, that without resting one hand on a table near him, and the other on the shoulder of an attendant, he could not have stood. I was so grieved at seeing him in such a pitiable state, that my eyes overflowed with tears, and I could with difficulty forbear sobbing aloud. He saw how shocked we were, and tried to make light of it, saying, he was sure the good O'Meara would soon cure him; but my mother observed, when we had left, that death was stamped on every feature. He, however, rallied from this attack, to pass nearly three more years in hopeless misery; for it became more evident to him that the anticipation in which he indulged (on first coming to St. Helena) of quitting the island, became fainter as health declined, and time wore on.*[435]

Betsy's assessment of Napoleon's increasing awareness that he would never leave St. Helena was completely accurate. His mind was coming to the growing realization that maybe Europe would not call for him to return. Maybe he was not needed to save the nation of France. Or were the English just preventing the message from reaching him? Either way, his body might not hold on until any proclamation could be issued for his triumphant return. Although his body began to shut down, his mind never relented.

While Betsy was visiting Napoleon, he took the Balcombe family into his bedroom to show them the new bust of his son, the King of Rome, which had just arrived at Longwood. The Empress Marie Louise sent it to Napoleon. Betsy could tell that the Emperor was "*much moved...and gazed upon it with proud satisfaction, and was evidently much delighted at our warm encomiums upon its loveliness. My mother told him he ought indeed to exult at being the father of such a beautiful creature as that boy must be. Smiles seemed to light up his face, and my mother often said, she never saw a countenance at the time so interestingly expressive of parental fondness.*"[436]

The visit by the Balcombes to Longwood did not go unnoticed to Governor Lowe. His suspicions were becoming heightened regarding the closer relationship between Mr. Balcombe and the exiles at Longwood. Following this visit, Dr. O'Meara recounted that Mr. Balcombe was "*interrogated and cross-examined both by the governor and by his privy counsellor, Reade, touching what they had heard and seen at Longwood, and that the father replied, that his daughters had come here to have the honor of visiting us, and not as spies.*"[437]

There was a great controversy that surrounding this bust of Napoleon's son, the King of Rome. It had arrived on board the ship the *Baring* and the sculptor had asked for 2,000 francs for the cost of making the piece for the Emperor. The Governor held the bust for some time to ascertain if there were any other intentions for giving the bust to the Emperor. Governor Lowe told Grand Marshal Bertrand that he believed the bust was mediocre and that the price demanded was "*exorbitant and unacceptable claim. The grand marshal replied that the Emperor alone could decide that matter, and that seeing the features of his son which had been deprived him for so many years was priceless; he therefore urged the governor to send it to him that same day.*"[438]

Governor Lowe had it sent to Longwood the next day, and the Emperor was completely overjoyed at viewing it for the first time. He said to Marchand, *"How can it be," he said, "that on this rock there is a man savage enough to order this bust thrown in the ocean? He is certainly not a father. For me, this bust is worth more than millions. Put it on the table in the drawing room, so that I may see it every day."*[439] Shortly afterward, Napoleon had it moved to his bedroom.

On board, this same ship was a crate that contained a beautiful chess set which was sent to the Emperor by an Englishman named Mr. Elphinstone. This man's brother had been wounded at the Battle of Waterloo and Napoleon ordered his men to provide Captain Elphinstone treatment, which ultimately saved his life. His brother, as a thank you for the Emperor's kindness, sent this chess set. Governor Lowe also held onto this chess set from Napoleon for over a week due to the fact that the chess set had an Imperial 'N' on it.

The Emperor was furious at Lowe's holding of the bust, chess set and other articles from him and instructed Bertrand to send the Governor a letter stating as such.

Governor:

I have received the five crates you took the trouble to send me... In the ministry restrictions it is specified that letters must come through its channels, but not objects of apparel, busts, furniture, etc... This cannot and could not have authorized you to hold back objects such as busts, furniture, books, and any other effects having no relation whatsoever to the security of the detention... Would it be because there is a crown on the tokens? But there can exist no regulation that is not brought to our attention; and there is to our knowledge nothing to prevent us from owning an object bearing a crown. In that case it would also be necessary to manufacture new decks of cards, because there are crowns on the ones provided... From whom could come this ruling that you say is in force? The Emperor asks me to pro-

test against the existence of any restriction or rule that has not been legally communicated to him prior to its execution.[440]

Governor Lowe was quick to respond to the Emperor's complaint. In the lengthy response, the Governor stated that his only goal was to "*prevent the impression that I tacitly recognized or approved the use of the imperial rank in the crown placed everywhere over the initial of Napoleon...Presents as well as a letter may threaten the security of the detention...A letter can be hidden under the squares of a chessboard or in the cover of a book as well as in the lining of a waistcoat, and I am under no obligation to trust the person sending them, whoever it may be.*"[441] The two men were now battling over the very symbol used to represent Napoleon and his reign. One clung to it as the very emblem of his successes, the other feared it as a means to enable Napoleon's potential escape.

Montholon wrote in his memoirs of the incident and used sarcasm to take aim at Lowe's apparent paranoia over the Emperor's potential escape.

It was perhaps all a conspiracy! The bust might contain a correspondence of the very highest political interest! Not to suffer it to go to Longwood, and break it in pieces, was in his opinion the advice of sound reason; but what recriminations, and what an echo would these recriminations find in public opinion, should we become acquainted with these facts, and happen to divulge them!...So much cunning and malevolence of purpose cruelly wounded the Emperor.[442]

Regardless of the Emperor's deteriorating health and as well as the passage of time on St. Helena, Governor Lowe's obsession with Napoleon potentially escaping the island only grew as the months passed. Though reports were coming to the Governor's office at Plantation House that the Emperor was in poor health, Lowe just could not put out of the realm of possibility that Napoleon had something up his sleeve. Again, Napoleon had escaped from his first exile on the island of Elba. A person could never be too careful around the mind of Napoleon Bonaparte. But this distrust and concern over the Emperor's potential escape, with his failing health, had become a misplaced notion by the Governor.

As the battle with Lowe and his government continued to rage on, Napoleon still had to mediate the ongoing struggle of personalities between his own followers in Longwood. Gourgaud's paranoia at not being Napoleon's center of attention was now reaching a breaking point. The Emperor knew of Gourgaud's desire to feel needed, so Napoleon would look to him for dictations, conversations, and games of chess. Napoleon would even call him "*Gorgo, Gorgotto*" in jest and as a means of affection.[443] But this accomplished little in settling the mind of Gourgaud.

Throughout his memoirs, Gourgaud continued to dwell on how Napoleon was ignoring him and focusing all his attention and praise for everyone but him. In one entry in March, 1817, Gourgaud wrote that the Emperor "*is playing chess with Bertrand, and says "Ah!" as I enter. Then he plays with Montholon. Not a word is spoken to me! Dinner. He continues to ignore my presence...*"[444] In June of the same year, Gourgaud continued his self-pity stating, "*I am sinking lower and lower in His Majesty's estimation. If the changes which have taken place during the last two years are any criterion, I can see what is in store for me...I prefer to suffer with my family, than to suffer here. I tell all this to Bertrand. He runs after me, seizing me by the arm, but all to no purpose. I cry out that now I understand everything; I have no illusions left.*"[445]

Even through these moments of selfishness by Gourgaud, Napoleon still turned to him for conversation to pass the time in exile. The Emperor also had a genuine caring for General Gourgaud as a person and even spoke many times about a proper marriage for him. Gourgaud was rarely silent on the fact that not only was he not married yet, but was without a woman on the island. Even Marchand had a mistress on the island named Esther with which he had a child.[446]

In June 1817, Napoleon informed Gourgaud that he needed a wife.

> *For to be without one at my age is indeed a privation. "Yes," says the Emperor, "or else you need a mistress, such as Esther. I didn't want Marchand to go and see her because I was afraid that her father might force him to marry her." The Emperor adds, that I ought to make friends with Madame*

Bertrand's mulatto servant. Now, I have never spoken a word to this girl, because the Grand Marshal had begged me not to. Even so, the Bertrands' behavior is very extraordinary; whenever I arrive at the house, the maid is sent out. The Emperor laughs, and asks Bertrand whether this is so. The latter excuses himself, on the grounds of his wife's delicacy of mind![447]

It is amusing to read that Napoleon and other members of the French suite thought that getting Gourgaud a female companion might address his anxieties and calm his thoughts. Though their intentions may have been well placed, they did not work in reassuring Gourgaud's concerns over his lack of attention from the Emperor.

*   *   *

On July 14, 1817, the Emperor received the officers of the 53rd British Regiment because the 66th Regiment was replacing them. When they entered the drawing room to have an audience with the Emperor, Napoleon talked with each and every one of them individually inquiring about their battles, wounds, and experiences. He explained to them that he "*shall always learn with great pleasure of any good fortune encountered by the 53rd, for whom I have only praise.*"[448] Gourgaud recorded that Napoleon turned to their commanding officer, General Bingham, and asked him how many years he had been with the 53rd, to which he replied some thirteen years. "Ah!" says the Emperor. "*As a consolation, you ought to give Lady Bingham a little Bingham.*" Bingham blushes."[449]

It was witty exchanges like these by Napoleon that made his personality so captivating. The British officers, soldiers, and citizens on St. Helena were instantly taken with Napoleon's conversation and charm. Governor Lowe paid great attention to this fact, which added to his fear that one or more of these people would aid in Napoleon's escape from the island. This was one of the reasons that Governor Lowe was so strict about who visited Longwood and why he would order reports by these visitors of everything that transpired between them and the French suite.

"The Soul Is Beyond Their Reach" 211

Dr. O'Meara was becoming Governor Lowe's next target in regards to his wanting information about what was transpiring behind the walls of Longwood. Because the Emperor would not see the Governor, Lowe was anxious about news of his health and any other issues he was complaining about. The Governor would often scold O'Meara for how attached he was getting to the French exiles, particularly Napoleon, and even questioned his allegiance at times. Dr. O'Meara was quick to stand his ground against the accusations by the Governor and insisted that he himself was neither in exile nor a prisoner. "*I replied, that I was not included in the act of parliament, as I had made an express stipulation that I should not be considered or treated as one of the French, and would immediately resign my situation, if I were required to hold it upon such terms.*"[450]

Marchand also discussed in his memoirs the interrogations that O'Meara endured at the hands of the Governor. There was no doubt in the minds of the French at Longwood that O'Meara was not only faithful to all of them, but the English doctor was considered their devoted friend as well. This is what Lowe feared.

> *Being a faithful reporter, Dr. O'Meara reported to Longwood his conversations with the governor, and whatever they might be, he lost nothing in the esteem of the Emperor, who had always trusted him. Such was not the case when he repeated the Emperor's words at Plantation House. The governor flew into rages in which he accused Dr. O'Meara of having sold out to the French. He threatened to have him taken to the Cape bound hand and foot, if he managed to get his illegal correspondence. "Your General Bonaparte pretends to be sick and he is not. You back up his statements; his complaints against me are infamous lies. He knows it well, but it is a system to substantiate his complaints and interest Europe in his person. He should know that the truth regarding his situation is known, and that I treat him too well! Tell him so."*[451]

When Napoleon was told about these exchanges with Governor Lowe, the Emperor "*would laugh about it, and when he was told about Hudson Lowe's fits of temper, wished that he might someday die of anger.*"[452] But Napoleon also warned O'Meara to be careful of Lowe for he had the power to send him back to Europe. The Emperor explained to the doctor that if Lowe could do so, "*he would not take such great care with you. You annoy him enough through your relations with the island inhabitants and the squadron sailors for him to send you away. You may be sure that if Lord Bathurst wants Lowe to kill me, he does not want it said that he killed me with a doctor of his choice, and that the first thing his government recommended to him was not to take you away from me without my consent.*"[453]

O'Meara heeded Napoleon's advice, but the interrogations by Lowe continued to get worse for the doctor. On July 22, 1817, another argument ensued between the doctor and Lowe. O'Meara recorded that Lowe ordered that he "*was not permitted for the future to hold any conversation with General Bonaparte, unless upon professional subjects, and ordering me to come to town every Monday and Thursday, in order to report to him General Bonaparte's health and his habits.*"[454]

O'Meara reported in his memoirs that he was questioned in a similar fashion not two days later. The doctor stated, "*a long and very disagreeable discussion took place, with which I shall not fatigue the reader, further than by stating, that I requested of him to remove me from my situation.*"[455]

Governor Lowe would soon grant Dr. O'Meara his wish.

But there was another person on St. Helena who had caught the watchful eye of Governor Lowe: Admiral Malcolm. The Admiral was a well-respected man who tried to mediate between the Governor and the Emperor, but the Governor believed that Admiral Malcolm was concealing information about the conversations he had had with Napoleon. Lowe wanted those reported to him in detail, but the Admiral was a person of such good character that he would not betray the honor that he had given Napoleon concerning their unguarded conversations. Malcolm was well aware of Lowe's pettiness and paranoia regarding Napoleon, and the Admiral did not believe that he had to 'report' to the Governor on every conversation that he had with members of the French suite at Longwood.

"The Soul Is Beyond Their Reach" 213

Regardless, the time had come for Admiral Malcolm's replacement to arrive at St. Helena. On July 3, 1817, Admiral Plampin arrived and Malcolm was to set sail for London.

Napoleon was again to lose another companion on St. Helena.

*   *   *

August 15, 1817, brought another birthday to the Emperor while in exile on St. Helena. As usual, Napoleon enjoyed spending his birthday surrounded by the children of his entourage. He invited the whole of his suite for dinner, but the Emperor took the most enjoyment in giving presents to the children. *"All the children, excepting the two infants of Counts Bertrand and Montholon, who were brought in and shown for a short time. To each of the children he gave a present, and amused himself, for some time, playing with them."*[456] Children had a soothing effect on the Emperor. He thoroughly enjoyed their playfulness, honesty, and innocence.

But as the days slowly continued through August, Napoleon was starting to become more fatigued and pained. He often *"complained about his side, and about his legs being swollen."*[457] Napoleon directly blamed the choice of St. Helena and its climate for making him ill. *"I would have lived to the age of 80,"* he said to the doctor, *"if the poor treatment I endure here and the abominable climate where I have been placed were not killing me sooner."*[458]

In contemplating his fate, Napoleon again placed the blame at the feet of the British government. *"They will see,"* said he, *"the folly and injustice of keeping me in this island; an island so bad, that I can compare it to nothing else than the face of the wretch they have sent out as governor."*[459] Napoleon said that the British would have been better off executing him on the *Bellerophon* the moment he surrendered. The Emperor said they would *"have excused themselves by saying, 'It is necessary for the tranquility of Europe to put this man out of the way.' This would have at once freed them from all alarm, and saved millions to their treasury, beside being much more humane."*[460]

On December 14, 1817, Governor Lowe sent for Dr. O'Meara again for a report on the Emperor's health. The doctor went to Plantation House and gave a similar assessment as before stating that the Emperor is in desperate need of exercise so that he could improve.

O'Meara added that the restrictions prohibit Napoleon from getting the exercise that he needs. Lowe

> *observed that it was very extraordinary he did not take exercise; that if he expected, by confining himself, to obtain any further relaxation in the system adopted, he was mistaken. He then inquired if the want of sleep was caused by mental, or by bodily disease. I said, that I thought it was chiefly caused by the want of exercise; that no man, leading such a life as Napoleon did, could possibly remain long in a state of health. The governor said, with a sneer, that he believed laziness was the cause of his not taking exercise.*[461]

Governor Lowe never really agreed with the assessments that O'Meara gave on the Emperor's health. Lowe believed that the doctor had come under Napoleon's control and was being used as a puppet of the French. At another meeting at Plantation House on January 2, 1818, Governor Lowe directly questioned O'Meara's loyalty. This meeting took an ugly tone right away. The Governor asked

> *whether I conceived myself independent of him, and if it were not in his power as governor, and having charge of Napoleon Bonaparte, if he thought that my conduct was not correct, to send me away if he pleased?" I told him that he could reply to that himself, as he best knew what the extent of his authority was. This answer did not please him, and after walking about the room for a little time, exclaiming against my conduct, he stopped, crossed his arms, and after looking at me with an expression of countenance which I shall never forget, said, "This is my office, sir, and there is the door leading to it. When I send for you on duty, you will come in at that door; but do not put your foot in any other part of my*

house, or come in at any other entrance. I calmly replied, that it was not for my own pleasure, or by my own desire, that I ever set foot in any part of his house; and after suffering this paltry abuse of authority, departed.[462]

Governor Lowe was stuck in a quagmire of a situation with Dr. O'Meara. If he kept the doctor at Longwood, Lowe knew that Napoleon would continue to pull O'Meara under his sphere of influence. But if Lowe sent him back to England, O'Meara would fill the newspapers and books with stories of Lowe's cruel torture of Napoleon. Lowe knew the doctor would meet with members of Parliament and travel from drawing room to drawing room throughout London pleading the Emperor's case of removal from St. Helena.

Governor Lowe would quickly have to act regarding Dr. O'Meara.

Thus began the year 1818 on the island of St. Helena. It would be a year that would most affect the Emperor in a detrimental way. Montholon recalled, "*The year 1818 began its course under sad auspices. Time, instead of alleviating the sufferings of our captivity, aggravated them every day, and the decline of the Emperor's health gave us serious uneasiness.*"[463]

But the Governor was growing concerned over the continuing deterioration of the Emperor's health. Even Russian Commissioner Count Balmain knew of his uneasiness over the situation. Balmain reported to his government "*the Governor is terribly disturbed over his prisoner's health and does not know which way to turn. The doctors prescribe horseback riding, but the patient refuses, swears that he will never stir from his room unless they cancel the present regulations and reestablish Admiral Cockburn's.*"[464] Balmain himself quickly discovered how the climate of St. Helena could harm his own health. In another letter to Moscow, the Russian Commissioner explained that his "*health continues bad. I suffer from nerves, and this climate weakens them. St. Helena is really unhealthy. The doctors are not of the opinion that I should stay twenty months longer.*"[465]

As Napoleon sought peace from the Governor so that his health would recover, Montholon and Gourgaud continued their feud while vying for the Emperor's attention. When Napoleon was informed about their latest argument, he flew into a rage. Gourgaud pleaded his side to the Emperor saying, "*Sire, you abuse my position. How could I go away? People would say it is from boredom. Howev-*

er, if Your Majesty requires it, I will go." Napoleon responded by saying *"You can't tolerate this, you can't tolerate that, or any of the normal things one says to you."*[466]

After sulking for a few days, Gourgaud went back to see the Emperor.

> *"Sire," I reply, "what is intolerable, is not St. Helena itself, but the bad behaviour of Your Majesty." "I do not treat you badly," answers the Emperor. "And what is more, I do not wish to be angry with you. It is as a friend that I speak to you, and if you don't calm your imagination, you will go mad. You must not believe that we are hatching plots behind your back. Try to forget all your discomfort. Don't probe into things too deeply, and don't seek to find out what people wish to conceal...I am devoted to you, and you certainly behaved loyally in coming here with me."*[467]

But these kind words of Napoleon still did not calm the doubt in Gourgaud's mind about his standing with the Emperor. On January 20, 1818, Gourgaud made a comment to the Emperor that he felt the Montholons had too much influence over Napoleon. Gourgaud went as far as to say *"the Montholons do order the Emperor's life, that it is true that he does love them, and would do anything for them."*[468] Napoleon responded by not doubting the Montholons' love and devotion to him. The Emperor added, *"If you were really devoted to me, you would court them. You see for yourself, that theirs is a real devotion. You and I are diametrically opposed. Both you and the Governor make my life a very hard one."*[469] It seemed as though Napoleon had to battle both the Governor and the juvenile temper tantrums of his officers.

On February 2, 1818, the final argument took place between the Emperor and Gourgaud. Napoleon was informed of Gourgaud once again challenging Montholon to a duel. Gourgaud made the challenge and Montholon merely ignored it. This was Montholon's usual tactic with Gourgaud, knowing full well that the lack of a response infuriated him further.

As Gourgaud entered the drawing room where Montholon and Napoleon were seated, the Emperor inquired why Gourgaud looked so sad. Napoleon said, "*Come, come; cheer up.*"[470] But Gourgaud just could not bring himself to that point and responded that he was just too ill-treated by the Emperor to be cheerful. This was too much for Napoleon to bear. "*The Emperor whistles in an angry manner, whereupon he dismisses Montholon under the pretext of finding out how many sentries are posted. Jumping up, the Emperor says to me: "What is it you want?"*"[471]

Gourgaud then went into a long diatribe about how he had been mistreated and overlooked by the Emperor after all the things he has done to protect him over the years. The Emperor went into a further rage demanding that he make up with Montholon and put an end to their feud. Napoleon went as far as to yell at Gourgaud and referred to him as a "*blackguard*" and an "*assassin*" if he disobeyed the Emperor and carried out the duel with Montholon.[472]

Once he calmed down, the Emperor apologized to Gourgaud and instructed him to claim illness and to request to Governor Lowe that he be allowed to return to Europe. Napoleon said that Dr. O'Meara could certify the illness to make it official for the Governor. Then Napoleon gave him his final strict orders as his Emperor. "*But listen to my advice. You must not complain to anyone. You must not talk about me, and once in France, you will soon see the chess-board on which you are to play.*"[473]

The following day, Napoleon embraced Gourgaud and thanked him for his honored service to the Emperor and the nation of France. Napoleon patted his General on the back and said, "*We shall meet again in another world. Come now, Good-bye. – Embrace me.*"[474]

Saddened and weeping, Gourgaud left Longwood for the last time and rode to Plantation House to report to the Governor and then went to Jamestown to stay until a ship arrived that could return him to Europe.

Napoleon had lost another member of his suite and a companion who even though he tried the Emperor's patience on many occasions, at least he had helped in passing the time of Napoleon's exile on St. Helena. He would not be the last person close to the Emperor to be sent away.

*   *   *

In February of 1818, Napoleon experienced a loss that would be difficult for him to bear. His long time friend and servant, Cipriani, had been experiencing severe intestinal pain that he eventually succumbed to and died towards the end of the month. Napoleon was completely distraught. Shortly after his death, Napoleon went to O'Meara and asked him, "*Where is his soul? Gone to Rome, perhaps, to see his wife and child, before it undertakes the long final journey.*"[475]

Cipriani was Napoleon's right-hand man since they had been young in Corsica. During the Emperor's reign, Cipriani served as Napoleon's body double for security purposes. At other times, he was the Emperor's spy who would search out clandestine information and report back. It was Cipriani that was sent out by Napoleon from Elba to spy on the Congress of Vienna to find out what their intentions were with the Emperor during his first exile. When Cipriani reported back that the Allied Powers were going to move him from Elba to a farther location, perhaps St. Helena, Napoleon made the decision to escape Elba and march back to Paris in 1815.

In fact, Cipriani had a prior 'engagement' with Governor Lowe back when the British officer was leading the Corsican deserters, as Napoleon described it. In 1806, Lieutenant-Colonel Lowe had hired a Corsican man by the name of Antonio Suzzarelli to spy for him and the British. During one mission, Suzzarelli met another Corsican named Cipriani Franceschi in a tavern. Cipriani persuaded Suzzarelli to act as a double agent and feed incorrect information that Cipriani had given to Lowe. Suzzarelli would, in turn, provide copies of Lowe's dispatches to Cipriani and other people seeking the removal of the British presence on the island of Corsica. Lowe quickly became aware of the name 'Franceschi' and knew that this individual was causing problems for him. Because of this history, Cipriani did not use the name 'Franceschi' while on St. Helena so that Lowe would not know of his prior history with the man.[476]

Montholon recorded in his memoirs how the French suite found this 'history' between Governor Lowe and Cipriani amusing. "*We always felt inclined to laugh when we saw Sir Hudson Lowe and Cipriani in each other's presence at St. Helena – two men who had played such different parts in that affair without the former having suspected the latter had cruelly mystified him.*"[477]

In the last moments of Cipriani's life, Napoleon wanted to be at his bedside, but O'Meara warned against it saying that "*he was still conscious enough that his love and veneration for him might bring about an emotion that would hasten his death. The following day Cipriani was no longer."*[478] This was a difficult loss for Napoleon.

More losses were to come.

* * *

With the sudden death of Napoleon's favorite servant and close friend, Cipriani, the Emperor was left with two officers and their families, a doctor, and a few servants. Napoleon was becoming depressed, grief-stricken, and very much alone. But there was another departure that was about to come that would level him a most destructive blow.

Mrs. Balcombe's health had taken a dreaded turn for the worse and doctors had advised that she return to England to recover from the illness. At the same time, Governor Lowe had become more suspicious of the close relationship that Mr. Balcombe had with Napoleon. As in other situations with people close with Napoleon, Lowe instantly believed that Mr. Balcombe was aiding the Emperor in sending clandestine letters to Europe. Though Mrs. Balcombe was ill at the time, this very well could have been the reason that Mr. Balcombe used to leave St. Helena before Governor Lowe could seek to damage his reputation back in Europe. In March 1818, Mr. Balcombe booked passage for the family on the next ship to leave Jamestown.

The departure of Betsy Balcombe from St. Helena was an emotional blow to Napoleon. She always had a way of making him laugh in the face of his suffering in exile. His happiest moments on St. Helena had been in her presence during their mischievous adventures.

But Betsy was not the young adolescent that she had been when Napoleon first came to stay in the Pavilion at The Briars. She was now sixteen and was continuously catching the admiring eyes of the British officers and sentries. Though her appearance and girlish manners had changed, she never passed up a moment to spend with the Emperor. She had become a woman, but she still was her same adolescent, playful self who enjoyed making the Emperor laugh.

At the same time, for Betsy, it was the end of her friendship with Napoleon Bonaparte. She would have to bid him goodbye with the dreadful understanding that she would never see him again. In her own words from her memoirs, Betsy recalled their final goodbye.

> *A day or two before we embarked, my father, my sister, and myself rode to Longwood, to bid adieu to the emperor. He was in the billiard room, surrounded by books, which had arrived a few days before. He seemed much depressed at our leaving the island, and said he sincerely regretted the cause; he hoped my dear mother's health would soon be restored, and sent many affectionate messages to her, she being too ill to accompany us to Longwood. When we had sat with him some time, he walked with us in his garden, and with a sickly smile pointed to the ocean spread out before us, bounding the view, and said, "Soon you will be sailing away towards England, leaving me to die on this miserable rock. Look at those dreadful mountains – they are my prison walls. You will soon hear that the Emperor Napoleon is dead." I burst into tears, and sobbed, as though my heart would break. He seemed much moved at the sorrow manifested by us. I had left my handkerchief in the pocket of my side-saddle, and seeing the tears run fast down my cheeks, Napoleon took his own from his pocket and wiped them away, telling me to keep the handkerchief in remembrance of that sad day. We afterwards returned and dined with him. My heart was so full of grief to swallow; and when pressed by Napoleon to eat some of my favourite bon-bons and creams, I told him my throat had a great swelling in it, and I could take nothing. The hour of bidding adieu came at last. He affectionately embraced my sister and myself, and bade us not forget him; adding that he should ever remember*

> *our friendship and kindness to him, and thanked us again and again for all the happy hours he had passed in our society. He asked me what I should like to have in remembrance of him. I replied, I should value a lock of his hair more than any other gift he could present. He then sent for Monsieur Marchand, and desired him to bring in a pair of scissors and cut off four locks of hair for my father and mother, my sister and myself, which he did. I still possess that lock of hair; it is all left me of my many tokens of remembrance of the Great Emperor.*[479]

The Emperor was quite solemn and depressed after the Balcombe family departed St. Helena. The presence of Betsy and her playful demeanor and mischievous ways had brought joy to Napoleon and they would never be replicated and would never again fill his heart the same way. His days with Betsy Balcombe and her family were the happiest he had during his entire exile on St. Helena. After she left, the Emperor remained in his bedroom for a number of days.

Even the Russian Commissioner Count Balmain recounted how the departure of Betsy and her family affected Napoleon and his suite. The Commissioner described that last visit of Betsy where she requested the lock of hair and how upset she became at leaving the Emperor. Balmain also explained how Mr. Balcombe had also treated the French exiles quite well. "*Balcombe's departure is much regretted at Longwood. His conduct toward the French was entirely correct, at the same time courteous and generous.*"[480] Montholon echoed those same comments in his own memoirs, but also added a tidbit of gossip as well. Montholon described Mr. Balcombe as "*a worthy man, and rendered as many services but without ever failing in his duty to his Sovereign. It was said in the island that he was the natural son of the Prince of Wales.*"[481] In other words, Mr. Balcombe was rumored to be the illegitimate son of the future King George IV.

The antics that Napoleon experienced with Betsy were not those of a deranged man losing his sensibility or those of the emotions of a doting suitor. These were the feelings of a grandfather figure who enjoyed the presence of children in his life and enjoyed them now more than ever for taking his mind away from this deteriorating situation.

Where the walls of Longwood and the shores of St. Helena reminded Napoleon of his perpetual exile, the laughter of the Balcombe children, especially that of Betsy, reminded Napoleon that there was joy in his mind and heart and that in the darkness of his exile, there was still time to live and laugh, even if for a few moments. Napoleon's time with Betsy served as the temporary ceasefire in his ongoing battle with the British government, particularly Governor Lowe. The childish laughter, the grandfatherly pranks that he committed, the compassionate caring that he felt for all the Balcombe children, provided the Emperor with a momentary light of happiness in a tunnel of darkness that was rapidly closing on his famous life.

Though possessing the heart and mind of a child, Betsy was able to penetrate the mental block that Napoleon had constructed and found the loving grandfather, father, and most of all, friend. Out of all the descriptions that have been made concerning the Emperor's personality, character, and warmth, Betsy Balcombe's description, written years later when she was middle aged, stands out as the most accurate of all composed.

> *Even a look, a tone of the voice, a gesture, in an unreserved moment, will give an insight into the real disposition which years of a more formal intercourse could fail to convey; and this is particularly the case in the association of a person of mature age with very young people. There is generally a confiding candour and openness about them which invites confidence in return, and which tempts a man of the world to throw off the iron mask of reserve and caution, and to assume once more the simplicity of a little child. This, at least, took place in my intercourse with Napoleon, and I may therefore perhaps venture to say a few words on the general impression he left on my mind after three months' daily communication with him...The point of character which has more than any other, been a subject of dis-*

pute between Napoleon's friends and his enemies, and which will ever be the most important of all, in the estimation of a woman, is, whether he furnished another proof of the "close affinity between superlative intellect and the warmth of the generous affections," or whether he must be considered only as a consummate calculating machine, the reasoning power perfect, but the heart altogether absent... he once said, "I have no friend except Duroc, who is unfeeling and cold, and suits me," and this may have been true in his intercourse with the world, and with men whom he was accustomed to consider as mere machines, the instruments of his glory and ambition, and whom he therefore valued in proportion to the sternness of the stuff of which they were composed. Even his brothers, whom he is said to have included in this sweeping abnegation of friendship, he taught himself to look upon as the means of carrying out his ambitious projects; and as they were not always subservient to his will, but came at times into political collision with him, his fraternal affection, which seldom resisted the rude shocks of contending worldly interests, was cooled and weakened in the struggle. But my own conviction is, that unless Napoleon's ambition, to which every other consideration was sacrificed, interfered, he was possessed of much sensibility and feeling, and was capable of strong attachment...I think his love of children, and the delight he felt in their society, - and that, too, at the most calamitous period of his life, when a cold and unattachable nature would have abandoned to the indulgence of selfish misery, - in itself, speaks volumes for his goodness of heart. After hours of laborious occupation, he would often permit us to join him, and that would have fatigued and exhausted the spirits of others, seemed only to recruit and renovate him. His gaiety was often exuberant at these moments; he entered into all the feelings of young people, and when with them was a mere child, and, I may add, a most amusing one.[482]

Betsy Balcombe would never seen Napoleon Bonaparte again.

* * *

Governor Lowe was not done removing people from Longwood who were close to the Emperor. He had one more that he believed needed to be removed; Dr. Barry O'Meara.

The relationship between Governor Lowe and Dr. O'Meara continued to deteriorate at a rapid pace. The more the Governor pushed O'Meara into reporting every word of Napoleon, the more the doctor refused. This only fed Lowe's paranoia that O'Meara was helping Napoleon to either communicate with Europe or even plan an escape.

An incident occurred where Napoleon had received word that a bulletin concerning his health had reached the Allied Commissioners. Napoleon questioned O'Meara who adamantly denied writing any medical reports without the Emperor's approval. It now became clear that due to O'Meara's refusal to report constantly to Lowe concerning Napoleon's health, the Governor ordered fake health reports to be given to the Commissioners so that they could report to their respective governments on the 'good' health of Napoleon. A couple of the Commissioners reported to Longwood about what reports they had been given. This sent Napoleon into a rage at the actions of the Governor.

This also angered O'Meara as well. In his memoirs, O'Meara explained, "*that every conscientious reader will be of opinion that those bulletins ought to have been shown to me, I being the only medical man who saw the patient, and consequently the only person capable of judging of their correctness.*"[483] When Lowe realized that these bulletins were being challenged, he ordered O'Meara to remain at Longwood and not leave the house. "*The governor had imposed upon me restrictions even more arbitrary and vexations* than those which he had inflicted upon the French; for confining me to Longwood, within the precincts of which he allowed no persons to enter without a pass, he deprived me of English society."[484]

Even some of the Allied Commissioners themselves were beginning to question the actions of Governor Lowe towards Napoleon. Austrian Commissioner Baron Strumer warned Governor Lowe that if Napoleon died without a doctor attending him, rumors would flood Europe that the English let the Emperor die without proper care.[485] Russian Commissioner Count Balmain directly warned Governor Lowe about the exact same concern. Addressing the Governor, Balmain said, "*May I speak to you frankly? Tell you my candid opinion, not as Russian Commissioner – for I haven't the right – but as a friend?...Remember that if Bonaparte dies without having seen a doctor, as he seems determined on doing, the English will be accused of having poisoned him, and it will be easy for Bonapartists in France and other places to produce false witnesses against you. And millions of men will henceforth look upon you as his assassin.*"[486] Russian Commissioner Count Balmain went further in his criticism of the Governor in a letter to his government on April 15, 1818.

> *I have always believed that Dr. O'Meara was a spy, an agent of the Governor at Longwood. It was generally believed at St. Helena, and the Governor himself has allowed me to think so. But to-day I am convinced that it is not true. O'Meara has never allowed himself to be so degraded. He gave the English news of Longwood as a matter of interest, just as he gave it to me, a stranger. They have done their best to persuade him to adopt that disgraceful role. But he has conducted himself as an honest man. The Governor has become his enemy, and, by submitting him to the same humiliating conditions, is trying to make him one of the French, which has forced him to resign. O'Meara, however, enjoys the esteem of his Government and has not failed in his duty in any respect. What the Governor is doing to him he would do to any man in the same circumstances – any man who enjoys Bonaparte's es-*

> teem. *The Governor fears what O'Meara may say of his ridiculous conduct and his indecent attitude toward the Commissioners of the Allied Powers.*[487]

This was a blistering attack, not by a member of the French suite at Longwood, but by an Allied Commissioner whose government was no fan of Napoleon Bonaparte.

While confined at Longwood at the order of the Governor, Napoleon refused to see O'Meara as his doctor until the order was lifted. Napoleon also urged O'Meara to quit his post as his doctor and to return to England before the Governor could do him more harm. With the refusal of the Emperor and the growing anger by the Allied Commissioners, Governor Lowe lifted the order of house arrest on O'Meara after confining him for 27 days.[488]

Following the lifting of the order, O'Meara resumed attending to Napoleon's medical needs. But Napoleon knew that the situation would never get better between Lowe and O'Meara. The Emperor said to O'Meara, "*You no longer have the necessary independence to take care of me; I would rather see you go than know you are treated that way. I have lived too long for them; what they want is for me to die in my bed, without help.*"[489]

Dr. O'Meara suggested to Napoleon that he see another English doctor who was on St. Helena named Dr. Stokoe. But this did not last long as Dr. Stokoe visited Napoleon a few times and wrote a report declaring that Napoleon "*had acute hepatitis and was extremely weak.*"[490] But once Napoleon realized that Governor Lowe wanted Dr. Stokoe to attend to him, the Emperor refused to see the doctor again and had Montholon send Lowe the following letter:

> *You think that because he (Napoleon) summoned Dr. Stokoe to a consultation he will receive his services as his usual physician. I have to assure you, unfortunately for his situation, that, even with death before his eyes, he will receive no assistance, nor take remedies, except from the hands of his own physician; if he is deprived of him, he will receive assistance from no one, and will consider himself assassinated by you.*[491]

As May 1818 approached, Governor Lowe made his move on O'Meara and had a letter delivered to the doctor ordering him to "*leave Longwood immediately after receiving this letter, without any further communication whatsoever with the persons residing there.*"[492] Governor Lowe then sent a letter to Longwood to inform the Emperor of his decision.

> *...Regarding Mr. O'Meara's departure, further instructions from Count Bathurst are that I must place Dr. Baxter in charge of providing his care, as a doctor, to Napoleon Bonaparte, whenever it is required; and particularly to recommend that he should consider at all times Napoleon Bonaparte's health as the principal object of his attention. When informing Napoleon Bonaparte of this arrangement, I must not fail to inform him at the same time that should he for any reason be dissatisfied with Dr. Baxter's care as a doctor, or if he should prefer that any person in the same profession present on the island, I am prepared to acquiesce to his desire on this point and allow the care of any doctor chosen by him, providing that he strictly conforms to the applicable regulations. Having informed Mr. O'Meara of the order of his departure, I have given Mr. Baxter the necessary instructions. He shall consequently be ready to proceed to Longwood at the first invitation, and when the slightest wish is expressed to him. At the same time, until I can be informed of the personal wishes of Napoleon Bonaparte on this subject, I shall see to it that a medical officer remains at Longwood, in the event there should be a reason to call upon him suddenly.*[493]

When it was time for Barry O'Meara to depart Longwood, he visited the Emperor for the last time. Typical of Napoleon, he gave the doctor a few gifts to remember him by. He presented O'Meara with "*a superb snuff-box, and a statue of himself; desired me, on my* arrival in Europe, to make inquiries about his family, and communicate to the members of it, that he did not wish that any of them should come to St. Helena, to witness the miseries and humiliation under which he labored."[494]

The Emperor then gave him special secret instructions for the doctor to contact Napoleon's older brother, Joseph. O'Meara was to inform Joseph that the Emperor desired Joseph to give to the doctor

> the parcel containing the private and confidential letters of the Emperors Alexander (Russia) and Francis (Austria), the King of Prussia, and the other sovereigns of Europe with me, which I delivered to his care at Rochefort. You will publish them...When I was strong, and in power, they courted my protection and the honor of my alliance, and licked the dust from under my feet. Now, in my old age, they barely oppress, and take my wife and child from me. I require of you to do this, and if you see any calumnies published of me during the time that you have been with me, and that you can say, 'I have seen with my own eyes that this is not true" contradict them.[495]

If the leaders of the Allied Nations would not come to his aid now, Napoleon would expose how they begged him for mercy when he was on the throne of France and had power. In his mind, Napoleon would use an Englishman to expose the hypocrisy of the sovereigns of Europe.

Next, the Emperor gave O'Meara instructions concerning Napoleon's second wife, the Empress Marie Louise, and his son, the King of Rome. *"You will express the sentiments which I preserve for them,"* added he, *"You will bear my affections to my good Louise, to my excellent mother and to Pauline (Napoleon's sister). If you see my son, embrace him for me; may he never forget that he was born a French prince!"*[496] The Empress was not worried about Napoleon's condition on St. Helena. The Empress Marie Louise had all but forgotten Napoleon and was now in a relationship with a man by the name of Count Neipperg. She practically deserted her son, the King of Rome, and left him with his grandfather, the Emperor of Austria.

Through his spies, Napoleon knew about Count Neipperg, but he never knew about the treatment of his son. This is probably why Napoleon's feelings constantly returned to Josephine, and not Marie Louise. The marriage to Josephine was out of love; the one to Marie Louise was for a political alliance.

Napoleon told O'Meara to "*testify to Lady Holland the sense I entertain of her kindness, and the esteem which I bear to her.*"[497] Here Napoleon is referring to the wife of Lord Holland who, along with her husband, was an outspoken critic in England of Napoleon's treatment in exile on St. Helena. Lady Holland sent numerous supplies to the Emperor including many books.

Lastly, the Emperor said his final goodbye to his English doctor and friend. "*The emperor then shook me by the hand and embraced me, saying, "Adieu, O'Meara, we shall never see each other again. May you be happy."*"[498]

Dr. O'Meara issued a final report to Governor Lowe on the health of Napoleon. It was not what Governor Lowe wanted to hear about his prisoner. O'Meara outlined the worsening condition of Napoleon. "*During the last days of September symptoms developed indicating a disorder in the functioning of the liver...his legs and feet become swollen...Since this time, the illness has not left him*"[499]

Dr. O'Meara continued his report by discussing his recommendations for Napoleon. The report also served as a blistering attack on Governor Lowe and his treatment of the Emperor.

> *I also advised horseback riding, massaging the abdominal area each day with a brush, wearing flannel, taking hot baths, some medications, diversions, following a diet, not going out in bad weather or exposing himself to extremes of weather. He neglected the two most important elements of exercise and diversions...Two years of inactivity, a murderous climate, rooms poorly ventilated, extreme ill-treatment, isolation, abandonment, everything that crushes the spirit acted in concert. Is it surprising that it is a liver dysfunction? If anything is astonishing, it is that the illness has not progressed more rapidly. This*

is only due to the power of the patient's spirit and the strength of a constitution that has never been weakened through debauchery, etc.[500]

Governor Lowe sent Dr. Barry O'Meara back to England with the hopes that it would end the doctor's 'mischief' on St. Helena and that his removal from Longwood would stifle any attempts to tarnish the reputation of Sir Hudson Lowe. The Governor was incredibly mistaken. Once back in England, Dr. O'Meara unleashed his attack on Governor Lowe. The doctor's most vicious attack would come in the form of a two-volume memoir entitled, *Napoleon in Exile*.

* * *

The days following Dr. O'Meara's departure were some of the worst for the Emperor. He began to experience severe vomiting. Marchand was at first going to call for Dr. Verling who had officially replaced O'Meara, but the valet knew that Napoleon would not see the new doctor. Marchand then explained to Napoleon that he *"had prepared pills that the doctor had left me, as well as what was needed to rub his legs. "As for that," he said, "fine; but as for everything that must enter my stomach, you can toss it into the fire."*[501]

These vomiting fits would continue for the Emperor until his death. That day was coming. The Emperor was dying. The painful and intolerable decline of Napoleon Bonaparte had begun. In the course of less than a year, the Emperor lost his secretary, his faithful officer, two servants from his years as Emperor, his dear friend and confidant from Corsica, his trusted English doctor, the English purveyor who sought to supply the Emperor with what he needed to be comfortable, and most importantly, Napoleon lost his adolescent playmate who brought laughter and joy to a man who had no real reason to experience either emotion again.

Throughout his final months on St. Helena, Napoleon would do everything possible to protect his name, his legacy, and his family in Europe against the Allied Powers with every breath he had left in him. More importantly, he would battle to cling to life; this was a battle that the Emperor would ultimately lose in the most agonizing way possible.

Our last hour is written above.

Napoleon

Chapter 7

Digging The Ground

The last weeks of the year 1818 saw the Governor easing some of the restrictions on Napoleon and actually extending some of the boundaries around Longwood where the Emperor could walk, of which the Emperor took advantage. He would often leave his bedroom for a stroll in the garden and back again. Word had also come from Lord Bathurst in England that Napoleon's uncle, Cardinal Fesch, had sent from Italy "*two priests, a doctor, a butler, and a cook...The Emperor and all of us were filled with joy. The Emperor was thus going to receive the medical help of which he had been deprived and some food for his mind.*"[502]

But there was still no doubt that the Emperor was failing. His servant, St. Denis or Ali as Napoleon called him, was very distraught over the declining state of the Emperor's health.

> *What a sad future presented itself to the Emperor's eyes! A number of those who had accompanied him into exile had left, and he saw the years flowing by without his gaolers thinking of loosening his chains. Had he not been unhappy enough? Would he have to drink the chalice to the dregs? What mortal could experience greater vicissitudes of fortunes than he had? Once he had seen all the princes and all the nations of Europe at his feet, and to-day he was reduced almost to himself, abandoned on a rock which was separated from the rest of the universe...He looked with a calm air on everything about him. Apparently he had nothing more to fear from this earth which saw him still standing erect; but all his woes were concentrated at the bottom of his heart, and it was not in his power to drive them*

away, do what he might. So, when he was plunged in reflections he was swamped by them; hope alone held him up.[503]

Towards the end of December 1818, Napoleon took ill again with a severe cold. Instead of calling for a doctor, Napoleon used his own remedy; licorice. Though Marchand insisted in his memoirs that the use of this candy was not effective, the Emperor was steadfast in his insistence that he would rely on the licorice, which was constantly in his pocket.

With the dawn of January 1, 1819, the Emperor was still ill and not able to hold the usual family festivities to celebrate the New Year. But he did not want to disappoint the children. Napoleon asked Marchand "*for some gold coins, and gave this to them for their New Year's presents.*"[504]

As Napoleon continued to battle severe pain in the area of his liver, he ordered Montholon to write a letter to Lowe requesting that Dr. Stokoe be allowed to remain at Longwood to treat his ailments. But the letter was laced again with accusations against the Governor. The letter concluded stating: "*What has happened in the last six months causes us to fear he may have one attack a month, and if he calls for Dr. Stokoe, he will arrive too late. Should the patient someday die of this, who will have killed him? The world and history answer that question loudly.*"[505]

The Governor's response was straight to the point and just as petty as Napoleon's letter. Lowe stated, "*no communication relative to Napoleon Bonaparte can be received, if it does not bear his signature or that of one of his officers, who, in that case, must clearly state he is writing and signing by his order.*"[506] Once again, Napoleon's stubbornness and Lowe's paranoia did nothing but worsen the Emperor's health.

The Governor did relent and allowed Dr. Stokoe to attend to Napoleon on January 22, 1819, but not without informing the doctor about his own viewpoint on the Emperor's illness. After ordering Dr. Stokoe to report to the Governor on the conversations that took place at Longwood, Lowe explained to Stokoe "*he did not believe any of this alleged illness, that he was only trying to fool him, and that it was nothing but a play to support Dr. O'Meara's statement regarding General Bonaparte's illness.*"[507] Stokoe found the Emperor still weak from his recent sickness but gaining strength.

As Russian Commissioner Count Balmain described it, the "*war of correspondence*" continued between Napoleon and Governor Lowe over the Emperor not wanting the doctors that the Governor had assigned to him.

> *The "war of correspondence" centered, naturally, around the "neglect" of the Emperor's health after O'Meara's departure. Doctors Verling and Baxter were constantly in readiness to give him aid, but the former met with no greater favor than the latter. Montholon returned to the governor a letter from Sir Thomas Reade, because "the Emperor, as you know, receives no communication unless signed by you." This letter was in turn sent back because it was written in the name of the "Emperor." So the childish and futile exchange continued.*[508]

Napoleon dictated another letter to Governor Lowe blasting the British government for not allowing him to have a doctor of his choosing. The Emperor blamed this fact for causing his health to continue to worsen and laid the guilt at the Governor's feet.

> *For a period of two years I have been afflicted with a chronic disease of the liver, endemic in this country. For the last year I have had no physicians, because O'Meara and Stokoe have both been designedly removed from St. Helena; for some days past I have been in a crisis – abandoned, and without receiving any relief from medical skill. Yet, as if this disease were not sufficiently hurtful in this climate and in the unhealthy situation of my residence, this moment is taken for redoubling the mean proceedings, the insults, the outrages, the insinuations, perfidies, and threats, in short all modes of violence. What! Peace has reigned in Europe during four years, and the vengeance of England is not yet satisfied! What baseness!*[509]

Over the course of a few days, the Emperor appeared to feel somewhat better. Marchand informed Napoleon of this, but the Emperor knew it would not last. Playfully he grabbed the ear of his valet and exclaimed, *"Don't believe it, my son, I haven't long to live. It is right here," he said, showing me the area of his liver; "this is only a moment of rest granted me by nature; the illness will again gain the upper hand and do me in."*[510] The Emperor was correct.

Another emotional blow was about to strike the Emperor. Madame Montholon had become ill and was not getting better. Dr. Verling suggested that she return to Europe for the betterment of her health and that the climate of St. Helena would only worsen her condition. Napoleon ordered that Montholon leave with his wife and children and return to Europe as to not split up the family. But out of honor and loyalty to Napoleon, Montholon refused to leave but allowed his family to return to Europe. This loss of even more members of the French suite took its toll on Napoleon. *"This departure would deprive the Emperor of a person whom he valued, and his social life was to be completely disrupted. Through her wit, to which the Emperor had become pleasantly accustomed, she provided some distraction to his work, and the time he spent with her played a large part in his daily routine. Her children, through their games, broke up the monotony of Longwood; a great void was to follow, for him and for the colony."*[511]

The day they were to leave became an emotional scene. Madame Montholon cried as she bid farewell to Napoleon. Her children also sobbed as they hugged the Emperor goodbye. Napoleon was very moved by the outpouring of emotion towards him and explained to Marchand, *"these tears hurt me."*[512]

There was a special connection that Napoleon had to Madame Montholon. It was widely believed amongst everyone at Longwood that Napoleon was often intimate with Madame Montholon. In fact, Madame Montholon's daughter, Helene, who was born on St. Helena in 1816, was described as having a striking resemblance to the Emperor. When the young infant would cry, Napoleon appeared to be the only person who was successful at cuddling and calming the child. The Emperor's emotional adieu to the family may have been made even more difficult with the fact that he may have been saying goodbye to his very own daughter.

*   *   *

On August 15, 1819, the Emperor spent another birthday in exile on the island of St. Helena. As in years past, he again celebrated it with the children. Though some sadness crossed his face knowing that the Montholon children were gone. He was now 50 years old.

Shortly after his birthday, another severe 'battle' of wills took place between the Emperor and Governor Lowe. The Governor was angered by the fact that Napoleon was not complying with the order that he permit himself to be seen daily by a British officer in order to ascertain the Emperor's continued presence at Longwood. This daily contact with the Emperor would ensure that he had not escaped. Due to his illness and determination not to obey Governor Lowe, Napoleon was refusing to leave the house, thus making it impossible for the British orderly to see him daily.

In order to enforce his directives, Lowe had the following letter sent to Napoleon:

> *...the undersigned [Lowe] finds himself under the painful but inevitable necessity of informing Napoleon Bonaparte, that, conformably to the instructions contained in Lord Bathurst's letter of the 6th of October, 1818, he has granted to the orderly officer permission to use such means as he may judge necessary to employ in order to remove any obstacle which may be opposed to his obtaining daily access to a place where Napoleon may be seen...*[513]

Napoleon was ready to respond to the Governor's latest order. He told Marchand that the Governor did not "*have the audacity to force my door.*"[514] The Emperor dictated the following letter to Montholon to be immediately delivered to the Governor.

> *Alone, ill, debarred from all communication with the universe, or even with the English officers and inhabitants on this rock, he presents his throat to the poniards of his murders; they need seek for no pretext...I reiterate what I told you a fortnight ago, that the Emperor would prefer the refuge of a tomb to suffering ignominious treat-*

> ment; that he can acknowledge no restrictions, even drawn up in terms of your law, if they do not emanate either from the Prince Regent or from the Privy Council. He has sacrificed everything, abandoned everything, and reduced himself to the most miserable life, in order to satisfy the hatred of his enemies. If their vengeance is not yet disarmed, let them strike him down at a single blow; it will be a benefit, since it will put a termination to the agony which has lasted since the 11th of August, and in which pleasure seems to be taken in holding him under the knife.[515]

Out of concern that the Governor would actually have the door to Longwood broken down, Napoleon ordered his servants to load their guns and barricade the doors to Longwood. The Emperor even ordered his sword to be placed near his bedside in case the residence was attacked. Napoleon would not have to wait long.

The next day, a British Colonel and another soldier requested a meeting with the Emperor. When the servants refused the request and went to see the Emperor, the British soldiers attempted to break down the door. When their efforts did not work in gaining them entrance to the house, they left and reported the incident to the Governor. The following morning, the Governor, his staff, and three dragoons came directly to Longwood. Governor Lowe walked right up to the bedroom window of the Emperor and attempted to look through, but was prevented due to the fact that Napoleon had closed the blinds. Frustrated, Lowe and his staff left and returned to Plantation House.

*   *   *

By September 1819, the new house being built for Napoleon was finished. Secretly, Napoleon went with a few members of his entourage and examined the house. Not surprisingly, Napoleon did not like the layout of the house. He informed the other Frenchmen that he would refuse to reside there. Napoleon also hoped Governor Lowe would never find out that he came and saw the house.

But the Governor knew everything that happened on St. Helena, including this.

On September 21, 1819, Napoleon received word that he would be having some new members join the suite at Longwood. His uncle, Cardinal Fesch in Rome, had gained permission from the English government to send a group of men to serve the Emperor at Longwood. They included two priests, Fathers Buonavita and Vignali, a surgeon, Francesco Antommarchi, a butler named Coursot, and a cook named Chandelier.

Once they arrived in Jamestown, Governor Lowe had dinner with them, mainly in the hopes of winning over their loyalty before they ventured to Longwood. As always, Lowe feared that they would fall under the spell of Napoleon.[516] Dr. Antommarchi explained in his memoirs that Governor Lowe also ordered each of the new men to be examined by his aide, British Major Gorrequer, to ensure that they did not carry any secret messages to Longwood. *"He informed us of it and apologized; but he was, he said, a sworn enemy to correspondences, and waged war against them without mercy. We immediately emptied our pockets, and opened our pocket-books."*[517] This move by the Governor towards the men who were sent to St. Helena to serve Napoleon and not the English Governor greatly angered the Emperor. Napoleon even went to the extent of delaying receiving the men at Longwood for another day.

Napoleon was grateful to his family for sending him these people, but he questioned why they would send him these particular people. One priest was so old that he had one foot in the grave and the doctor was completely unknown to Napoleon. The Emperor thought it would have been better had they sent him one of his former doctors from France, not a completely unknown person to him from Corsica. But as Marchand observed in his memoirs *"no one could foresee that eighteen months later one of these priests, Father Vignali, would walk before his [Napoleon's] coffin and bless his grave."*[518]

The Emperor did not receive the priests and doctor the day they arrived. But he did want to see the cook and servant. Coursot, the butler, and Chandelier, the cook, came to Longwood to be introduced to the Emperor. The first questions he posed to the two men were concerning his family, particularly his mother. Napoleon asked about her health and daily habits. Coursot responded to the questions stating that she was well but longed to see her exiled son.

The butler told of whenever dinner was served to her, she would respond, "*If only I could send this supper to my son!*"[519]

On the following day, the Emperor received the two priests. When the men entered the room they quickly approached the bed where Napoleon lay, knelt and kissed his hand. Again, the Emperor's first questions were of his family, particularly his mother. Marchand could see that Napoleon was quite moved by his mother's mourning for her son. As strong a man as Napoleon was as a general and Imperial Emperor, there was no hiding the eternal love that he felt for his family, especially his dear mother. Napoleon explained to Abbe Vignali that "*his mother had always loved him very much, he and Princess Pauline [his sister] had been the spoiled children of the family.*"[520]

Whenever the Emperor discussed his family or read the letters from them that Governor Lowe permitted to reach Longwood, Napoleon would again slip into a depressed state. There was no masking this grief. These sporadic bouts with depression that weighed upon the mind of Napoleon led him one time to say "*his enemies would have been less barbaric had they had him shot rather than brining him to Saint Helena.*" As Marchand pointed out in his memoirs, "*his mental sufferings must have been great.*"[521]

Napoleon did explain to the two priests that he wanted to start celebrating Mass on Sundays. He instructed the two men to decide amongst themselves how it was to be done, and that it was to be celebrated in the drawing room. Abbe Vignali and Abbe Bounavita were both pleased with this decision by Napoleon, as well as being pleased with their first meeting with Napoleon. Both men would reside at Longwood, taking the vacant rooms once held by General Gourgaud and Dr. O'Meara.

Dr. Antommarchi was next brought in to meet the Emperor. Napoleon was never very trusting of medicine and doctors and this time was not different. It had taken time for the Emperor to trust O'Meara, and when he did, the doctor was removed. Napoleon was now being sent a doctor with whom he had absolutely no familiarity. Dr. Antommarchi also did not know what to expect from his new patient.

The room was small and very dark, and Napoleon was in his bed, so at first I did not see him. I approached silently, with a kind of religious awe:

> he perceived it, and addressing himself to me most graciously, - "Approach, Capo Corsinaccio" [Cape Corsican – Resident of Cape of Corsica], said he in Italian, the language he ever afterwards used in our conversation, "approach, that I may see you more distinctly; and above all that I may hear you better, for on this miserable rock I am become quite deaf."[522]

The doctor did as he was instructed and the Emperor began his typical series of questions. Because Antommarchi was from Corsica, Napoleon peppered him with questions about the island, where the doctor was from, and even his childhood. Napoleon paused for a moment of reflection in the conversation and then remarked, "*But this is saying quite enough of a country which I shall never see again.*"[523]

Napoleon would always dive into questioning a new arrival because he loved the knowledge he would gain from meeting this new person. He wanted to learn new information while at the same time learn about the person. Even when a statement by someone or a memory might throw the Emperor into a depressed state, he could turn right around and shift right back into a jovial mood and recommence his line of questioning. These questions and inquiries were not done to interrogate, but rather they were done for the sheer reason of wanting information. And Napoleon did this to everyone he met.

The Emperor's series of questions went to the doctor's age and family. When Antommarchi told Napoleon he was thirty years old, the Emperor lightheartedly remarked, "*oh, oh, you might be my son. If I had known your mother, I should have left Macinajo, and landed at Morsiglia...Was she pretty, graceful, bewitching?*" Antommarchi answered that she was beautiful. Napoleon jokingly responded "*Just the thing! Oh I should certainly have landed at Centuri, and should have gone to Morsiglia to pay my court to an Capo Corsina, to Madame Antommarchi.*"[524] Typical of Napoleon, he could not pass up the opportunity to 'meet' a beautiful woman.

Napoleon questioned Antommarchi about why he would forsake lovely Corsica for the awful exile of St. Helena. What was his motive for making such a decision? The doctor responded by saying he sought "*neither gold nor favours; I have set no price on my services, I* have stipulated no conditions. It was proposed to me to approach your person, and that glory sufficed me."[525] Upon hearing this, the Emperor paused and again asked questions about his mother and his favorite sister, Pauline.

At the end of September, Dr. Antommarchi did a complete examination of Napoleon to assess what he believed sickened the Emperor. He found Napoleon to be in a weakened state.

> *I went to see the Emperor, and found him lying on a camp bed. The room was lighted so that I could observe the progress of the disorder. His ear was hard, his complexion unhealthy, his eyes livid, the white part of the eye of a reddish hue tinged with yellow, the whole body excessively fat, and the skin very pale. I examined the tongue, and found it slightly covered with a whitish substance. He was seized with violent and prolonged sneezing, sometimes accompanied by a dry cough...The nostrils were discoloured and obstructed; the secretion of saliva abundant at intervals, and the abdomen rather hard. Pulse low but regular, giving about sixty pulsations per minute. All these symptoms appeared to me alarming.*[526]

Following the examination, Napoleon began his usual barrage of questions. Most importantly, and with humor, the Emperor asked the doctor what he thought of his new patient's health? Napoleon added, *"Am I yet destined to disturb for a long time the digestion of the rulers of the earth?"* Antommarchi responded saying, *"You will outlive them, Sire."*[527]

Still leery of his new doctor, Napoleon took to using humor to test the Corsican doctor's resolve. A few weeks after his arrival, Antommarchi came to check on Napoleon after the Emperor had completed his bath and breakfast. The doctor found the Emperor reading a volume of French author Jean Racine. Antommarchi asked the Emperor about the famous passage he was reading. Napoleon laughed and said, *"You expect me to recite that passage so much admired by wiseacres in general, but my dear Dottoraccio*[528], *I shall*

Digging The Ground 243

do no such thing: it is all foolery clothed in poetry too elegant. Let us turn to this other passage."[529]

> *And he began to read with a delicacy and truth of expression, and inflexion of voice, which would have done honour to an actor. He, however, soon grew weary, threw down the book, fell back into his arm-chair pronouncing the name of his mother in an undertone, and sunk into a kind of stupor. I endeavoured to recall him to himself; I felt his chest heave, and as it were some great effort agitating his whole frame. He looked at me, but spoke not, and I did not know what to think of the state in which I saw him. Suddenly a crisis took place, and he was relieved. "Doctor," said he, "I am dead; what do you think about it?" Then rising from his chair and advancing towards me, he looked at me from head to foot, and took hold of me by the ears and whiskers, and pushed me against the wall, exclaiming, "Ah! You rascal of a Doctor Capo-Corsino, you are come to St. Helena to physic me, are you? – Do you know that I will have you hanged at your own house at Cape Corsica?" In speaking thus he laughed, gesticulated, and said the drollest things imaginable.*[530]

The Emperor loved to use humor with people to keep them alert and, in a sense, always on their toes. With Dr. Antommarchi, things would be no different. But in a very short time, their relationship would become far from cordial.

Part of the reason for this deterioration in their relationship was due to one major reason: Dr. Antommarchi was an anatomist and had never actually practiced medicine on the living. The Emperor's family had sent him a completely unqualified doctor to attend him. Napoleon would quickly see this in the care the doctor would provide him, or rather, the lack thereof. Russian Commissioner Count Balmain wrote to Moscow about the situation with the new doctor. He wrote, "*It would have been difficult to find a technically qualified* man more unsuited to a post where by this time skill and experience and tact had become so vitally necessary. He had not even the social qualities required, being merely an ignorant provincial from a village in a wild and remote corner of Corsica."[531] Count Balmain was absolutely correct on his assessment of Antommarchi. Napoleon would quickly realize this himself and would eventually unleash his anger upon the new doctor.

Napoleon was dying within the walls of Longwood with no one medically qualified to help him.

*   *   *

The last few months of 1819, found the Emperor drifting back and forth between periods of depression and bouts of anger at the Governor, but there were also moments of humor and enjoyment. The latter moments came with his time spent with the Bertrand children. They were the only ones who remained at Longwood since the departure of Madame Montholon and her children. As Napoleon's body continued to deteriorate and his strength diminished, his love still grew for those children. He absolutely adored their innocence and honesty.

Antommarchi recorded in his memoirs a few episodes of the Emperor basking in the enjoyment while playing with the Bertrand children.

> *The Emperor sent for the children of the Grand Marshal; - they had not seen him for some days past. They hastened to him full of joy, and immediately began to play and sport around him. To him they appealed as arbiter of their discussions: - "Is it not true, Sire, that my cup and ball goes best?"- "No, it is mine." – "It is mine," said a third: "I refer it to you – your Majesty shall decide." The Emperor laughed, gave his decision, laughed louder still, and the tumult went on as before. "You are too noisy, children: I shall not keep you to dinner."- "Yes, do! we will not make any more noise:" and they were quieter. Napole-*

> on kept them, and placed little Hortensia next to
> him, and ordered dinner to be served. But their
> appetite satisfied, the discussions began again:
> each contended for the palm of victory, - each
> pretended to have been the most skillful. The
> Emperor was again established judge, and ap-
> pealed to, right and left. "Is it not true, Sire?
> Your Majesty has seen; - have you not?" Napole-
> on, almost stunned with the noise, did not know
> whom to answer, and laughed more and more.
> "Hold your tongues," said he to them at last; "you
> are little chatter-boxes. True, but be quiet; you
> make too much noise." And they all began again,
> accusing each other mutually of crying out too
> loud, until, dinner being over, the Emperor sent
> them away. "You will send for us to-morrow,
> Sire; - will you not?" - "You are, then, very fond
> of playing with me?" - "Yes! yes!" exclaimed they
> all together, and withdrew in the hopes of coming
> again.[532]

The Emperor took immense joy in their laughter and mirth. Their little voices, playfulness, and jest engulfed him and made all other cares of exile, St. Helena, and Governor Lowe subside, even if just for a few moments. His own roars of laughter were healthy for him, even if they exhausted him. But to Napoleon, it was worth every minute.

> "How happy they are when I send for them or play
> with them!" said the Emperor;

> "all their wishes are satisfied. Passions have not
> yet approached their hearts: they feel the pleni-
> tude of existence; - let them enjoy it! At their age,
> I thought and felt as they do: what storms
> since!...But how much that little Hortensia grows
> and improves! If she lives, of how many young

> *elegans [bachelors] will she not disturb the repose! I shall then be no more: what say you Doctor?"*[533]

Even in his joy of playing with the children, Napoleon's own mortality crept back into his mind. The Emperor was well aware that his time with them was limited and he would not see these children grow to adulthood.

A few days later, Napoleon kept his promise and brought the children back to play. The Emperor did everything he could to get them as noisy as possible in their frolicking. He roared with laughter at all they were doing. He especially revealed a great affection for the little boy named Arthur Bertrand. Antommarchi described that at one point during their playing, the little boy began to get "*out of temper.*"

> *"What is the matter with you, little urchin? – What do you say?" said the Emperor to him, making him jump and laugh at the same time in spite of himself. – "This little fellow," said Napoleon to me, "is as independent as I was at his age; but the fits of passion to which I often gave way, proceeded from more excusable motives."*[534]

Remarkably, this led Napoleon to reveal a sensitive story about himself when he was a child. He explained to the doctor about how when he was little his parents placed him in a school filled with young ladies. This led him to be chastised by other boys of the neighborhood. Napoleon described that as "*a pretty boy, and the only one there, I was caressed by every one of my fair schoolfellow.*"

> *"I might generally be seen with my stockings down, and covering half my shoes; and in our walks I constantly held the hand of a charming little girl, who was the cause of many broils and quarrels. My malicious comrades, jealous of my Giacominetta,*[535] *combined these two circumstances together in a song which they made, and whenever I appeared in the street they followed*

> me, singing, "Napoleone di mezza calzetta, fa l'amore a Giacominetta!" [Napoleon the wimp makes love to Giacominetta!] I could not bear to be laughed at; and seizing sticks or stones, or any thing that came in my way, I rushed into the midst of the crowd: fortunately it always happened that somebody interfered, and got me out of the scrape; but the number opposed to me never stopped me – I never reckoned how many they were."[536]

Even as a child of five years, Napoleon would not back down from a battle.

*   *   *

New Year's Day, January 1, 1820, came and was celebrated in the usual fashion with Napoleon surrounded by the children. Again he gave them each gold napoleons bearing his Imperial image and laughed at their enjoyment and excitement.[537]

A few days later, Napoleon was reflecting on his life, his decisions, and actions. Much of this reflection was brought about even more by his attending the Masses celebrated by the two priests. The realization that death was near, coupled with little hope of returning to France made Napoleon think more about the future and his own mortality. In conversing with Montholon, the Emperor said,

> *My actions and events answer all the libelous statements made against me. I am innocent of the ordinary crimes of dynasty heads. I have nothing to fear from posterity, history will perhaps even accuse me of having been too good. Montholon, my son,"* he said to the general, grabbing him by the ear, *"I can present myself with confidence before God's judgment seat.*[538]

Napoleon would die with a clear conscience.

But he also enjoyed his time spent at these new improvised Masses celebrated by Abbe Vignali and Abbe Buonavita. He attended them every Sunday. After one of the Masses, Napoleon said to his suite, "*I hope the Holy Father will not find fault with us; we have become Christians again. If he could see our chapel he would grant us indulgences. If any of you has a conscience overburdened with sins, Buonavita is there to take them and give you absolution.*"[539] It makes one wonder whether Napoleon himself had made his own confession to the old Abbe.

During one of Napoleon's physical exams by Dr. Antommarchi, the doctor remarked that Napoleon was in desperate need of exercise. The Emperor snapped back at Antommarchi as if unaware of his surroundings at Longwood. "*What am I to do, Doctor?*" – "*Take exercise.*" – "*Where?*" – "*In the gardens – in the fields – in the open air.*" – "*What! in the midst of the red-coats?*" – "*No, Sire.*" – "*How then?*" – "*You must dig the ground, turn up the earth, and thus escape from inactivity and insult at the same time.*" – "*Dig the ground! yes, Doctor, you are right, I will dig the ground.*"[540] The Emperor instantly knew how to accomplish this task.

Throughout his time at Longwood, Napoleon enjoyed walking and sitting in his garden. But he loathed the fact that the British sentries could see him there and would report back to Governor Lowe all that they had witnessed. To prevent this from happening, the Emperor had discussed erecting a large berm to create a barrier that would obstruct the view of the British soldiers. Napoleon also desired to create a fountain in the garden. Towards the end of January 1820, Napoleon decided the time was now to take on the task and 'dig the earth.'

The creation of the berm and the enlargement of the garden took place from the end of January through the early spring of 1820. The Emperor approached these tasks as if he were planning out his next great battle. The undertaking of this new project injected a dose of excitement and purpose into the Emperor. It not only helped to break the boredom of his exile, but it also served as a means for providing him with a form of exercise that he desperately needed, even if it was just a little.

Governor Lowe was notified about the commotion taking place in the garden outside of Longwood but was informed that the berm was being created to shield the garden from the wind. Believing what he was told, Governor Lowe did not interfere in the work that was taking place.[541]

Once the Emperor made the decision to work in the garden, all he could do was focus on the task at hand. The servants gathered the tools and the Emperor outlined where exactly each part of the garden was going to be located, especially the fountain that was to be positioned in the middle. When working on the garden outside, "*the Emperor had adopted for dress a nankeen jacket like a farmer's and a pair of trousers of the same fabric, with red slippers and a wide-brimmed straw hat to protect him from the sun, with the shirt collar over that of the jacket. So as to be less recognizable, he had ordered Saint-Denis and Noverraz to dress the same way.*"[542] Napoleon also carried a rake and spade, which he mainly used as walking sticks.

The Emperor was always in a good mood when working on the garden. He would wake at five in the morning and would wait impatiently for the sentries to withdraw from their nighttime positions. Napoleon would then pace outside near the windows of Longwood carrying a big bell, which he would swing vigorously to awaken his 'workers.' If the bell did not work, the Emperor would pick up a stone, or large clumps of dirt and throw them at the windows. He would go right down the house hitting all the windows, starting with St. Denis' and ending with Marchand's.

On one of these mornings when the Emperor was doing this early morning work ritual, he came to St. Denis' window, threw a rock and then sang, "*Ali, Ali, you sleep! You will sleep more comfortably when you have gone in again.*" When the valet opened the window, the Emperor yelled, "*Come lazybones, don't you see the sun?*" Napoleon then sang, "*Ali! Ali! ah! ah! Allah! It is day!*"[543] A stone next found its way against Marchand's window, followed by the voice of the Emperor singing.

While working on the garden, the Emperor would supervise and yell out commands just as if he was on the battlefield again. When one of the members of his suite would smile or laugh at him, Napoleon would run over to them, laughing himself, and would pinch their ear and say they were not working hard enough. This just caused them to laugh more. Other times, the Emperor would sarcastically say, "*Gentlemen, you are incapable of earning a shilling a day!*" which was always met with laughter.[544]

Montholon took great joy in observing the Emperor in such high spirits. "*It was a picture worthy of being represented by the most celebrated artists, to see the conqueror of so many kingdoms, him who had dictated laws to so many sovereigns, at dawn of day, with his spade in his hand, a broad straw hat on his head, and his feet clad in red slippers, directing our labours, and those, assuredly more useful, of the Chinese gardeners of the establishment.*"[545] It was as if he was just this typical little Corsican man back on his home island in the Mediterranean Sea directing his servants in the construction of his beloved garden.

Antommarchi noticed that when Napoleon came close to the Chinese laborers, the men began to laugh. The Emperor was curious as to their amusement and asked the doctor if they were laughing at the attire Napoleon was wearing. "*Probably, Sire, they are surprised to see you dressed like a workman, like themselves.*"[546] Napoleon found their laughter humorous as well. The Emperor said, "*It must be my costume that causes their mirth; and it is, indeed, odd enough. But with all their laughing they must not be burnt up by all the heat: every one of them shall also have a straw-hat, as a present from me.*"[547] Napoleon enjoyed seeing those around him take delight in his 'unusual' appearance.

Marchand recorded in his memoirs that this physical activity by the Emperor caused him to regain part of his once healthy appetite. Sometimes the food grown in his new garden would appear on his plate during a meal. St. Denis explained how the Emperor would feel a sense of pride when they would dine and eat something that came from their garden.

> *When the Emperor saw something on his table which came from his garden he would say, "After all, our trouble has not been wholly lost. Our gardens are feeding us." We could not help smiling. "What, rascal, are you smiling?" the Emperor would say, looking at one of those who were waiting on him, and he would smile himself.*[548]

As the group constructed the fountain in the middle of the garden, Napoleon took special interest in its location and design. When it was completed, the Emperor took childish joy as it was turned on for the first time.

> *In order to enjoy this pleasure, which one might call infantile, the Emperor would stand between the basin at the fence and the grotto and would*

watch the water run down and reach there. The noise and movement would amuse him for a few moments. He would laugh at himself for being amused at so little.[549]

The Emperor's entourage stood in awe, not because of the creation, but because of the reaction of its very creator.

This work and exercise on the garden must have sparked a burst of energy in the Emperor because at one point while they were enjoying the garden, Napoleon walked off and then appeared on horseback to everyone's surprise. He rode off, followed by a servant on horseback. It appeared he was headed towards Deadwood, a plain near Longwood. After taking a view out his spyglass, he hurriedly galloped back to Longwood. This little excursion set off an enormous panic across the island. What made the British nervous was the question as to why there was a 'laborer' riding swiftly on horseback?[550]

When Napoleon realized that his riding on horseback dressed the way he did set Governor Lowe into a panic, the Emperor decided to have a little fun. Antommarchi described in his memoirs how Napoleon carried out his plan.

The Emperor, who was highly amused by his [Lowe's] fears, took it into his head to increase them. For that purpose he made Vignali put on a dress similar to his own, gave him his horse, his piqueur [servant], and his glass, ordering him to ride fast, and appear to be making observations. The missionary went, was seen and noticed, and the tranquility of the whole island was immediately disturbed; signals were made and Hudson, Gorrequer, Reade,[551] *- all instantly turned out and proceeded to Longwood."*[552]

The Governor was completely irate at the incident and proceeded to curse out the doctor of Longwood. After Antommarchi's scolding, for an incident that he was not even involved with, the doctor went back to the garden. Napoleon was anxious to know the Governor's response. The Emperor said, "*Well! What did Hudson say to* you? Is he afraid that I shall some day get wings and fly away, and escape the grave?"

> *"I know not, Sire: I was relating to him how you had usurped victory and public admiration; the sketch displeased him, and he retired." Napoleon was very much amused at this new misadventure, he laughed, pitied Hudson, and thought he had been too much teased for one day.*[553]

Though Napoleon hated Governor Lowe, he still took mercy on him, unlike the Governor himself towards his prisoner.

With pride in his new creation, Napoleon also was incredibly protective of his garden and fountain. Shortly after planting the garden, peas and string beans began to show themselves. One morning in the spring of 1820, Napoleon was out taking a stroll in the garden in his bathrobe to check on his crops, when he noticed a few hens that were 'attacking' his garden. Enraged by what he saw, Napoleon ordered St. Denis to fetch his guns. Marchand recorded the punishment the Emperor inflicted on the invaders.

> *The poor chickens continued doing their damage, not suspecting that lead was about to put an end to it. They were close together. Aim was taken, three fell with one shot, the others flew away, and a fourth was hit with the second shot on the wall where it had perched... "I forbid you to pay for them," he said, no matter who the owner is!" It so happened they belonged to (Napoleon's) cook, who was careful not to complain, and found a way to lose nothing by offering a good chicken broth!*[554]

The Emperor also put an end to an ox that had wandered into the garden. This animal belonged to the East India Company and the manner by which its life ended did not please the Governor. When the animal was shot, Little Arthur Bertrand was present and "*was so frightened at seeing this enormous animal fall under the impact of the shot that he threw himself between the Emperor's legs, not want-*

ing to turn his head toward the ox. The Emperor often referred to that child's fright, and when he saw him would say: "Well, Arthur, what about the ox?"[555] Napoleon never missed an opportunity to jest with the children.

*   *   *

As the Emperor's valet, Marchand was privy to Napoleon's most intimate moments. During the spring of 1820, the valet recorded in his memoirs the morning routine of the Emperor in much detail.

When the Emperor got out of his bathtub, two very hot sheets were ready. One would be thrown over him and he would wrap it around himself and go from the bathroom into his bedroom, where a bright fire was prepared; the second sheet was placed on his shoulders, and this way he was well dried. If the Emperor was feeling well, he would dress immediately. He would put on silk stockings and buckled shoes, then don a pair of white cloth trousers and remain stripped from the waist up to do his beard; but in Saint Helena he shaved only every other day. All the details of his preparations were seen to with great care. His teeth had remained very fine and quite shiny, although he had not had any opiate for a long time, and had to content himself with a little brandy mixed with water. After having run a brush over his head and combed his hair, he had his shoulders and body brushed, insisting that we press hard on the liver side while brushing briskly as well on the right shoulder where he felt some pain. He then had cologne poured in his hand, and would rub his side and chest with it, and put some under his arms, after having washed his face in a larger silver basin contain-

ing water mixed with cologne. For his hands and nails he used a lemon. When all this washing was done, he completed his dress.[556]

Though this was the Emperor's daily routine, he was always curious as to how others prepared themselves in the morning. As he was completing this morning ritual a few days later, Grand Marshal Bertrand entered the bedroom to converse with the Emperor. As Bertrand began to speak, Napoleon interrupted him to ask him if he too used a brush on his body to prevent diseases.

"No, Sire," replied the grand marshal.

"You are mistaken, Bertrand, it prevents diseases."

"Sire, I have reached the age of nearly fifty without using it, and I am none the worse for it."

"Well, rubbing my liver is good for me; you don't believe it?" asked the Emperor. And the grand marshal was smiling while looking at him: "You don't believe that I am ill, you are like your wife who does not want to believe it either!"

"Sire, Your Majesty will not allow me to say that he does not appear to be in bad health."

"You dare to argue, Bertrand!" Taking the grand marshal by the throat and pinning him against the wall he said: "Your money or your life! – Aristocrat!" he said, releasing him.

"Your Majesty will permit me to say that all his strength does not seem to have left him, for he was certainly holding me tightly."

> "Without being tall, I never failed to be quite strong," said the Emperor. "I remember when I was in military school we minor nobles would have fights with sons of great noblemen, and I always came out victorious!" Knowing the very liberal ideas of the grand marshal, the Emperor called him "aristocrat!"[557]

Napoleon constantly longed for word about his son. Any letter or word about the King of Rome brought about immense emotion from the Emperor. Once the two priests were settled into Longwood, they unpacked their belongings and brought to the Emperor a portrait of his son held in a green leather portfolio. When Napoleon took the portrait of the King of Rome into his hands, one would think he was actually holding the boy himself. Tears ran from Napoleon's eyes as he said to Marchand, *"Poor child, what a destiny! Here, place it open on my desk, so that I may see it every day."*[558]

This portrait made him miss his son even more than before. Being with the Bertrand children always lifted his spirits, so he sent for them. During this visit, Napoleon invited Madame Bertrand and the children to stay and eat with him. While the children were eating, Napoleon started to throw bread balls at them and would look away when they turned towards him to catch him in the act. The Emperor could not keep a straight face for long and burst out into loud laughter. As the children joined in on the fun, Napoleon took one of the children on his knees and kissed and teased him as he was playfully pulling the child's ears. Marchand's eyes filled with tears as he remembered the Emperor playing the same way with the King of Rome when he was an infant.[559]

Napoleon thought little Hortensia was the sweetest little child. He really wanted her ears to be pierced and had an inclination that Madame Bertrand would not approve. But as in all things, this did not stop the Emperor. Antommarchi described the scene in his memoirs when the Emperor found the right moment to implement his plan.

> *The children of the Grand Marshal perceived him [Napoleon], and were soon round him. He had not seen them in some days, and purposing to send for them, was not sorry to find them before-*

> *hand with him. – "Send for the Doctor," said he to General Montholon, "I want his ministry; he must bore these pretty little ears" (showing those of little Hortensia, and opening a paper, in which a pair of coral ear-rings were folded-up). I prepared accordingly to perform the little operation, but the sight of the instrument produced the usual effect,-the child cried, and the Emperor, fearing lest mamma should not be pleased, hesitated. His presence, however, and that of the ear-rings, soon dried up her tears. We retired under the shade of an oak-tree. General Montholon supported the patient; Napoleon looked on, and little Arthur stamped and stormed, crying out that he would not allow his sister to be hurt! Napoleon was highly amused by the anger, threats, and English phrases, of the little fellow, who only grumbled the more. "What do you say, little rogue?" said the Emperor to him; "if you do not stay quiet I will have your ears bored also: come, will you be obedient?" – The operation over, and the ear-rings put on, Napoleon embraced the amiable little creature, congratulating her on her courage, and sent her away: "Go and show your ears to mamma, and if she is not satisfied, and does not approve of the operation, tell her that it was not I, but the Dottoraccio who did it!" – "Yes, Sire;" and she bounded away and disappeared in an instant.[560]*

Napoleon walked away and kept laughing to himself about the behavior of little Arthur Bertrand. Still amused, Napoleon turned to Antommarchi and said, "*The little urchin!...I was just as resolute at his age!*"[561]

The Emperor took joy in spoiling this little boy. Arthur Bertrand often reminded him of himself. A few weeks after the ear-ring incident in the summer of 1820, Arthur spotted a pony that he wanted the Emperor to purchase for him. The owner had ridden it to Longwood and the sight of the pony completely captured the heart of the young boy. Not wanting to disappoint the boy, Napoleon told the owner to come back at noon and he would purchase the pony. He then went to his bedroom and took a nap. As the cannon sounded the noon hour, little Arthur went to the Emperor's bedroom to wake him so he could buy the pony as he promised. Marchand found the boy pleading with Noverraz to let him in to wake the Emperor, who outright refused. Marchand, afraid the boy would cry, took the boy by the hand and asked him if he wanted to wait for the Emperor to awake from his nap; Arthur answered that he would.

> *I took him by the hand, he went near the bed where the Emperor was resting, saw he was sleeping, then sat on the rug and stayed with me almost an hour, playing alone and noiselessly. When the Emperor awoke, he was quite surprised to find him there: "There you are, Arthur, what do you want, my boy?"*
>
> *"You tell me gun fire." I was not aware of the promise made to him. "What does he say?" the Emperor asked. "He is telling Your Majesty that he told him to come back when the gun went off." "Take him to Montholon, to find out what he wants." At that very moment, Count de Montholon was announced at the Emperor's bedroom; he learned that during lunch he had told the child to come at noon, and he would buy him the little pony. "Gun fire" was the cannon announcing that hour, and he came to claim the promise made to him.*
>
> *"Indeed! What a memory," said the Emperor, "is the horse still there?" Count de Montholon, who had discussed the price with the owner, assured*

him that it was. "But," said the Emperor, caressing the child and embracing him,

"do you have any money?" "Yes, I have two dollars." "That is not enough."

"Papa give you everything!" "But Papa Bertrand has no money." "I have plenty of gold." "Will you be good?" "Yes." "How much does he want for this horse?" the Emperor asked General Montholon. "Fifty Louis [1000 francs], Sire."

"Give this boy 1,200 francs," said the Emperor to me. I went upstairs to get the money that was locked up in a bag. The child was four years old, and on seeing me arrive, he held out his pinafore to catch the money. "You won't be able to carry it." "Yes, yes." I put the money gently in his pinafore to test his strength. He turned rapidly and, accompanied by Count de Montholon, he went to purchase the horse he wished to buy.[562]

Because Marchand served as Napoleon's personal valet, he most often witnessed the Emperor in the presence of the children. The valet recorded that Napoleon was extremely fond of children "*and there was nothing he wouldn't do to please them.*"[563]

But yet again, these moments with the children focused his mind back on his own son. All of the people who surrounded the Emperor knew very well the depression and grief that filled his heart over being separated from his son. St. Denis recorded that "*his misfortunes would have been greatly softened, he would have borne them with still more resignation, if he had his son with him. This consolation had been refused him; consequently he would often say: "How much happier is a cobbler than I am! He at least has his wife and son with him!""*[564]

Dreams of Josephine, the Emperor's second wife Marie-Louise, and his son also tormented Napoleon immensely. He would call out their names in the night and awake with tears in his eyes. Marchand recorded one of these emotional moments in the latter part of 1820.

> *I stood in front of his bed awaiting his orders. He was looking at me as if preoccupied by something other than the object he was staring at. Suddenly he told me he had dreamt of Empress Marie-Louise and his son, whom she was holding by the hand. It was a new experience for me to hear the Emperor mention a dream. "She was as fresh," he said to me, "as when I saw her in Compiegne; I took her in my arms, but no matter how hard I tried to keep her, I felt her escape me; and when I wanted to hold her again, everything had disappeared and I was awakened." "Your awakening must have been cruel, Sire, but I witnessed Your Majesty's dream; I even thought from the agitation I heard that you were ill, and I was about to awaken you when you called Saint-Denis." "Ah," he said, jumping out of his bed and taking me by the throat, "it is you, miserable wretch, who are the reason I could not remain any longer with my wife and son! What does your crime deserve? Confess."*
>
> *"May heaven grant me the power to place both of them in Your Majesty's arms, to atone for the error, and obtain my forgiveness." "It is enough for me to bear the burden of my misery alone without having them for witnesses," he replied letting me go.*[565]

But Napoleon's depression over his separation from family would only worsen as his time on St. Helena continued. While perusing the newspapers from Europe in the latter part of 1820, the Emperor came across an obituary that sent shock waves through his heart; that of his beloved sister, Eliza. A few members of Napoleon's suite were present to witness his reaction to the emotional news. Dr. Antommarchi recorded Napoleon being *"thrown into a state of* stupor. *He was in his arm-chair, his head hanging down on his breast, motionless, like one a prey to violent grief: deep sighs escaped at intervals from his breast; he raised his eyes, cast them down again, fixing them alternatively upon me and the ground, and looking fixedly at me without uttering a single word."*[566] Napoleon then put out his arm for the doctor to take his pulse. Antommarchi found his pulse to be weak. The Emperor knew this news was taking a toll on his heart.

Later that night, Napoleon talked with St. Denis and expressed his feelings on the death of his sister.

> *"There is the first member of my family who has set out on the great journey; in a few months I shall go to join her. I shall be the second, certainly, since I am not the first. The end of my sufferings is only postponed." "Ah, Sire, we must hope that Providence will re-establish Your Majesty's health, and that your friends will not have to weep for your loss so soon; it is too much for them now to know that you are in chains. And we, Sire, what would become of us if we were to lose Your Majesty, we who are so happy at having accompanied you, at being with you and at serving you?" "You will have the happiness of serving your family again, your friends, your country, beautiful France." Tears rolled from my eyes, and if I had dared they would have moistened the hands of my master.*[567]

* * *

Governor Lowe sent word to Grand Marshal Bertrand that the new Longwood house was ready for Napoleon. The new house was large and well constructed but was surrounded by an iron gate that Governor Lowe insisted be placed around the house. Napoleon had already informed the Governor that he would not reside in this house, but Lowe still informed Napoleon that it was ready. In response, the Emperor instructed Montholon to write a letter to the Governor stating that Napoleon would "*never, unless forced so to do, enter the iron cage which was being constructed by the English government.*"[568]

Part of this decision by Napoleon was to refuse to do anything that was either commanded by Lowe or that would help the Governor in his reputation back in Europe. Remaining at Longwood, in its present condition, would ensure that the Emperor could continue to wage his public opinion war in Europe over his living conditions in the damp residence. While remaining at Longwood, Napoleon could continue to complain about his situation in the hopes that Europe would pressure the English into returning him to the continent. Two things were certain; Napoleon would not reside in the new Longwood House and he would not return to Europe alive.

August 15, 1820, brought another birthday for the Emperor on the island of St. Helena. He insisted on being surrounded by the children and again took joy in their happiness at receiving gifts from him. Montholon described this day in his memoir.

> *He appeared to be truly happy, as a good father might in the midst of his family, when at dinner, he was surrounded by our children, or when he amused himself by exciting their gaiety and drawing forth their little secrets. His great pleasure was to constitute himself judge between them and us: he had accustomed them to this, and really I know not how we should have contrived to pressure our parental authority had he not always founds means to adjudge us in the right, at the same time that he persuaded the children that his justice was impartial; but whenever the question agitated related to a piece of bread and jam, or a party of pleasure, his judgment was always in favour of the children, to the great despair of the mother.*[569]

The Emperor always took great pleasure in sharing his birthday with the children. As the clouds of sadness and depression loomed over St. Helena, the laughter of the children served as rays of sun to break up the anguish of exile.

Napoleon was 51 years old. He would not see another birthday.

What would I see upon returning there?
My fellow country men bound in chains?...

There is only one thing left for a true patriot
to do: die.

Napoleon

Chapter 8

Purification Through Suffering

As the final days of 1820 came to a close, the Emperor's health was seriously worsening. His legs became so swollen that they would no longer support him. Napoleon would either use a billiard cue as a walking stick or resort to taking the arm of one of the members of his suite as a means of support for his ailing legs. Continuous fits of vomiting began to take over his daily activities, leaving him practically bedridden. Napoleon would take rides out in the calash when the weather was good, but it would often leave him tired and in a more weakened state.

As New Year's Day came, Marchand entered the Emperor's bedroom to open the curtains. Napoleon asked, "*Well, what are you giving me as a present?*" Marchand responded, "*Sire, the hope of seeing Your Majesty get well very soon and leave a climate so bad for his health.*" In a somber voice, the Emperor replied, "*It won't be long, my son, my end is near, I cannot go on much longer.*"[570]

Montholon could see the rapid decline in the Emperor's health.

> *The night between the 31st of December 1820, and the 1st of January 1821, was one of the last passed in intimate conversation of the recollections of a better time. The disease, which was some months later to deprive us of the Emperor, made, after this time, rapid progress. He daily felt himself less disposed to activity either of mind or body; a general feeling of fatigue oppressed him, he said; he remained sometimes for hours listlessly seated in a bergere, and perfectly silent; he who before had passed the greatest part of the day in pacing the apartment, at the same time either dictating, or recalling recollections and collecting materials for his work. I now often remained standing for hours near him, expecting the termination of a*

phrase, or waiting till he should decide upon rousing himself from his state of torpor, otherwise than by these few words: "Well, my son! What have you now to say? What should we do?"[571]

For the past couple of months, the health of Madame Bertrand declined and the Grand Marshal sought permission from the Emperor to have his wife and children return to Europe. Napoleon advised that the Grand Marshal return as well to aid in returning his family to the comforts of Europe. Napoleon only requested of the Grand Marshal that the date of departure would be left up to the Emperor himself.

Marchand knew of the emptiness that would be left in the Emperor if the family were to leave St. Helena. *"If the grand marshal left Longwood with his wife, four children, and the servants, who all brought a certain animation to the colony, an immense void would ensue for the Emperor…In the months that followed, it led to some coolness, less with the grand marshal perhaps than with the countess."*[572]

This coolness towards Madame Bertrand may have occurred for other reasons as well. Many believed that Napoleon was intimate with Madame Montholon while she was on the island. But many also suspected that the Emperor's sexual overture to Madame Bertrand may have been rebuffed to his anger and dismay. Adding to this was Madame Bertrand's great interest in spending long hours conversing with Dr. Antommarchi, often times at the expense of the doctor's time attending to the sick Emperor. Both Madame Bertrand and Antommarchi shared the same opinion that the Emperor was not *"ill to the extent that his days were in danger."*[573] This only enraged the Emperor more.

When it came to Antommarchi's care for the Emperor, it seemed to get worse as well. He often times could not be found when Napoleon was ill and when he was located, he was with Madame Bertrand. During one illness that occurred during the month of February, Antommarchi placed vesicatories on both the Emperor's arms, which literally prevented him from eating. When Marchand tried to look for the doctor, he was nowhere to be found. Antommarchi later returned and Napoleon let loose his rage. *"Leave me alone. You place vesicatories that have no shape, you do not shave the place before you apply them: this would not be done to the poorest man in a hospital; it seems to me that you could have left one of my arms free, without affecting both arms! That is no way to tie up a poor man...Go away, you are an ignoramus, and I a greater one for having let you do this."*[574]

The Emperor's rage at Antommarchi caused the doctor to ask permission to be sent back to Europe. At first, Napoleon was completely in favor of the decision and dictated a letter to be delivered to Antommarchi that stated, "*During the fifteen months which you have spent in this country, you have given his Majesty no confidence in your moral character; you can be of no use to him [Napoleon] in his illness, and your residing here for some months longer would have no object; and be of no use.*"[575] Though incompetent, to say the least, the doctor was needed to attend to Napoleon. Through the intervention of most of the Emperor's suite, Napoleon agreed to let the doctor remain.

One piece of medical advice that Antommarchi provided which the French suite agreed with was the need for Napoleon to strengthen the muscles in his legs. To achieve this, Montholon, Bertrand, and the valets constructed a 'see-saw' in the drawing room of Longwood for the Emperor to use for exercise. When the Emperor first saw the contraption, he asked if it was some war machine or a swing for the children. But knowing the pain in his legs was worsening, Napoleon agreed to use the see-saw. To his amusement, the Emperor enjoyed having the Bertrand children seated on the other side of the see-saw and would howl with loud laughter when he would purposely give the board a quick jerk, causing the children to fall to the ground giggling.[576]

Madame Bertrand laughed heartily when she saw Napoleon on the see-saw. Grand Marshal Bertrand describe how she believed that "*someone really ought to make a cartoon showing the Emperor on one end, and all the crowned heads at the other end unable to raise him off the ground, and the caption should be: a cure for liver. The truth is that the Emperor is very heavy; he weighs more than Noverraz, who is over six feet.*"[577] Napoleon's weight gain had made it even more difficult for him to maneuver around Longwood.

The exercise did not last long, for the Emperor's legs became so swollen and weak that he could no longer use the see-saw. This lack of mobility left the Emperor bedridden where he would vomit continuously throughout the day and night, much of which was black in color and as thick as tar. Napoleon told Bertrand the end was near.

Napoleon told the Grand Marechal that he is much worse. "If I should end my career now," he said, "it would be a great joy. At times I have longed to die, and I have no fear of death. It would be a great joy to me if I were to die within the next two weeks. What have I left to hope for? Except, possibly, an even more miserable end.[578]

Various reports were being passed to Longwood concerning the prospects of moving the Emperor from St. Helena. Napoleon's mother had been sending letters to members of Parliament and other British officials begging them to bring her dying son back to Europe. Her pleas won over some support and rumors began to spread that Napoleon may be brought back or even sent to the United States. Though the discussions gave some hope to the French exiles, for Napoleon the reality had already sunk in that St. Helena would probably become his grave.

Due to illness from the climate, both Abbe Buonavita and servant Gentilini were to leave St. Helena aboard the next ship to Europe. Days later, cook Chandelier requested to return as well. To Montholon, he believed this reduction in members of the Emperor's suite only pleased Governor Lowe. *"It really seemed as if the isolation of the Emperor were an idee fixe* [fixation] *of the man's hatred, and that to seize or make any opportunity of persuading any one of us to quit the Emperor, was an enjoyment which he could not resist."*[579]

As Napoleon's entourage was getting smaller, his depression and loneliness only grew. These men possessed what Napoleon did not: the choice to go home.

*   *   *

The month of March 1821 saw the Emperor's health worsen rapidly. More fits of vomiting occurred and Napoleon came down with a severe fever. Montholon recorded that the vomiting was so violent and looked as if *"something like a clot of blood...We had only taken a few steps when the vomiting returned. I immediately led or rather carried the Emperor back to his apartment, for he could scarcely stand, so violent was the pain below the left breast. Antommarchi's evil star willed that again he should be absent from Longwood."*[580]

Towards the end of March, Montholon described the Emperor's condition in his memoir, particularly the fact that his vomit was now black in color. Antommarchi administered Napoleon a bowl of emetic lemonade as a medicine. *"But scarcely half an hour later after the Emperor had taken a glass, he made frightful efforts to vomit, and rolled on the ground uttering groans."*[581]

When he recovered, the Emperor again expressed his rage at the doctor. *"Keep your physic: I will not have two diseases – that with which I am afflicted, and that which you would inflict upon me."*[582] When Antommarchi recommended another emetic, the Emperor responded by stating, *"Why don't you go jump in the lake and take the emetic yourself?"*[583] The doctor later tried to persuade Marchand of the importance of the emetic and desired that the valet secretly put it in the Emperor's drink. Marchand outright refused.

As ill as the Emperor was, he was still sharp enough to foresee the possibilities of someone putting the medicine in his drink. He questioned Marchand about this and the valet confessed that he was asked, but that he refused the request. Napoleon responded, *"I certainly hope no one has taken the liberty of adding anything to my licorice."*[584]

As Napoleon's condition worsened, even the routine task of relieving himself left him tired and weak. Medicine was given to the Emperor to induce a critically needed bowel movement, which Bertrand recorded as causing *"him fifteen hours of suffering and discomfort, which had exhausted him."* As Dr. Antommarchi congratulated himself on the success of the remedy, a tired and sarcastic smile appeared on Napoleon's face as he turned to him and said in a humorous tone, *"Shut up, you bore me."*[585]

Being that the Emperor was bedridden for over two weeks, the Governor came to Longwood to express his concern to Montholon that a British officer had not seen Napoleon during this time. Montholon explained that he was very ill and that requiring him to be seen would only agitate the situation. The Governor was not convinced. Grand Marshal Bertrand recorded the exchange between the two men in his memoirs.

"The Emperor is ill," Montholon had replied, "he is unable to go out, therefore he cannot be seen. Do you wish to break down the door of his room?"

"Yes," replied the Governor. "If it should be necessary, the door of his room will be battered down and an entry made by force."

"But that would kill him."

"No matter, I would have it done."

"But you are responsible for him."

"I am responsible for him in the eyes of the Courts. I not only am the agent of the English Government, but I also represent the Powers."

According to Montholon, Sir Hudson Lowe spoke with a harshness Montholon had not yet heard him use.[586]

The following day, the British orderly officer was given written orders to break down the door to Longwood if the Emperor did not allow himself to be seen. Montholon explained to the orderly "*that given the Emperor's state of health, violating his domicile was a murderous act, and furthermore, he would be received by His Majesty with a pistol in his hand.*"[587] The orderly believed General Montholon and refused to carry out the Governor's order. A few days later, Lowe replaced the orderly officer with Captain Crockatt.[588]

The Emperor's suite found these latest actions by the Governor intolerable. To think that he would break down the Emperor's door in his sickened state to ensure that he had not escaped boggled their minds. Of all his previous acts of paranoia concerning the prevention of Napoleon's escape, this one seemed to reach the pinnacle of sheer lunacy. To Montholon, this latest action by Lowe was maddening.

This man's character was a very singular one; he required constant nourishment for the uneasy and restless workings of his imagination, and when this nourishment was not the natural result of the danger of his prisoner's escape, he sought for it everywhere, as the bloodhound seeks for the track of the stag on whom a pack of hounds is waiting to rush.[589]

As April 1, 1821, approached, Napoleon lost more confidence in Dr. Antommarchi. In previous months he had resisted seeing any other British doctor fearing he *"will go report my condition to that executioner. It will give him far too much pleasure to learn of my agony."*[590] Even in his weakened state of health, Napoleon was still fighting the battle against Governor Lowe.

But knowing that his condition was rapidly declining, coupled with the fact that he believed Antommarchi to be completely incompetent, the Emperor relented and requested that the British doctor, Dr. Arnott, consult with Antommarchi before he examined him. Once the consultation took place, Napoleon allowed Dr. Arnott into his bedroom.

When Arnott entered the room, he was shocked by the Emperor's appearance and condition. *"The Emperor's face, always noble and handsome, nevertheless showed the signs of long suffering. A beard of several days added even more to the paleness of his complexion, and his eyes so full of expression showed the calmness of perfect resignation."*[591]

After a few moments of general health questions between the two men, Napoleon explained to the doctor his symptoms. *"I have an acute pain here that seems to cut me like a razor. Do you think it might be the pylorus that is affected? My father died of this disease at the age of 35; could it not be hereditary?"*[592] Dr. Arnott proceeded with his examination and stated that Napoleon's illness was *"very serious; he discovers great inflammation in the region of the stomach; but he must see the vomited matter before decidedly giving his opinion."*[593]

Dr. Arnott would not have to wait long for the desired evidence. On April 5, the Emperor vomited a considerable amount of blackish matter. Montholon recorded that *"Dr. Arnott perceives from its nature that there is ulceration in the stomach...has warned Bertrand and myself of the danger which threatens the Emperor."*[594] Napoleon could see that Dr. Arnott was holding back with his patient about his condition. The Emperor instructed the doctor to be honest with him. *"Don't be afraid to speak, Doctor; you have to do with an old soldier who likes frankness. Tell me, what do you think of me?" The doctor continued to speak in the same way as at first, trying to remove from his patient's mind every foreboding of his approaching end."*[595]

During the next few nights, Napoleon was becoming more weakened. He summoned for Antommarchi to assist him in dressing a blister that he had placed on Napoleon's entire abdomen as a treatment, but the doctor was nowhere to be found. He had also administered purgatives as well. Montholon wrote in his memoirs that *"Antommarchi is in disgrace...I received orders to declare to him that the Emperor would see him no more."*[596]

When it came to Antommarchi, the Emperor had had enough. Napoleon's rage hit its pinnacle and he unleashed a brutal verbal lashing to the Corsican. What made the incident worse was that Napoleon accused the doctor of having an affair with Madame Bertrand instead of attending to his needs. This angry onslaught took place in front of Grand Marshal Bertrand. The Grand Marshal himself recorded in his memoirs the rage put forth by the Emperor.

> *Antommarchi went to the Emperor at half-past seven in the morning. Napoleon flew into a rage with him. He said that "Antommarchi should be in attendance on him by six o'clock in the morning, instead of spending all his time with Mme. Bertrand." The Emperor sent for the Grand Marechal, who arrived at a quarter to eight. Napoleon repeated what he had just said to Antommarchi and added that the doctor was only interested in his whores. "Very well, let him spend all of his time with his whores," Napoleon said, "Let him fuck them back and front, in the mouth and in the ears, but get rid of that man for me, he is stupid, ignorant, pretentious, and utterly devoid of any sense of honor...The Emperor repeated five or*

six times that Mme. Bertrand was a whore and he added: "I have made a will: in it I have left Antommarchi twenty francs to buy himself a length of rope with which to hang himself!"[597]

Though enraged at the Corsican doctor, Napoleon continued to permit Antommarchi to attend him out of necessity. For the Grand Marshal during this tirade, he merely stood there speechless.

But even after the brutal words towards his wife by the Emperor, Bertrand was still emotional over the sight of the dying and deteriorating man who had once ruled over much of Europe. On a number of occasions, the Grand Marshal asked Napoleon if he could now serve as his personal valet alongside Marchand, but the Emperor refused. As Bertrand watched Napoleon sleep one afternoon, the Grand Marshal had tears come to his eyes as he gazed upon the Emperor's face and discovered that he saw a *"profile more emaciated and altered than I had ever seen."*[598]

The agonizing suffering for the Emperor was not yet over. His inner battle for life would fiercely continue.

During the first week in April, Napoleon mustered enough strength to dictate a letter to Montholon that was to be sent to the Prince Regent in London. Napoleon was requesting that his body be placed in Paris, not London, where he feared it was to be sent. Little did he know that the British government had no plans whatsoever to allow his remains to ever enter into any European country.

*   *   *

As those first days of April slowly passed, the Emperor began to suffer from severe sweating throughout the night. His linens had to be changed three to seven times per night. Even the Emperor's handkerchief that he wore on his head had to be changed.[599]

Napoleon was exhausted in the morning. Marchand tried to cheer up Napoleon a little by explaining to him that they had seen a comet streak across the sky. But the valet's efforts were to no avail. Napoleon's response pained Marchand. *"Ah," he said to me, "my death shall be marked, as was Caesar's." Struck by the Emperor's words, I hastened to say that it did not threaten us with such a catastrophe! It was showing the course towards France: "Ah, my son! I no longer have any hope of seeing Paris again." Those words were said with so much conviction that they hurt me."*[600] St. Denis described in his memoirs how a great storm formed over the island just days after the comet was seen. The servant explained that during the storm *"it seemed as though heaven and earth wished to mark the end of a great life by something extraordinary."*[601]

Dr. Arnott visited Napoleon a few days later to check on his condition. Arnott reiterated his diagnosis as an ulceration of the stomach and prescribed certain pills to alleviate the pain, but the Emperor waved off the medicine and *"remained as defiant to medicine from him as he had been with Dr. Antommarchi."*[602]

Dr. Arnott did inform the Emperor that the new Longwood house was completed and that the larger rooms would be better for his health. Napoleon would not hear of it. *"Doctor,"* replied the Emperor, *"it is too late; I informed your governor when he submitted the plans for the house to me, that it would take five years to build, and by then I would need a grave; you can see they are offering me the keys, and I am finished!"*[603]

The fits of vomiting and perspiration never relented for the Emperor. Antommarchi recorded on April 5, that the Emperor passed *"a night of extreme agitation."*

> *He had four successive vomitings, and the fever continued to rage with violence until two in the morning, when it began to abate. He was considerably weakened by abundant clammy perspirations about the head, the back, and the breast. The tension of and pain in the abdomen, and the general sensation of uneasiness and anxiety, had not ceased for a single minute. Napoleon was quite overpowered by his sufferings, and exclaimed several times – "Ah! since I was to lose my life in this deplorable manner, why did the cannon-balls spare it?"*[604]

Bedridden for weeks, Napoleon had not shaved in twenty days and his beard became quite cumbersome for him. The Emperor usually shaved himself but was now so weakened; it was impossible for him to do so. Napoleon finally permitted a member of his suite to shave his face clean. Everyone thought this might help in making him feel a little better. But the vomiting and defecations in his bed continued. St. Denis found the Emperor so ill and heavy in weight that he had to lift Napoleon up from the bed while Marchand removed the sheet on which the Emperor had just moved his bowels. Because the Emperor's body had become so large, St. Denis had to squeeze Napoleon tight to get enough leverage to pick him up. This would cause the Emperor pain, to which Napoleon would yell, "*Ah! rascal, you are hurting me!*"[605]

Dr. Arnott came on April 14th to examine Napoleon again. The Emperor never let pass an opportunity to jest with the Englishman even in his sickened condition. Napoleon took the opportunity to poke fun at Dr. Arnott's Protestant religion. "*Tomorrow is Palm Sunday, the Sunday before Easter,*" Napoleon said to the doctor. "*But, of course, you are a heretic and will go to hell.*" Everyone laughed. "*Oh! Very well, Dr. Arnott, there are good people of every kind of religion.*"[606]

As the examination continued in a more serious tone, the doctor observed that Napoleon had a twitching of his lips. The doctor inquired with the Grand Marshal if this was a typical characteristic of the Emperor's, to which Bertrand responded that it was not. Being that this was something new, it greatly concerned Dr. Arnott. He advised that Napoleon take more nourishment.[607]

The Emperor did try to take some small amounts of food, either a spoonful of jelly or soup or even a biscuit. He drank small amounts of tea or little sips of wine. Napoleon even took to his armchair instead of his bed during moments when he felt better. But these intervals of energy and gaiety did not last long and the pain in his stomach quickly cast him back into periods of melancholy and vomiting.

Antommarchi continued to prescribe the daily enemas for the Emperor as well as some pills. This constant regiment seemed to only weaken Napoleon even more, putting his body through constant work that culminated in more vomiting.

> *The Emperor got up at one P.M. and was supported to his arm-chair; but in a half an hour afterwards he experienced an icy coldness in the lower extremities, and was obliged to get into bed again. At two, enema. The patient was very*

> *much agitated the remainder of the day, and the short intervals of light sleep which he had were interrupted by a sensation of suffocation. Nausea, followed by abundant vomiting of glairous matters. Sleep, during which his whole frame was convulsed – kind of continual mastication.*[608]

Though weakening, Napoleon continued to battle for life.

* * *

It was during this second week in April when the Emperor took to the serious matter of finalizing his Last Will and Testament while his mind was still sharp. He shut himself up for a number of hours with Montholon who was vested with the charge of recording down the Emperor's final wishes. The document achieved a variety of the Emperor's goals besides merely dividing up his monetary possessions.

First, and foremost, Napoleon laid the blame for his death squarely at the feet of the British government and Governor Lowe. *"I die prematurely, assassinated by the English oligarchy and its deputy: the English nation will not be slow in avenging me."*[609] He also used his Will to lay blame to those who, in his belief, betrayed France during his reign. The Emperor even left money to the man who attempted to assassinate the Duke of Wellington, Napoleon's nemesis at the Battle of Waterloo.[610] Napoleon went on to thank his mother and family and left instructions for his son to never take arms against France.

> *My son should not think of avenging my death; he should profit by it. Let the remembrance of what I have done never leave his mind; let him always be, like me, every inch a Frenchman...He should propagate, in all those countries now uncivilized and barbarous, the benefits of Christianity and civilization. Such should be the aim of all my son's thoughts; such is the cause for which I die a*

martyr to the hatred of the oligarchs, of which I am the object.[611]

Napoleon even left instructions for his two illegitimate sons that he had bidden farewell to back in France at Malmaison. *"I should not be displeased that the little Leo should enter the magistracy, if such should be his taste. I should wish Alexander Waleska to be drawn into the service of France, into the army."*[612]

To the people of France, Napoleon declared that he had *"saved the revolution which was about to perish; I raised it from its ruins, and showed it to the world beaming with glory...I was their true representative. My dictatorship was indispensable; and the proof of this is, that they always offered me more power than I desired."*[613] His final instruction, and the most important to him, was to be buried amongst his people in the French capital of Paris. If this was not to be permitted and if the body was to remain on St. Helena for eternity, then he wanted to be buried *"under the shade of the willows where I have rested at times."*[614] These words were crushing to Marchand who wrote, *"these words, spoken with so much calm and resignation, implied the possibility of abandonment on this accursed rock, which wrenched the soul."*[615]

This completion of his Will caused Napoleon to remain melancholy and depressed. On April 18, he asked Montholon to send for Abbe Vignali with the specific instructions that no one was allowed to know he was meeting with the priest. Montholon recorded that they met privately for over an hour with Montholon believing that Napoleon was making his final confession.[616]

The following day, Dr. Arnott came to the Emperor to attend to him. After the examination and the usual questions back and forth between the doctor and the Emperor, Napoleon explained his grievances against the British government and the Governor in a respectable manner to the doctor. He wanted Dr. Arnott to know who was to blame for the Emperor's premature death.

I had come to seek the hospitality of the British people; I asked for a generous protection, and, to the subversion of every right held sacred upon the earth, chains were the reply I received. I should have experienced a different reception from Alexander [of Russia]; the Emperor Francis would have treated me with more respect and kindness; and even the King of Prussia would have been more generous. It was reserved for England to deceive and excite the Sovereigns of Europe, and give to the world the unheard-of spectacle of four great powers cruelly leagued together against one man. Your Ministers have chosen this horrible rock, upon which the lives of Europeans are exhausted in less than three years, in order to end my existence...And how have I been treated since my arrival here? There is no species of indignity or insult that has not been eagerly heaped upon me. The simplest family communications, which have never been interdicted to any one, have been refused to me. No news, no papers from Europe, have been allowed to reach me; my wife and son no longer existed for me; I have been kept six years in the tortures of close confinement. The most uninhabitable spot on this inhospitable island, that where the murderous effects of a tropical climate are most severely felt, has been assigned to me for a residence; and I, who used to ride on horseback all over Europe, have been obliged to shut myself up within four walls, in an unwholesome atmosphere. I have been destroyed piece-meal...Hudson has been the executioner of the high deeds and exploits of your Ministers.[617]

Napoleon weakened again throughout the night and summoned for Abbe Vignali again. He asked the priest if he had ever officiated a Mass where the body of the deceased lies in state, a *chambre-ardente*. When Abbe Vignali answered that he had, Napoleon requested that he officiate over his. Dr. Antommarchi was in the room during his exchange between Napoleon and his priest and was amazed at both the detail of his request, but also at the emotion that crossed his features.

> *His face was animated and convulsive, and I was following with uneasiness the contraction of his features... "I believe in God, and am of the religion of my father...I was born a Catholic, and will fulfill the duties prescribed by the Catholic religion, and receive the assistance it administers."*[618]

The Emperor then gave specific instructions to Abbe Vignali on how his ceremony was to be conducted.

> *You will say mass every day in the chapel, and will expose the holy sacraments during forty hours. After my death, you will place your alter at my head in the room in which I shall lie in state; you will continue to say mass, and perform all the customary ceremonies, and will not cease to do so until I am under ground.*[619]

Napoleon then discussed various religions with Antommarchi for a little while, concluding with the statement *"for, after all, if men had no religion, they would murder each other for the best pear or the finest girl."*[620]

*   *   *

The last few days of April 1821 found Napoleon drifting between bouts of severe sickness and moments of jovial conversation. The attacks of illness were met with vomiting and painful bowel movements both consisting of black bile and tar-like substances. This left him in a state of powerlessness with him lying in bed or exhausted in his armchair.

The days of conversation found him either dictating his final thoughts to his Generals or in enjoyable banter with Dr. Arnott. The Emperor came to enjoy his talks with Arnott in a similar way that he had with Dr. O'Meara. Again, Napoleon turned his questions to how many times Englishmen get drunk and what kind of alcohol they preferred. With good humor, Arnott answered all of his questions on the subject.

Napoleon then turned his questions to that of medicine and anatomy desiring to know everything he could from the doctor's expertise. He asked the doctor how food was digested and reached the bowls and how urine left the stomach. Napoleon turned his questioning to that concerning reproductive organs. He wanted to know how fluid would be blocked from leaving the body. Dr. Arnott answered his question and explained that tubes connected the organs allowing it to pass.

> *"So that if the first two tubes and the last two were tied up, one could no longer pass either water or sperm?" "Quite so. The same thing arises in the female ovary. If the tubes leading to it are tied up, women are no longer able to conceive. This is, in fact, done, so as to prevent a woman from having children..."*
>
> *"My father had a tumor of the pylorus. Can it be cured after it has formed?"*
>
> *"No. It cannot be cured even if it is formed in the breast."*[621]

Even as he lay dying, between fits of vomiting and pain, Napoleon still desired to learn. Partially it was done to diagnose his own illness, but also simply to learn from someone who knew. No matter who was around the Emperor, if someone had information and knowledge that he did not, Napoleon would question them to learn all he could. When Napoleon again asked Dr. Arnott what he believed ailed him, the doctor replied the stomach.

April 26, brought back the vomiting with a vengeance. Bertrand recorded that *"the vomiting recommenced, and up until half-past two the Emperor again vomited four or five times, bringing up phlegm and mucus tinted with red by the wine."*[622]

Grand Marshal Bertrand was in an extremely difficult situation; while he was entirely devoted to the Emperor without question, he had to listen to Napoleon belittle and degrade his wife for refusing to become Napoleon's mistress. The Emperor took no reservation from continuously reminding Bertrand of this. The Grand Marshal recorded these incidences in his memoirs. All Bertrand desired was for Napoleon to see his wife and accept her devotion and honor, but the Emperor repeatedly refused, telling the Grand Marshal "*I resented her refusal to become my mistress, and also I wanted to teach her a lesson.*"[623] When Bertrand begged again, the Emperor responded, "*this is not the moment.*"[624]

Even when faced with these harsh words, Grand Marshal Bertrand remained devoted, even blaming himself. Writing in third person in his memoirs, Bertrand recorded, "*Possibly the Grand Marechal has forfeited some of the Emperor's confidence and affection: but he nonetheless has certain claims on him. Bertrand has a reserved nature which has become greatly accentuated through his natural seriousness of mind.*"[625]

The Grand Marshal also witnessed the mind of Napoleon beginning to fade. The Emperor became confused at times or his memory would fail him in conversation. Bertrand recorded in his memoirs that on April 29, Napoleon called servant, Pierron, to ask him about his trip to Jamestown. Pierron gave the Emperor one of the oranges he purchased, and Napoleon sucked the juices for a moment, but quickly found that it irritated his stomach. Napoleon then posed a series of questions to the servant about a recent ship that had anchored in the harbor to resupply the island.

"*Did this boat bring any limes?*"

"*No.*"

"*Any almonds?*"

"*No.*"

"*Pomegranates?*"

"*No.*"

"*Grapes?*"

"*No.*"

"Wine?"

"No, at least not in bottles, but in casks."

"It brought nothing then?"

"It brought cattle."

"How many oxen?"

"Forty."

"How many sheep?"

"Two hundred."

"How many goats?"

"None."

"How many chickens?"

"None."

"On the whole, one could say that it brought nothing. Did it bring any walnuts?

"No..."

"Did it bring any limes, pomegranates, almonds?"[626]

Napoleon repeated these questions to Pierron three times and made him go over the same things, "*like a man who had completely lost his memory.*"[627]

Everyone around the Emperor could see the changes in him. Bertrand realized "*the Emperor could only be recognized by the multitude of incessant questions which he asked. Dr. Arnott noticed the change in his voice and the fact that he repeated questions to which*

Purification Through Suffering

the doctor had already replied. He had never before noticed this lack of memory."[628]

At first, it had been Napoleon's body that was beginning to deteriorate and shut down; now it was his mind.

It was decided that the Emperor's camp bed would be moved from his bedroom to the drawing room for better ventilation. This is where he would remain until his death. When the servants were preparing to carry Napoleon into the drawing room he stopped them saying, "*No...you may do that when I am dead; for the present it will be sufficient that you support me.*"[629]

Bertrand and Montholon would come to the drawing room for further dictations but found the Emperor's memory fading at such a rapid pace that further dictations would not happen. The mind that had strategically planned numerous battles, dictated volumes of governmental legislation, was now laboring to remember the simplest of things. Such a drastic change in the Emperor led many of his trusted men to leave the room in tears over the sight he had become. Bertrand took it especially hard.

> *In the morning the Emperor had asked at least twenty times whether he might be able to have some coffee. But every time the answer had been: "No, Sire." "Won't the doctors allow me just a spoonful?" "No, Sire. Not at present. Your stomach is over-irritated, and it might cause you to be sick a little sooner." He had been sick perhaps eight or nine times in the course of the day. What thoughts spring to mind at the sight of so great a change! Tears came to my eyes, as I looked at this man, formerly so terrifying, who had commanded so proudly and in a manner so absolute, now reduced to begging for a spoonful of coffee, asking permission, obedient as a child, asking permission again and again without obtaining it. Repeatedly asking permission, and always unsuccessful, yet without any signs of bad temper. At other periods of his illness he had sent his doctors to the devil and had done as he pleased. But*

> at present he was as docile as a child. That was what the Great Napoleon had become, a humble and an unhappy man.[630]

The emotional torment that plagued Napoleon's mind as the illness ravaged his body during the last few days of his life was unimaginable. At the end of April, Montholon was awoken at four A.M. by the Emperor who told him he had dreamt of Josephine.

> *I have just seen my good Josephine, but she would not embrace me; she disappeared at the moment when I was about to take her in my arms. She was seated there; it seemed to me that I had seen her yesterday evening: she is not changed; still the same-full of devotion to me. She told me that we were about to see each other again, never more to part; she assured me that – did you see her?"* I took great care not to say anything which might increase the feverish excitement, too plainly evident to me. I gave him his potion and changed his linen, and he fell asleep; but on awaking, he again spoke to me of the Empress Josephine, and I should only have uselessly irritated him, by telling him that it was only a dream.[631]

It was as if Josephine, visiting from beyond the grave, was there on St. Helena to call her Napoleon home.

*   *   *

It was now May 1, 1821, and the Emperor was clinging to life. His mind contemplated thoughts on instructions he believed still needed to be given. To Antommarchi, Napoleon instructed him that upon his death, the doctor was to conduct an autopsy and *"to make careful examination of the stomach, in order to save his son from a disease that had led his own father and himself into the grave."*[632] He made Antommarchi promise that no English doctor be permitted to touch his body. If Governor Lowe required it, then

Purification Through Suffering

the Emperor wanted Dr. Arnott present at the autopsy. Napoleon also instructed Antommarchi to remove his heart and "*place it in spirits of wine, and carry it to Parma to my dear Maria Louisa. You will tell her that I tenderly loved her – that I never ceased to love her.*"[633]

After the doctor left the room, Grand Marshal Bertrand remained with Marchand and the Emperor "*whose eyes remained closed.*"

> *On opening them he spotted Count Bertrand, and spoke a few words to him, among them: "...You are sad, Bertrand, what's the matter?" The grand marshal replied with one of those looks that revealed how much his heart was moved and saddened. I retired, so as to not disturb him in what he had to say to the Emperor, who at the time was asking him for news of the countess. That lady had remained without seeing His Majesty until then: she had talked to me about it, and I therefore knew how distressed she was. The grand marshal suffered greatly himself; he no doubt talked to the Emperor about it, as when he came out, he told me with a cry of satisfaction the Emperor had told him to bring his wife and children.*[634]

May 3 had come and the Emperor could speak only with extreme difficulty. When he did speak, in was in short statements that exhausted him. All the members of the Emperor's suite could do was watch his facial expressions and try to make out his words.

The valets and servants found that Napoleon stared at the painting of his son for hours at a time as tears streamed from his eyes. Some in the room felt that the portrait depressed the Emperor and made his condition worse, so they had it removed from the room. St. Denis wrote that Napoleon looked around the room, searching for it for quite a while. Unable to locate it, the valet sadly described how the Emperor looked devastatingly at those around him as if to say, "*Where is my son? What have you done with my son?*"[635]

Bertrand wrote how that evening found the Emperor suffering more from hiccups and difficulty urinating.

> *Between six o'clock in the evening and eleven o'clock, the Emperor was at times fairly quiet and could breathe easily, while at other times he had hiccups, sighed heavily, and had the eyes of a dying man. He could barely articulate his words, saying nevertheless, "Let me piss." Between half-past six and seven o'clock when the Grand Marechal went to remove his little piece of china, the Emperor said: "Leave it there, my friend."*[636]

Napoleon had been afflicted with a great difficulty in urination for most of his adult life. Bertrand recalled the Emperor on numerous occasions trying in vain to urinate when they were back in France. Napoleon would "*lean his forehead against a tree or wall, and standing there would wait patiently.*"[637] Even on his deathbed, he struggled merely to empty his bladder.

On May 4, as the minutes ticked by, all present knew the end had come. Antommarchi wrote of the painful moments when the Emperor's devoted followers came to pay their final respects and say their *Adieus*.

> *His end was now approaching; we were going to lose him, and every body redoubled his zeal and attention, anxious to give him a last mark of devotedness. His officers, Marchand, Saint-Denis, and myself, had exclusively taken upon ourselves the duty of sitting up at night; but Napoleon could not bear the light, and we were obliged to lift him up, and to administer all the cares his state required, in the midst of a profound obscurity. Anxiety had added to our fatigue: the Grand Marshal was exhausted; General Montholon was equally so, - and I was not much better.*[638]

Napoleon began to have violent hiccups that refused to cease. Montholon had left him the night before sleeping peacefully, "but I had scarcely had time to throw myself on my bed, when some one came in haste to fetch me; the rattling in the throat – the forerunner of death – was beginning!"[639] Abbe Vignali was sent for and Last Rites were given to Napoleon. "An hour afterwards, the chapel was prepared, and the almoner had commenced the forty hours of prayer."[640]

Madame Bertrand came and remained at the Emperor's bedside sobbing. Now that the end was imminent, she sent for her children to come and say goodbye to their beloved Emperor and friend. Antommarchi captured the painful scene in his memoirs.

No words can express the emotion of these poor children on witnessing this spectacle of death. They had not seen Napoleon for about fifty days, and their eyes full of tears sought, with terror, upon his face, now pale and disfigured, the expression of greatness and goodness which they were accustomed to find in it. As if by common accord, they rushed towards the bed, seized the hands of the Emperor, kissed them, and sobbed aloud, covered them with tears. Young Napoleon Bertrand could no longer bear this heart-rending scene; overcome by his emotion, he fell back and fainted. We were obliged to tear these youthful mourners in the midst of their grief from the Emperor's bedside, and to take them into the garden...the impression also produced upon us all, on witnessing the moving adieu of these children to their august protector, is beyond the power of words to express.[641]

For these children, this was as if their cherished grandfather was leaving them. The man who had loved them, played with them, and cared for them was dying before their eyes.

While sitting with the Emperor in his last moments, Napoleon's men heard him utter his last words: "*Who retreats at the head of the army?...King of Rome...Josephine.*"⁶⁴² His beloved Josephine was in his mind and his heart until the very last moments of his life.

For Montholon, this moment was the most painful he had ever felt.

> *From this moment, until half-past five in the evening, when he breathed his last, he remained motionless, lying on his back, with his right hand out of the bed, and his eyes fixed, seemingly absorbed in deep meditation, and without any appearance of suffering; his lips were slightly contracted, and his whole face expressed pleasant and gentle impressions. Whenever Antommarchi attempted to relieve me, in moistening his lips with the sponge, he repulsed him with his hand, and turned his eyes upon me. As the sun was setting, the Emperor quitted this earthly life, and I lost more than a father. I piously fulfilled the duty which his kindness confided to me – I closed his eyes!"*⁶⁴³

Napoleon Bonaparte was dead, with no family members at his side. His wife, his son, his mother, brothers, and sisters were all kept away from him by the European powers, due to politics and as punishment. The only ones to comfort him during these final moments were his beloved Generals and servants. With tears in his eyes and his hat in his hand, Grand Marshal Bertrand rendered his last service to his beloved Emperor Napoleon by stopping the hand of the clock at 5:50 P.M. on May 5, 1821.⁶⁴⁴

*You may make my body prisoner,
but my soul is free.*

Napoleon

Chapter 9

A Temporary Resting Place

Napoleon Bonaparte laid on his camp-bed, lifeless and still. The body of the Emperor was surrounded by his entourage, which had shared his exile those past six years. Abbe Vignali remained with the body overnight in constant prayer.

Word was sent to the Governor that the Emperor had died. In the letter written and signed by General Montholon as dictated to him by Napoleon during his last days, the brief letter concluded with the statement, "*Please let me know what arrangements have been dictated by your government for the return of his body to Europe, as well as that of the people in his retinue.*"[645] Governor responded in writing, "*he had been ordered not to allow the mortal remains of General Bonaparte to leave the island, but that he did not care where they were placed. That choice was in our hands.*"[646] The Emperor's suite chose the Valley of Willows on the island. Napoleon had enjoyed this spot while alive.

Governor Lowe and the British government were just as afraid of Napoleon's dead body as they were of the living Emperor. To bring his remains back to France with almost certain fanfare would cause resurgence in French Nationalism among the Bonapartists that the newly restored Bourbons would not tolerate. Nor would the British government want this type of celebration. A rise amongst the supporters of Napoleon could lead to a civil war in France; neither England nor the Bourbon King in France wanted to take the chance.

Governor Lowe wanted to view the body himself so that he could verify to his government that the Emperor was truly dead. The following morning, May 6, the Governor, his staff and French Commissioner Montchenu entered Longwood to view the body. Montholon wrote that "*Lowe bowed respectfully when I showed him the inanimate corpse of the Emperor, and his example was followed by all the persons of his suite. They all defiled before the bed with religious silence and respect.*"[647] Governor Lowe requested that Dr. Arnott guard the body and be present during the autopsy.[648]

Later that same day, Dr. Antommarchi used plaster to make a mold, or 'death mask,' of the Emperor's face. Roughly twenty hours after the Emperor's death, Antommarchi began the autopsy. Present during this procedure were Generals Bertrand and Montholon, Marchand, some British staff officers including Sir Thomas Reade, Doctors Shortt, Arnott, and few other medical men that Antommarchi had requested be present.[649] Governor Lowe feared Napoleon's escape when he was alive, Lowe now feared his dead body would prove that the Emperor's exile caused his death. The Governor wanted to ensure that the cause of death was not reported as being due to the island of St. Helena.

During the late morning of May 6, the autopsy commenced. The autopsy was very thorough and revealed a number of interesting details surrounding the Emperor's condition that led to his death. The man who measured 5'2" at death had a liver that was "*affected by chronic hepatitis.*"[650] The stomach had a slight obstruction and a perforation that caused much of the Emperor's pain. A closer examination of the mucus substance in the stomach revealed a cancerous ulcer on the inner part of the stomach.[651] The bladder was found to be small in size, thus leading to the Emperor's difficulty in urination.

Dr. Antommarchi was desirous of examining Napoleon's brain. "*The state of that organ in such a man as the Emperor, was an object of the highest interest; but my proceedings were unfeelingly arrested, and I was obliged to yield.*"[652] None of the Frenchman were going to allow this doctor to cut open the brain of their beloved Emperor just because the doctor was 'curious.'

Antommarchi later sent a copy of his autopsy findings to Governor Lowe, who in turn, did not agree with their findings and sent his own autopsy report back to Antommarchi that had been completed by the British doctors who observed Antommarchi's procedure on Napoleon's body. This infuriated the Corsican doctor who had spent the last countless months attending to the dying Emperor.

> *These gentlemen had, as I have already mentioned, been present at the autopsy, ex officio, but they had not taken any active part in the operation. It had, however, suddenly occurred to them that it was their duty to frame the report of it: they had consequently written that report, and*

> *now brought it to me for my signature, which I refused to give. What had I to do with English and English reports? I was Napoleon's physician; I had performed the operation of the autopsy, and it was for me to state this fact, and the circumstances attending it. I could neither disguise any thing, nor listen to any suggestions; I offered a copy of my own report, but it did not answer the desired purpose, and was therefore rejected.*[653]

Once again, Governor Lowe was concerned about his reputation and that of his government when it came to the death of Napoleon. They had to ensure that his death did not appear in a way caused by their detention of him on St. Helena or due to any lack of appropriate care during his time in exile. The battle over this issue would extend far beyond the shores of St. Helena and the year 1821.

At the conclusion of the autopsy, the Emperor's head was shaved so that the hair could be given to the members of his suite as remembrances. Napoleon also instructed that a bracelet of his hair be made for his wife, Empress Marie Louise. The body was then washed and clothed in "*the uniform of the Chasseurs de la Guarde with his boots, spurs, orders, medals, decorations, and his hat. The body was laid on the cloak that he had worn at Marengo, and which had been spread over the camp bed on which he died.*"[654] The Emperor was not buried with his own sword. Out of fear that Governor Lowe may confiscate it, Napoleon's sword was replaced with Bertrand's instead.[655]

During the afternoon on May 6, Napoleon's body lay in state for the public to pay their respects. "*The bed was surrounded by candelabra and torches, with a chandelier in the middle. The Grand Marechal stood at the head of the bed, General de Montholon at the foot, with Marchand behind him. Also at the head of the bed were Mme. Bertrand and her children, and behind her Monseigneur the Abbe Vignali knelt before the alter.*"[656]

Not only did the public on St. Helena pass through, but so did most of the British soldiers from the 66th Regiment. One of the officers brought his young son with him and stopped before the body of the Emperor and said, "*Take a good look at Napoleon, he is the greatest man in the world.*"[657] Some of the British officers "*en-*

treated to be allowed the honour of pressing with their lips a corner of the cloak of Marengo, with which we had covered the Emperor's feet."[658] Most were grief-stricken at the sight of the fallen Emperor; for many, this was their first actual time seeing him. Others passed through to witness the sad reality that Napoleon was gone.

That evening, the official word of the Emperor's death written by Governor Lowe was given to Captain Crokatt, the duty officer at Longwood. The Captain boarded the British vessel, *Acheron*, to deliver the news of his death and the minutes of his autopsy to England.[659]

Antommarchi followed the Emperor's instructions and preserved the stomach in one container and his heart in another. In completing Napoleon's instructions, the doctor was going to take them to Europe to personally deliver his heart to Empress Marie Louise. Governor Lowe declared that his instructions were not to allow anything to be removed and that all must be placed in Napoleon's coffin. There was no negotiation on this topic.[660]

However, Governor Lowe was not finished yet with his declarations concerning his prisoner. "*I assume that you will not wish to place an inscription upon the tombstone, because it would be necessary to use titles and that I cannot allow,*" the Governor told the Grand Marshal. "*No, we only want to put, Napoleon, born in ___ died in ___*" "*I cannot allow you to put Napoleon alone. You must put Napoleon Bonaparte.*"[661] Since the two sides were unable to compromise on the name to be placed on the tombstone, the slab that was to cover the tomb remained blank without any inscription.

The grave of the French Emperor Napoleon Bonaparte would be unmarked.

The time had come to place the Emperor in his coffin. Marchand provided a detailed description.

> *The Emperor, placed in a tin casket lined with white quilted satin, could not have his hat on his head for lack of space. The head had to rest on a pillow of the same material, and the hat was placed on his legs. Various coins bearing the Emperor's effigy and a few pieces of silver...were added. The same man who had soldered the vases carefully soldered this first casket. It was placed*

> *inside another mahogany casket, which in turn was placed inside a third leaden shell that was also soldered. Finally, it was set within a fourth mahogany casket, which was sealed with silver-headed iron screws. The casket was put back on the camp bed, covered with a purple, velvet pall on which we spread the Marengo cloak. Candles were kept lit on the alter near the casket, on which a crucifix was placed.*[662]

On May 9, the funeral procession of Napoleon Bonaparte began at Longwood and brought the Emperor's remains to the grave site near the willows he loved down in the valley. *"If the Emperor's most implacable enemies could have seen his funeral procession passing before the English soldiers sighs would have escaped from their breasts and tears would have moistened their eyelids,"* wrote St. Denis in his memoirs.[663] Some soldiers of the British 66th Regiment transported the body to the carriage, followed it to the gravesite, and again carried it to its final resting place.

When the Emperor's remains were lowered into the ground, the French suite found the moment almost impossible to bear. Marchand wrote *"this was the place where, even after his death, the Emperor's ashes were to remain captive. Our emotion was deep and intense...There the mortal remains of the Emperor were to lie, locked up for centuries."*[664]

But Bertrand thought differently: *"They say the body of the Emperor will not remain there for long."*[665]

Grand Marshal Bertrand was absolutely correct.

There is nothing like having friends in time of war, my dear Bertrand. One doesn't need many. Above all there must be friends. They take the place of so much more!

Napoleon

Chapter 10

Absolution And The Journey Home

Upon the burial of the Emperor, the French entourage packed up their belongings and boarded a ship to return to Europe without the remains of the man they had served with so much devotion for many years. Tears were shed as the island of St. Helena disappeared in the distance. They were all going home. Little did they know that some of them would return.

When they reached Europe, Montholon, Bertrand, and Marchand immediately set out to petition the various governments for the return of the Emperor's remains. They wrote formal requests to Lord Liverpool in London and the King of England himself. London's response stated that their government could only return the body to France if the French government requested it. The Bourbons refused to make the request.[666]

With their Emperor back on St. Helena, the members of Napoleon's suite settled back into their lives, but always dedicating themselves to his memory. Marchand settled in France and married. The valet sent letters and bracelets of the Emperor's hair to Empress Marie Louise and Napoleon's mother. *"This wish had been expressed to me by the Emperor. The most flattering letters were sent back to me, bearing witness to the feelings that dictated them and honoring the hearts that wrote them."*[667] Marchand's entire adult life was dedicated to Emperor Napoleon and his memory.

General Montholon returned to France as well. Late in 1840, Montholon joined the failed coup of Louis Napoleon against the Bourbons and was briefly imprisoned. Once Louis Napoleon succeeded in gaining power, Montholon served in the government of the newly crowned, Napoleon III, nephew to Napoleon I and son to Queen Hortense.

General Gourgaud went to London after leaving St. Helena and wrote letters to the various heads of state throughout Europe pleading for the Emperor's return to the continent. When British authors wrote works attacking Napoleon, Gourgaud was rapid in his response to counter and defend his Emperor. He later served in the French Legislative Assembly.

Las Cases had spent time in Brussels when he was not permitted to return to France. Upon Napoleon's death, he returned to France and published his memoirs. In 1822, young Las Cases, now an adult, found Hudson Lowe walking down a street in London and assaulted him for the former Governor's treatment of Napoleon and Las Cases.[668]

Grand Marshal Bertrand returned to France and also continued to dedicate his life to the memory of his Emperor. For Bertrand, his service to Napoleon never ended. In the 1830s, Bertrand also served in the French Government.

Dr. Barry O'Meara returned to England after being removed from St. Helena and continued his attacks in writing against the treatment of Napoleon by Governor Sir Hudson Lowe. O'Meara published both his memoirs and a book containing the clandestine letters he successfully smuggled off of St. Helena while attending the Emperor. O'Meara was useful to Napoleon in getting his message back to Europe of his suffering and humiliating regulations at the hands of the British government and their governor. Ironically, the publishing of these also proved Governor Lowe correct in his suspicions of Dr. O'Meara and his attachment to Napoleon. Once Lowe was back in London, O'Meara continued to lambaste the former Governor for his treatment of the Emperor while in exile on St. Helena.

Dr. Antommarchi returned to Europe for a few years, still practicing in the medical profession. By 1834, Antommarchi had set out for the United States and spent some time in New Orleans where he donated a bronze copy of Napoleon's death mask to the city. The remainder of his life was spent in Mexico and eventually Cuba where he died.

For Governor Lowe, his return to England was without fanfare. He did the job that was requested of him with many in London believing his obsession with following every detail of his instructions on St. Helena and his paranoia over Napoleon's possible escape did more harm to his reputation than good. He served in some other minor military capacities, but never really received the recognition for his service on St. Helena that he desired and expected. Hudson Lowe died in poverty in 1844 in London.

The Balcombes returned to England for a brief time before Mr. Balcombe was reassigned to a position in Australia. The voyage to the island was taxing to the family with Jane dying before they reached the continent. Betsy, who had become a very beautiful woman since her early days on St. Helena, married Edward Abell in 1822 in London. The marriage provided Betsy with a beloved daughter. But her husband turned out to be a pathetic excuse for a husband and deserted Betsy and her young daughter, leaving them in virtual poverty. Betsy taught music lessons to help support her daughter. Because Betsy provided so much joy to Napoleon in exile and their playful antics provided incredible stories throughout Europe, she drew the attention of Napoleon's family. The Emperor's older brother, Joseph Bonaparte, visited Betsy in London to talk with her about her time on St. Helena with Napoleon. Joseph was deeply touched by how Betsy kept the depressed man happy on St. Helena and he was moved by the descriptions she gave him about his younger brother's time in exile. Years later, Emperor Napoleon III, also thankful for Betsy's time with his uncle on St. Helena, rewarded her for her dedication by giving her hundreds of acres of land in Algeria. Betsy later wrote her memoirs about Napoleon, which also helped in supporting her and her daughter. Betsy Balcombe Abell died in London in 1871 at 69 years of age in poverty, comforted by her only daughter.

* * *

Napoleon Bonaparte's devoted officers and servants had one more duty to perform for their Emperor: bringing him home.

The restoration of the Bourbon family to the throne in France did not settle the unrest in the nation following Napoleon's abdication in 1815. Another revolution broke out in the French nation in 1830. The Bourbon King, Charles X, was replaced by his cousin, Louis-Philippe, the Duke of Orleans. But the unrest did not cease, and the Bonapartists sought to influence the newly formed government. Louis-Philippe wisely realized that the memory of Napoleon was something that he needed to embrace to secure his own throne. In 1840, in order to secure public opinion, the new King Louis Philippe I, sent "*his son, the Prince de Joinville, to Saint Helena to retrieve the Emperor's ashes and bring them back triumphantly across the seas*" to Paris.[669]

The King called upon Napoleon's trusted men to accompany his son and bring Napoleon's remains home. Joining Prince de Joinville on the voyage back to St. Helena were Grand Marshal Bertrand, General Gourgaud, Louis Marchand, St. Denis, Pierron, Noverraz, Archambault, Bertrand's son Arthur, who had been born on the island, and Las Cases' son, Emmanuel, who had spent so many hours with the Emperor recording his dictations. It had been 19 years since the Emperor had been buried on St. Helena.

Once they had reached the island of St. Helena, the Frenchmen returned to the Emperor's gravesite and readied themselves to view the man they were forced to leave behind those many years before. Upon bringing the large casket to the surface, it was decided that the coffins should be opened. As the casket was opened and the satin covering was pulled back, the Emperor's men were astonished at what they saw. Expecting to view the skeletal remains of Napoleon, "*they were confronted with the Emperor himself, virtually unchanged – looking as though asleep. Those who had experienced his exile had aged with the intervening years. He was as he had been when laid away in 1821.*"[670] Napoleon's men were completely overcome with emotion and were unable to hold back their tears. For them, the sight of this man instantly brought them back to the very day they placed him in that coffin. However, now, they were older men, and Napoleon looked as if he was trapped in time at age 51. Fearing that the air would cause the body to rapidly decompose, Gourgaud ordered the coffins to be sealed again for eternity in preparation for the voyage back to Paris.

France prepared for the return of their Emperor. The National Residence of the Invalids, better known as Les Invalides, had been a hospital and residence for wounded soldiers. It was now being converted to house the remains of Napoleon Bonaparte.

News of Napoleon's return put the city of Paris into vibrant celebration. After leaving St. Helena in October 1840, the remains of the Emperor arrived in Paris two months later. On that cold day in the nation's capital when Napoleon Bonaparte was finally laid to rest, people from all over France lined the streets to get one last sight of the man who had brought the nation glory, riches, as well as war. Thousands gathered as the carriage bearing the Imperial remains was paraded down the crowded streets of Paris, under the Arc de Triomphe and down the Champs-Elysees towards his final resting place. The loud roar of cannon fire rang through the air as jubilant cries of 'Vive Napoleon' and 'Vive l'Empereur' rang throughout the city.

Assembled behind the horse-drawn carriage that carried the draped coffin were numerous soldiers, who had served in the Emperor's Imperial Guard. All showed the effects of time, but none were more proud than they to see their Emperor Napoleon returning home. They had been waiting for this day for over twenty-five years since he was exiled to St. Helena in 1815. Leading the procession of the Imperial Guard was none other than the Grand Marshal of the Palace, Henri Bertrand. Cradled in Bertrand's arms was the Emperor's sword. Four years later in 1844, the coffin of Grand Marshal Bertrand would be laid to rest within a few yards of the Emperor he had faithfully served for so many years.

The procession entered the front of Les Invalides and made its way to its center underneath the great dome. It was here that Emperor Napoleon Bonaparte was finally laid to rest in the fashion he would have wanted; a parade, cannon fire, his soldiers, thousands of his countrymen crying out his name, and being placed at the very spot he so desperately willed; along the banks of the Seine River, in Paris, amongst Napoleon's beloved citizens of France.

But even as the Emperor was being laid to rest, there was still one thing missing from Napoleon's final wishes that would make this event complete, and it would not be done until 1940. Actually, it was one person who was missing: Napoleon's son, the King of Rome.

Practically treated like a prisoner himself since his father's exile in 1815, the King of Rome (Napoleon II) was deserted by his mother and left under the care of his grandfather, the Emperor Francis of Austria. Emperor Francis ordered the young Napoleon II's name to be changed to Franz, Duke of Reichstadt, and he was taught German instead of his native French. Throughout his childhood, a number of Frenchmen made attempts to capture the boy with the goal of returning the young heir to his rightful throne in Paris. With Napoleon II exhibiting traits of his father's abilities and personality, the young man was limited on what military service he was allowed to engage in during his teenage years.

Napoleon II, the King of Rome died in 1832 at the age of 22 from tuberculosis. When Napoleon's remains were brought back to Paris in 1840, Austria refused to allow his son's body to be brought to France to be reunited with his father's. This would not happen until one hundred years later.

In 1940, France again had a new leader, who possessed both Austria and newly conquered France. As a gift to his new people, this leader ordered that the body of Napoleon II be removed from Austria and brought back to Paris as a gift to the nation to be buried next to his father.

The ruler of Austria and France in 1940 was one of the most ruthless and cruel figures this world has ever known. His name was none other than Adolf Hitler.

The restoration of Napoleon Bonaparte to his beloved land of France was now complete.

But in the end, no matter what rank or title one holds in life, and no matter how much power one has or the number of people one controls; when breath escapes the body for the last time, the individual is placed in the ground and covered like every other human. Death avoids no rank or title, nor does it avoid the rich and powerful. When death arrives and the body is laid to rest just like all of those who have gone before, there is one description left for that historical figure to be called: human.

Author's Note

The research that has gone into this book has been an ongoing labor of love for me over the past 25 years. My interest in this human side of Napoleon began when I was 14-years-old. I had borrowed a book in 1988 from the Penn Yan Public Library entitled, *The Murder of Napoleon*, by authors Ben Weider and David Hapgood. I was completely taken by the historical account of Napoleon's playful antics with the 14-year-old Betsy Balcombe. I was amazed at this side of the famous man and it led me to want to research more into this topic. I spent the next 25 years working on my research whenever I could. When most of my adolescent friends were playing video games, I was proudly working on what I enjoyed.

As a young teenager living before the advent of the internet, who was unable to read French and extremely limited on funds to buy antique books, I spent many days and hours during my high school and college years in the library at Hobart and William Smith Colleges in Geneva, New York. Their library possessed many of the primary sources that I desperately needed to complete my research. Whether it was after school or after my baseball practice, I would walk down to the archive in the library to continue where I had left off the day before. I am immensely grateful to the librarians from the colleges who helped me over the years.

In college and a few years after graduation, I worked part-time jobs to save up the money to buy the needed books on his exile; many were printed in 1821-1850. Each time I received the new text, I would sit down during any spare moment to take down my written notes. As my professional life took me to serving as a Legislative Assistant in the New York State Senate, I still used my lunch hours and late evenings to continue my goal of completing this work.

When my public high school teaching career began in 1998, I was still able to squeeze in time between creating lesson plans and correcting papers to further my pursuit. At the State University of New York at Oswego, I was able to complete my Master's thesis on this topic of Napoleon's human side and achieve my MA in History.

As I married my childhood friend and we began to raise two beautiful children together, I stayed up many late nights after all went to bed to finish my research, all handwritten and completed on numerous legal pads. My hope was to finish a full-length book on the human side to Napoleon Bonaparte, but I just did not know when I would find the time.

I owe a sincere thank you to Michael Chirco. It was this man who finally encouraged me to sit down and finish the book. Michael Chirco was my Superintendent at Marcus Whitman High School in Rushville, New York where I am presently a high school Social Studies teacher. He and I got to know each other more after I became President of the Teachers' Association. Though many of our conversations surrounded labor relations, we enjoyed numerous side discussions on history and literature. As a former English teacher, Mike was always interested in the latest historical theories and written works and I thoroughly enjoyed our conversations.

Before Mike retired, he told me once again to 'finish the book.' This time he offered to edit the book when it was completed. I could not turn him down and it served as the necessary push I needed. His editing, advice, and friendship I will always be thankful for. Without his encouragement, I would still be sitting by countless boxes of handwritten research with the continued 'hope' of completing it in the near future.

I also owe a great deal of gratitude to Dr. David King, retired History professor and Dean of Graduate Studies and Research from the State University of New York at Oswego. As my professor, thesis advisor, mentor, and friend, Dr. King taught me how to write an academic work that was both well documented for historical accuracy and interesting to the reader. I am extremely grateful for his additional advice on my approach to finishing this book.

J. David Markham, historian and President of the International Napoleonic Society, was incredibly helpful in providing me with advice and guidance as I navigated the final stages of the publishing process. It is truly an honor and privilege to have the foremost Napoleonic scholar writing the introduction to this book. I wish to thank him for everything he has done. I am proud to be a member of such a distinguished academic society.

This book would not be where it is today without the support and expertise of Bernadette Serton. Her enthusiasm for the topic, her belief in me, and her support all through this process was invaluable and instrumental in its publication. I value her assistance and especially her friendship.

I also would like to thank my brother, Peter Barden, for his help and encouragement over the years. His final editing and advice greatly served in putting the final touches on the work. His eyes and words also helped me in fine-tuning what I have wanted to put forth for so many years on Napoleon Bonaparte.

I owe an enormous amount of gratitude to my wife, Stacey, and our children Tommy and Corinne. They were all so supportive as I spent hundreds of hours late at night in my office pouring over countless pages of research and books filled with sticky notes. All three of them would make their way through the 'mess' to get a quick hug or ask a question and they were so careful as to not knock over the pages or kick out the power cord to the computer. The breaks I took to check my children's homework or to read them a book kept me grounded and reminded me that they are always my main focus in life. As I read, played with them and listened to their giggles, I could easily understand why Napoleon so enjoyed the playfulness and mirth of children.

My parents George and Rita were also very supportive of me over the years as I continued this path. They supported my quest and rarely complained about the amount of books I was amassing in my bedroom. Both of them encouraged me in all of my interests in school and sports but knew that I would always come back to the topic of Napoleon.

I especially want to thank my grandmother, Helen Lou Barden, who is an author in her own right. She wrote two family biographies in her lifetime, is an amazing artist, and raised a beautiful family. She always encouraged me to continue my research and writing and enjoyed reading all that I wrote. Though Alzheimer's disease has taken her memory and trapped a lifetime of history deep into her mind, her heart remains full of love and I will always be thankful for all she has taught me about history and writing.

As odd as this may seem, I also have to thank the 'Thomas Barden' of 1990, 1995, 1998, etc. As I began to go back through my research files that I have not looked at in years and had accumulated since I began this at age 14, I discovered that I had left myself various notes in case I ever decided to write a final book on the topic. One note said, "Use this quote before the chapter about his decline." Another note told me to listen to a particular song when I wrote the chapter about his death. Each note was exactly what I needed at the time I was writing in that particular moment. It literally was like a 'Back To The Future' moment where 'Thomas Barden' of the past was telling the present 'Thomas Barden' what to do. It made me laugh every time I found another note.

In researching and writing this book for over 25 years, I found that I could never have done it without the presence of music. The sounds of notes, the melodies and rhythms, and especially the lyrics have such a way of pulling emotion from a person that really open a pathway to deeper thought. There were 5 songs from two artists that I must have played over and over thousands of times that brought out these emotions in me and made me connect to what I was writing about and the emotions that Napoleon was experiencing throughout his ordeal in exile. Three songs were by Elton John called, *The King Must Die*, *Madman Across The Water*, and *Have Mercy On The Criminal*. The two other songs were by Peter Gabriel called, *Curtains* and *Across The River*. These songs and their words helped me in my creative thought and enabled me to try and put into words the emotions of a man who has been dead for over 190 years. The world would be lost without the presence of music.

After more than a quarter-century of work, I have put everything I have and know into this book in the hopes of bringing forth this human side of Napoleon Bonaparte as described by the people who were with him in exile on St. Helena. I have grown up from a teenager in 8th grade to a father of two children with the history of Napoleon Bonaparte by my side. My sincerest hope and wish is that my words will serve in adding to his history in a positive way.

Thomas Barden
Penn Yan, New York
August 2015

Index

A

Alexander I, Czar of Russia, 35, 49
Antommarchi, Francesco
  becomes Napoleon's doctor, 239
Archambault brothers, 54
Arnott, Dr.
  attends Napoleon, 271

B

Balcombe, Alexander, 73, 92
Balcombe, Betsy
  departure from St. Helena, 219
  describes Napoleon's habits, 88
  first meeting Napoleon, 75
  Napoleon's poor singing, 84
  seeing Napoleon as a playmate, 91
  seeing Napoleon deteriorate, 165, 205
Balcombe, Jane, 73
Balcombe, William, 73
Balcombe, William Jr., 73
Balmain, Count, 8, 162, 195, 200, 202, 215, 221, 225, 235, 243, 244
Bellerophon, HMS, 34, 36, 38, 39, 40, 41, 43, 44, 48, 52, 54, 55, 82, 192, 213
Bertrand, Countess
  despair over exile to St. Helena, 50
Bertrand, Grand Marshal Henri
  Napoleon's anger at Countess Bertrand, 272
  seeing Napoleon deteriorate, 283
Bonaparte, Joseph
  offers to disguise himself as Napoleon, 33
Buonavita, Father, 239
  leaves for Europe, 268

C

Castlereagh, Lord, 42
Chandelier (cook), 239
  leaves for Europe, 268
Cockburn, Admiral Sir George
  concern over Napoleon's escape from St. Helena, 80, 116
  observations on Napoleon, 58
  placed in charge of Napoleon, 55
Coursot (butler), 239

E

Elba, 17, 20, 26, 29, 52, 54, 157, 208, 218, 313

F

Fesch, Cardinal, 158, 233, 239
Forgiveness, 17
Fouche, Joseph, 25, 313
Franceschi, Cipriani, 54

death of, 218
Francis II, Emperor of Austria, 29, 33, 82, 277, 303

G

Gentilini, 54
  leaves for Europe, 268
Gourgaud, General Baron
  carries Napoleon's letter to Prince Regent, 37
  jealous of others, 83, 161, 198, 215
  leaves for Europe, 217

H

Hortense, daughter of Josephine, 7, 27, 28, 29, 30, 31, 35, 299, 313

J

Josephine, Empress of Napoleon I, 26
  divorce, 26

K

Keith, Lord, 43, 44, 45, 55
King of Rome, Napoleon II, 7, 9, 25, 29, 30, 33, 74, 85, 113, 140, 157, 186, 206, 228, 255, 288, 303

L

L'Epervier, 38
Las Cases, Emmanuel, Count de
  discussions with Maitland, 36
  encourages Napoleon to write memoirs, 51
  removal to Europe, 195
  smuggling letters to Europe, 190
  teaching Napoleon English, 59
Lepage (cook), 54
Liverpool, Lord, 42, 299
Longwood
  description, 71, 112
Louis XVIII, 25, 34
Lowe, Lt. General Sir Hudson
  arrives to St. Helena, 126
  meeting with Napoleon, 128, 174
  restrictions on Napoleon, 157

M

Madame Mere, Napoleon's mother, 7, 31, 186
Maitland, Captain Frederick
  discussions with Las Cases over Napoleon's surrender, 36
Malcolm, Admiral Sir Pulteney, 137
Marchand, Louis
  devotion to Napoleon, 53
  reading to Napoleon, 49
  witnesses playfulness of Napoleon and Betsy, 79
Marie-Louise, Second Empress to Napoleon, 7, 29, 74, 258, 259
Medusa, frigate, 33
Montchenu, Marquis de, 162, 166
Montholon, Countess
  leaves for Europe, 236

rumors of affair with
    Napoleon, 236
Montholon, General Charles
    Tristan
  fighting with Gourgaud,
    161, 215
  witnesses playfulness of
    Napoleon and Betsy, 79
Montholon, Tristan (son),
    178

N

Napoleon I, Emperor of
    France
  abdicates to son, 25
  admiring beautiful
    women, 41, 98, 173
  anger at being considered
    prisoner, 81, 162
  anger at Lowe, 127, 160,
    207, 237
  British citizens at
    Plymouth cheer for
    Napoleon, 40
  burial of, 294
  contemplations of
    surrender, 33
  death of, 288
  depression, 122, 131, 157,
    240
  difficulty sleeping, 120
  dining habits, 58
  friendly with British
    soldiers on Bellerophon,
    43
  illegitimate sons, 29
  lack of exercise, 59
  lack of exercise, 164, 186,
    195

  love of children, 80, 87, 89,
    167, 178, 186, 201, 213,
    244, 248, 255, 261
  love of Josephine, 100, 140,
    284
  meeting with Lowe, 128,
    174
  moves to Longwood, 105
  physical pain, 179, 204
  plans to settle in United
    States, 28, 32, 47
  protests exile to St. Helena,
    45, 48, 52
  sense of boredom, 140
  sense of humor, 84, 90, 95,
    137, 141, 203, 242
  surrenders to England, 38
  teasing Betsy, 77
  thoughts of suicide, 50
Northumberland, HMS, 54
Noverraz (valet), 54

O

O'Meara, Barry
  chosen as Napoleon's
    doctor, 54
  questioned by Lowe about
    Napoleon, 211
  removal to Europe, 227

P

Pierron (butler), 54
Plantation House, 72, 95, 97,
    134, 137, 180, 191, 196, 208,
    211, 213, 214, 217, 238
Plymouth, 39, 40, 42, 47, 54,
    82
Poppleton, Captain, 7, 117,
    118, 119, 125, 178

Prince Regent, future King George IV, 34, 36, 37, 40, 43, 48, 82, 129, 238, 273

R

Rousseau (steward), 54

S

Saale, frigate, 33
Santini, 114, 187, 189
Santini (usher), 54
Slaney, 37
St. Denis 'Ali' (valet), 54
St. Helena, 313
   description, 66
Stokoe, Dr.
   treating Napoleon, 234
Sturmer, Baron, 162

T

The Briars
   Napoleon asks to stay in pavilion, 72

V

Verling, Dr., 236
Vignali, Father, 239

W

Walewska, Countess, mistress of Napoleon, 30
Waterloo, 17, 18, 19, 25, 33, 34, 47, 52, 53, 139, 207, 276, 313

Endnotes

[1] Napoleon's veteran soldiers.

[2] Elba was the location of Napoleon's first exile in 1814. Only after a few months and after rumors of assassination attempts and learning through his spy Cipriani that he was soon to be removed from Elba and exiled to St. Helena, he escaped, landed on the Southern coast of France and walked back to Paris. He regained the throne without firing a single shot.

[3] Napoleon knew that members of his entourage that followed him to exile like Las Cases, Marchand, and others were keeping journals and would write memoirs and letters detailing Napoleon's every move and thought. He would joke with Las Cases asking if anything in his journal would be of interest in Europe. Of course, Napoleon would say this with his usual grin.

[4] Hamilton-Williams, *The Fall of Napoleon*, John Wiley & Sons, New York, 1994 p. 251. Joseph Fouche was Napoleon's Minister of Police and was considered as being in control of Paris after the Battle of Waterloo and victory by the Allies. With the urging of the Allies, Fouche sought to put Napoleon on a run for the coast with the hopes he would be captured.

[5] Montholon, General Count, *History of the Captivity of Napoleon at St. Helena*, Henry Colburn, Publisher, London, 1846, Vol. I p. 26, St. Denis, Louis Etienne (Ali), *Napoleon From the Tuileries to St. Helena*, Harper & Brothers Publishers, New York, 1922, p. 142.

[6] Bruce, Evangeline, *Napoleon & Josephine: An Improbable Marriage*, Scribner Publishing, New York, 1995, p. 103. Napoleon found Josephine's real name of 'Rose' not romantic enough for her beauty, so he therefore decided to call her Josephine instead.

[7] Montholon, *History*, Vol. I, p. 56.

[8] Hortense, Queen, *The Memoirs of Queen Hortense*, J.J. Little and Ives Company, New York, 1927. Vol. II p. 236.

[9] Hortense, *Memoirs*, Vol. II p. 238., Montholon, *History*, Vol. I, p. 27, St. Denis, *Napoleon* p. 141.

[10] St. Denis, *Napoleon*, p. 141.

[11] Ibid, p. 153.

[12] Las Cases, The Count De, *Memoirs of the Life, Exile, and Conversations of the Emperor Napoleon*, W. J. Widdleton, New York, 1862, Vol. I, p. 15.

Napoleon was so certain of his desire to come to the United States if his reigned ended, that he sent a man by the name of Russell Atwater to Upstate, New York to buy him land in January, 1812.

[13] Ibid, p. 15., Montholon, *History*, Vol. I, p. 34.

[14] Montholon, *History*, Vol. I, p. 51.

[15] Hortense, *Memoirs*, Vol. II p. 236. Marchand, Louis-Joseph (Proctor Jones Editor), *In Napoleon's Shadow*, Proctor Jones Publishing, San Francisco, 1998, p. 261.

[16] Ibid, p. 238.

[17] Weider, Ben, *Assassination at St. Helena Revisited*, John Wiley & Sons, Inc. New York, 1995, p. 113.

[18] Hortense, *Memoirs*, Vol. II p. 240, Las Cases, Memoirs, Vol. I, p. 211-213. This young boy grew up to become Comte "Charles" Leon. It was his birth that proved the fertility of Napoleon and the infertility of Josephine.

[19] Hortense, *Memoirs*, Vol. II p. 242, Las Cases, *Memoirs*, Vol. I p. 211-213. This young boy grew up to become Alexandre Walewska and served the French Government during the 1850s and 1860s.

[20] Hortense, *Memoirs*, Vol. II, p. 243.

[21] Ibid., p. 243.

[22] Ibid., p. 242.

[23] Ibid., p. 244.

[24] Ibid., p. 244-245.

[25] Ibid., p. 247.

[26] Montholon, *History*, Vol. I, p. 67.

[27] Ibid., p. 68.

[28] Ibid., p. 69.

[29] Marchand, *In Napoleon's*, p. 282, Montholon, *Memoirs*, Vol. I, p. 83.

[30] Marchand, *In Napoleon's*, p. 282, 285.

[31] Montholon, *History*, Vol. I, p. 87.

[32] Marchand, *In Napoleon's*, p. 283.

[33] Montholon, *History*, Vol. I, p. 86-87.

[34] Ibid., p. 87-88.

[35] Ibid., p. 85-86.

[36] Las Cases, *Memoirs*, p. 21, Montholon, *History*, Vol. I, p. 82.

[37] Las Cases, *Memoirs*, p. 22-23.

[38] Ibid., p. 25.

[39] Ibid., p. 24, Marchand, *In Napoleon's*, p. 285.

[40] Weider, Ben, and Hapgood, David, *The Murder of Napoleon*, St. Martin's Press, New York, 1982, p. 27.

[41] Marchand, *In Napoleon's*, p. 299.

[42] Marchand, *In Napoleon's*, p. 285.
[43] Ibid., p. 285.
[44] Montholon, *History* Vol., p. 100.
[45] Las Cases, *Memoirs*, Vol. I, p. 26, Marchand, *In Napoleon's*, p. 307., Montholon, *History*, Vol. I, p. 92.
[46] Marchand, *In Napoleon's*, p. 307.
[47] Las Cases, *Memoirs*, p. 28.
[48] Marchand, *In Napoleon's*, p. 309, 312, Montholon, *History*, Vol. I, p. 101, St. Denis, *Napoleon*, p. 157.
[49] Marchand, *In Napoleon's*, p. 309, 312.
[50] Ibid., p. 314.
[51] Ibid., p. 330.
[52] St. Denis, *Napoleon*, p. 158.
[53] Montholon, *History*, Vol. I, p. 101.
[54] Ibid., p. 105.
[55] Marchand, *In Napoleon's*, p. 313, footnote.
[56] Montholon, *History*, Vol. I, p. 104.
[57] Las Cases, *Memoirs*, Vol. I, p. 46, Marchand, *In Napoleon's*, p. 313, footnote.
[58] Marchand, *In Napoleon's*, p. 313, footnote.
[59] Ibid., p. 314.
[60] Weider, *The Murder*, p. 28-30.
[61] Sir George Cockburn was the British Admiral who successfully burnt down the American White House and Capitol Building during the War of 1812 with the United States.
[62] Las Cases, *Memoirs*, p. 37-38, Marchand, *In Napoleon's*, p. 316-317.
[63] Montholon, *History*, Vol. I, p. 103.
[64] Marchand, *In Napoleon's*, p. 317.
[65] Ibid., p. 318.
[66] Ibid., p. 318-319.
[67] Ibid., p. 319.
[68] Napoleon actually crowned himself Emperor and then proceeded to crown Josephine Empress. The Pope was present, seated behind Napoleon.
[69] Montholon, *History*, Vol. I, p. 119.
[70] Las Cases, *Memoirs*, Vol. I, p. 52.
[71] Ibid., p. 40.
[72] Ibid., p. 40.
[73] Marchand, *In Napoleon's*, p. 322.
[74] Las Cases, *Memoirs*, Vol. I, p. 41.

75 Ibid., p. 41-42.
76 Ibid., p. 42-43.
77 Marchand, *In Napoleon's*, p. 323.
78 Weider, *Murder*, p. 33
79 Las Cases, *History*, Vol. I, p. 49, Marchand, *In Napoleon's*, p. 320, Weider, *Murder*, p. 34.
80 Marchand, *In Napoleon's*, p. 320, footnote.
81 Weider, *Murder*, p. 34.
82 Ibid., 34-35.
83 Marchand, *In Napoleon's*, p. 328-329.
84 Ibid., p. 321.
85 Ibid., p. 331, Montholon, *History*, Vol. I, p. 110, 123.
86 Ibid., p. 120.
87 Montholon, *History*, Vol. I, p. 110-111.
88 Ibid., p. 112.
89 Ibid., p. 111-112.
90 Cockburn, Sir George, *Buonaparte's Voyage To St. Helena; Compromising the Diary of Rear Admiral Sir George Cockburn*, Lilly, Wait, Colman, and Holden, Boston, 1833, p. 16.
91 Ibid., p. 17.
92 Montholon, *History*, Vol. I, p. 121.
93 Marchand, *In Napoleon's*, p. 331, Montholon, *History*, Vol. I, p.123.
94 Ibid., p. 122-123.
95 Ibid., p. 126.
96 Cockburn, *Buonaparte's*, p. 61.
97 Las Cases, *Memoirs*, Vol. I, p. 61.
98 Montholon, *History*, Vol. I, p. 125.
99 Las Cases, *Memoirs*, Vol. I, p. 71.
100 Marchand, *In Napoleon's*, p. 336-337.
101 Cockburn, *Buonaparte*, p. 61.
102 Ibid., p. 106-107.
103 Ibid., p. 93.
104 Ibid., p. 25.
105 Ibid., p. 68
106 Marchand, *In Napoleon's*, p. 338.
107 Ibid., p. 336-337.
108 Las Cases, *Memoirs*, Vol. I, p. 122, Montholon, *History*, Vol. I, p. 139.
109 Marchand, *In Napoleon's*, p. 337.
110 Ibid., p. 337.
111 Montholon, *History*, Vol. I, p. 133.

[112] Cockburn, *Buonaparte's*, p. 103.
[113] Montholon, *History*, Vol. I, p. 139.
[114] Marchand, *In Napoleon's*, p. 338.
[115] Ibid., p. 339.
[116] Ibid., p. 339.
[117] Las Cases, *Memoirs*, Vol. I, p. 154.
[118] Weider, *Murder*, p. 50.
[119] Gourgaud, General Baron, *The St. Helena Journal of General Baron Gourgaud*, Butler & Tanner Ltd., London, 1932, p. 1.
[120] Indian servant.
[121] Weider, *Murder*, p. 51.
[122] Montholon, *History*, Vol. I, p. 147.
[123] Las Cases, *Memoirs*, Vol. I, p. 163.
[124] Abell, Mrs. (Betsy Balcombe), *Recollections of the Emperor Napoleon at St. Helena*, John Murray, Albemarie Street, London, 1844.
[125] Marchand, *In Napoleon's*, p. 340.
[126] Weider, *Murder*, p. 51.
[127] Abell, *Recollections*, p. 14, Marchand, *In Napoleon's*, p. 340.
[128] Abell, *Recollections*, p. 15.
[129] Marchand, *In Napoleon's*, p. 343-344.
[130] St. Denis, *Napoleon*, 166.
[131] Ibid., p. 166.
[132] Marchand, *In Napoleon's*, p. 343.
[133] Ibid., p. 343.
[134] Ibid., p. 343.
[135] O'Meara, Barry, *Napoleon In Exile*, Worthington Co., New York, 1890, p. 5, Marchand, *In Napoleon's*, p. 344.
[136] Marchand, *In Napoleon's*, 344.
[137] Ibid., 343., Gourgaud, *The St. Helena*, p. 3, O'Meara, *Napoleon*, p. 6.
[138] Ironically, on his way back from India in 1805, Arthur Wellesley, spent a few nights in the pavilion at the Briars. Wellesley would later become the Duke of Wellington. It is believed that while the Duke of Wellington was in occupied Paris, he stayed in Napoleon's bedroom and sent a note to the Emperor on St. Helena stating that he hoped he found the pavilion to his satisfaction, for he found Napoleon's room at the Tuileries to be the most comfortable.
[139] Marchand, *In Napoleon's*, p. 347, Las Cases, *Memoirs*, Vol. I, p. 158, Montholon, *History*, Vol. I, p. 149-150.

[140] Alexander was the same age as Napoleon's son. The Emperor often played little games with him and remarked how similar he was to his own son, the King of Rome. Betsy recorded a number of times in her memoirs that Napoleon would appear depressed after talking of his son.

[141] Brookes, Dame Mabel, *St. Helena Story*, Dodd, Mead, & Company, New York, 1961, p. 3. Dame Mabel Brookes was the great-niece of Betsy Balcombe. Her grandfather was Alexander Balcombe, Betsy's little brother. Much of what she writes about in her book are stories and events that were passed down through the family. A considerable amount of stories about Betsy and Napoleon are known to Mabel through Betsy's daughter, Mrs. Johnston. "Betsy's memoirs, written in 1844, were of necessity guarded, but her daughter, Mrs. Charles Johnston, elaborated them and filled in the gaps that politics and the exigencies of the time made it expedient for her mother to leave unfilled. It was evident, she remarked, that Napoleon never ceased to be the preoccupation of her mother's life." Brookes, *St. Helena*, p. 88.

[142] Las Cases, *Memoirs*, p. 158.

[143] Marchand, *In Napoleon's*, p. 348.

[144] Ibid., p. 350.

[145] Ibid., p. 350.

[146] Ibid., p. 350.

[147] Abell, *Recollections*, p. 12.

[148] Brookes, *St. Helena*, p. 4.

[149] Ibid., p. 4.

[150] Abell, *Recollections*, p. 19-22.

[151] Ibid., p. 23-25.

[152] Ibid., p. 23-24.

[153] Ibid., p. iii-v.

[154] Ibid., p. 29-30.

[155] English card game.

[156] Marchand, *In Napoleon's*, p. 353-354.

[157] Montholon, *History*, Vol. I, p. 164.

[158] Ibid., p. 156-157.

[159] Marchand, *In Napoleon's*, p. 358-361.

[160] Ibid., p. 358.

[161] Montholon, *History*, Vol. I, p. 159-160.

[162] Ibid., p. 160-161.

[163] Ibid., p. 161-163.

[164] Marchand, *In Napoleon's*, p. 354.

[165] Ibid., p. 354.

[166] Abell, *Recollections*, p. 24-25.
[167] Ibid., p. 24-25.
[168] Ibid., p. 25-26.
[169] Ibid., p. 26-27.
[170] A Russian soldier.
[171] Ibid., p. 31-32.
[172] Unfortunately, these walks always had to be within a designated area where the Emperor could be seen by British soldiers.
[173] Ibid., p. 32-33.
[174] Jokes or pranks, Ibid., p. 30, 34-35.
[175] Brookes, *St. Helena*, p. 42.
[176] Ibid., p. 40.
[177] 'do not cry'
[178] Abell, *Recollections*, p. 35-38.
[179] Ibid., p. 39-40.
[180] Ibid., p. 40-41.
[181] Ibid., p. 41.
[182] Ibid., p. 41-42.
[183] Balcombe, here is Miss Betsy's theme, will it work.
[184] Ibid., 44-45.
[185] Ibid., 43.44.
[186] Plantation House was the residence of the former Governor, then Admiral Cockburn, and later Governor Lowe. It was a spacious house that was beautifully decorated, and in quite better condition than Longwood.
[187] Ibid., p. 47-48.
[188] Ibid., p. 48.
[189] Ibid., p. 48.
[190] A gold Napoleon was currency under the French Empire.
[191] Ibid., p. 48.
[192] Ibid., p. 48-49.
[193] jokes or pranks
[194] wicked or naughty
[195] Ibid., p. 49-50.
[196] Ibid., p. 50.
[197] Ibid., p. 51.
[198] Ibid., p. 51-52, Brookes, *St. Helena*, p. 57.
[199] Ibid., p. 55.
[200] Ibid., p. 56-57.
[201] Ibid., p. 149-151.
[202] Montholon, *History*, Vol. I, p. 164-165.

[203] Las Cases, *Memoirs,* Vol. I, p. 242, O'Meara, *Napoleon,* Vol. I, p. 12.
[204] Ibid., p. 242
[205] Abell, *Recollections,* p. 57-58.
[206] Gourgaud, *The St. Helena,* p. 27.
[207] Abell, *Recollections,* p. 82.
[208] Ibid., p. 82.
[209] Ibid., p. 82.
[210] Ibid., p. 82.
[211] Ibid., p. 82.
[212] Ibid., p. 204.
[213] Ibid., p. 204.
[214] Ibid., p. 204-205, Brookes, *St. Helena,* p. 81.
[215] Ibid., p. 204-205.
[216] Ibid., p. 206.
[217] Old Huff was believed to be crazy and had "taken many strange fancies into his brain; among others, that he was destined to restore the fallen hero to his pristine glory, and that he could at any time free him from thralldom. All argument with this old man upon the folly of his ravings was useless; he still persisted in it, and it soon became evident that old Huff was mad…" Abell, *Recollections,* p. 199-200.
[218] Ibid., p. 200-201.
[219] Ibid., p. 70-71.
[220] A game similar to Hide and Seek.
[221] Ibid., p. 72-75, Gourgaud, *The St. Helena,* p. 41, O'Meara, *Napoleon,* Vol. I, p. 8.
[222] Montholon, *History,* Vol. I, p. 172.
[223] Abell, *Recollections,* p. 114, Marchand, *In Napoleon's,* p. 365.
[224] Ibid., p. 93.
[225] Marchand, *In Napoleon's,* p. 367.
[226] Ibid., p. 367.
[227] Ibid., p. 367.
[228] Ibid., p. 369.
[229] Ibid., p. 369.
[230] Ibid., p. 369.
[231] Ibid., p. 371.
[232] Ibid., p. 370-371.
[233] Las Cases, *Memoirs,* Vol. I, p. 266, St. Denis, *Napoleon,* p. 170.
[234] Ibid., p. 268.
[235] St. Denis, *Napoleon,* p. 183.
[236] Ibid., p. 193-194.

[237] Ibid., p. 174.
[238] O'Meara, *Napoleon*, Vol. I, p. 13-14.
[239] Ibid., p. 14.
[240] Marchand, *In Napoleon's*, p. 387.
[241] Ibid., p. 386.
[242] Abell, *Recollections*, p. 60-63.
[243] Gourgaud, *The St. Helena*, p. 28.
[244] Ibid., p. 31.
[245] Montholon, *History*, Vol. I, p. 177.
[246] Ibid., p. 176-177.
[247] Marchand, *In Napoleon's*, p. 395.
[248] St. Denis, *Napoleon*, p. 186.
[249] Ibid., p. 186.
[250] Ibid., p. 186-187.
[251] Ibid., p. 187.
[252] Ibid., p. 190.
[253] Las Cases, *Memoirs*, p. 246.
[254] Ibid., Vol. II, p. 60.
[255] Ibid., p. 274.
[256] Ibid., p. 286-287.
[257] Ibid., p. 298.
[258] Gourgaud, *St. Helena*, p. 32.
[259] Marchand, *In Napoleon's*, p. 393.
[260] Ibid., p. 393.
[261] Marchand, *In Napoleon's*, p. 400-401.
[262] Ibid., p. 401, O'Meara, *Napoleon*, Vol. I, p. 17.
[263] Marchand, *In Napoleon's*, p. 401.
[264] Ibid., p. 401-402, Montholon, *History*, p. 180, O'Meara, *Napoleon*, Vol. I, p. 17.
[265] Marchand, *In Napoleon's*, p. 402.
[266] Gourgaud, *The St. Helena*, p. 47.
[267] Ibid., p. 47.
[268] Montholon, *History*, Vol. I, p. 181.
[269] Las Cases, *Memoirs*, Vol. II, p. 76, Marchand, *In Napoleon's*, p. 402-403, Montholon, *History*, Vol. I, p. 181, O'Meara, *Napoleon*, Vol. I, p. 17-18.
[270] Marchand, *Napoleon*, p. 403.
[271] Gourgaud, *The St. Helena*, p. 46.
[272] Ibid., p. 48.
[273] Marchand, *In Napoleon's*, p. 403.
[274] Montholon, *History*, Vol. I, p. 182.

[275] Marchand, *In Napoleon's*, p. 408.
[276] Ibid., p. 409, O'Meara, *Napoleon*, Vol. I, p. 20.
[277] Ibid., p. 409.
[278] Ibid., p. 409.
[279] Ibid., p. 410.
[280] Ibid., p. 410.
[281] Ibid., p. 411.
[282] Ibid., p. 412, Montholon, *History*, Vol. I, p. 193.
[283] Las Cases, *Memoirs*, Vol. II, p. 179.
[284] O'Meara, *Napoleon*, Vol. I, p. 26-27.
[285] Ibid., p. 27.
[286] Montholon, *History*, Vol. I, p. 190.
[287] Ibid., p. 191-192.
[288] Marchand, *In Napoleon's*, p. 412.
[289] Montholon, *History*, p. 215-216, O'Meara, *Napoleon*, Vol. I, p. 34.
[290] Marchand, *In Napoleon's*, p. 413.
[291] O'Meara, *Napoleon*, Vol. I, p. 29, Montholon, *History*, Vol. I, p. 213.
[292] Las Cases, *Memoirs*, Vol. II, p. 177.
[293] Ibid., p. 100.
[294] Malcolm, Lady, *A Diary of St. Helena: The Journal of Lady Malcolm*, Harper & Brothers, New York, 1943, p. 37.
[295] Ibid., p. 35.
[296] Lowe served under Prussian General Blucher at the battle of Waterloo.
[297] Malcolm, *A Diary*, p. 38-40.
[298] Ibid., p. 41.
[299] Ibid., p. 41.
[300] Marchand, *In Napoleon's*, p. 415-416.
[301] Montholon, *History*, Vol. I, p. 199.
[302] Ibid., p. 193-194.
[303] Josephine's adult son, sister of Hortense.
[304] Montholon, *History*, Vol. I, p. 193-194, Las Cases, *Memoirs*, Vol. II, p. 184.
[305] Marchand, *In Napoleon's*, p. 421, O'Meara, *Napoleon*, Vol. I, p. 36.
[306] Abell, *Recollections*, p. 87-88.
[307] Montholon, *History*, Vol. I, p. 210-211.
[308] Marchand, *In Napoleon's*, p. 423.
[309] Las Cases, *Memoirs*, Vol. II, p. 220.
[310] Gourgaud, *The St. Helena*, p. 61.
[311] Las Cases, *Memoirs*, Vol. II, p. 227.
[312] Montholon, *History*, Vol. I, p. 214-215.
[313] Ibid., p. 213.

[314] Gourgaud, *The St. Helena*, p. 59.
[315] Las Cases, *Memoirs*, Vol. II, p. 228.
[316] Montholon, *History*, Vol. I, p. 222.
[317] Marchand, *In Napoleon's*, p. 418.
[318] Ibid., p. 418.
[319] Ibid., p. 418.
[320] Montholon, *History*, Vol. I, p. 222.
[321] Las Cases, *Memoirs*, Vol. II, p. 246.
[322] Malcolm, *A Diary*, p. 43.
[323] Ibid., p. 43.
[324] Ibid., p. 44.
[325] O'Meara, *Napoleon*, Vol. I, p. 40.
[326] Marchand, *In Napoleon's*, p. 429.
[327] Ibid., p. 429.
[328] Ibid., p. 429.
[329] Abell, *Recollections*, p. 94.
[330] Ibid., p. 94.
[331] Ibid., p. 94-95.
[332] Ibid., p. 103-104.
[333] Weider, *Murder*, p. 66-67.
[334] Abell, *Recollections*, p. 103-104.
[335] Ibid., p. 103-106, the eagle, along with the bee, was the Imperial symbol of the Emperor Napoleon.
[336] Ibid., p. 111-113.
[337] Ibid., p. 114.
[338] Ibid., p. 114-116.
[339] Ibid., p. 117.
[340] Ibid., p. 119-120.
[341] Ibid., p. 121.
[342] Ibid., p. 122.
[343] Ibid., p. 122.
[344] Ibid., p. 122-123.
[345] Ibid., p. 123-124.
[346] Ibid., p. 123.
[347] Ibid., p. 134, Marchand, *In Napoleon's*, p. 461.
[348] Ibid., p. 135.
[349] Ibid., p. 135-136.
[350] Las Cases, *Memoirs*, Vol. II, p. 360.
[351] Ibid., Vol. II, p. 360, Marchand, *In Napoleon's*, p. 432-433, Montholon, *History*, Vol. I, p. 239.

[352] Marchand, *In Napoleon's*, p. 432.
[353] Ibid., p. 432, Gourgaud, *The St. Helena*, p. 73.
[354] O'Meara, *Napoleon*, Vol. I, p. 57.
[355] Montholon, *History*, Vol. I, p. 239-240.
[356] Malcolm, *A Diary*, p. 58-59.
[357] Ibid., p. 60.
[358] Ibid., p. 60.
[359] Ibid., p. 60-61.
[360] Ibid., p. 62-63.
[361] Ibid., p. 63-64.
[362] O'Meara, *Napoleon*, Vol. I, p. 57.
[363] Marchand, *In Napoleon's*, p. 433, Montholon, *History*, Vol. I, p. 240-241.
[364] O'Meara, *Napoleon*, Vol. I, p. 55.
[365] Marchand, *In Napoleon's*, p. 433, Montholon, *History*, Vol. I, p. 240.
[366] Ibid., p. 433-434, Montholon, *History*, Vol. I, p. 240, O'Meara, *Napoleon*, Vol. I, p. 66.
[367] Las Cases, *Memoirs*, Vol. III., p. 122.
[368] Ibid., Vol. III., p. 123.
[369] O'Meara, *Napoleon*, Vol. I, p. 55-56.
[370] Marchand, *In Napoleon's*, p. 442.
[371] Ibid., p. 442.
[372] Montholon, *History*, Vol. I, p. 261, Marchand, *In Napoleon's*, p. 447.
[373] Ibid., Vol. I, p. 264-265.
[374] Ibid., Vol. I., p. 270-271.
[375] Ibid., Vol. I., p. 271.
[376] Las Cases, *Memoirs*, Vol. IV, p. 15-16.
[377] Las Cases, *Memoirs*, Vol. III, p. 247.
[378] Montholon, *History*, Vol. I, p. 273.
[379] Las Cases, *Memoirs*, Vol. III, p. 304.
[380] It was rumored throughout Longwood and much of the island that Napoleon was intimate on a number of occasions with Madame Montholon while in exile on St. Helena.
[381] Ibid., Vol. III, p. 305-308.
[382] Ibid., Vol. III, p. 316-317.
[383] Ibid., Vol. III, p. 316-317.
[384] Upon removal from St. Helena, Rousseau and Archambault ended up settling in the United States.
[385] Marchand, *In Napoleon's*, p. 452.
[386] Montholon, *History*, Vol. I, p. 277, Marchand, *In Napoleon's*, p. 457.
[387] Marchand, *In Napoleon's*, p. 457.

[388] Ibid., p. 457
[389] Ibid., p. 453.
[390] Ibid., p. 453.
[391] Las Cases, *Memoirs*, Vol. III, p. 382-384.
[392] Ibid., Vol. III, p. 384.
[393] Ibid., Vol. III, p. 387-388.
[394] Ibid., Vol. III, p. 394.
[395] Marchand, *In Napoleon's*, p. 463.
[396] Gourgaud, *The St. Helena*, p. 85.
[397] Ibid., p. 85.
[398] Ibid., p. 85.
[399] O'Meara, *Napoleon*, Vol. I, p. 138.
[400] Ibid., p. 141.
[401] Ibid., p. 143.
[402] Marchand, *In Napoleon's*, p. 461.
[403] Montholon, *History*, Vol. I, p. 287.
[404] Marchand, *In Napoleon's*, p. 469-470, Montholon, *History*, Vol. I, p. 285.
[405] Ibid., p. 470, Ibid, Vol. I, 285.
[406] Balmain, Count, Editor Julian Park, *Napoleon in Captivity*, Books For Library Press, Freeport, New York, 1971, p. 68-69.
[407] O'Meara, *Napoleon*, Vol. I, p. 145.
[408] Ibid., p. 144-145.
[409] Ibid., p. 149-150.
[410] Ibid., p. 150.
[411] Ibid., p. 177.
[412] Montholon, *History*, Vol. I, p. 300-301.
[413] Gourgaud, *St. Helena*, p. 109.
[414] Montholon, *History*, Vol. I, p. 413.
[415] Ibid., Vol. I, p. 413-414.
[416] Gourgaud, *St. Helena*, p. 101.
[417] Ibid., p. 102.
[418] Ibid., p. 122.
[419] Balmain, *Napoleon*, p. 29-30.
[420] Ibid., p. 107.
[421] Ibid., p. 107.
[422] Marchand, *In Napoleon's*, p. 477.
[423] Montholon, *History*, Vol. II, p. 423-424.
[424] Ibid., Vol. II, p. 424.
[425] Ibid., Vol. II, p. 425.
[426] Ibid., Vol. II, p. 471.

427 Ibid., Vol. II, p. 474.
428 Balmain, *Napoleon*, p. 23-24.
429 Gourgaud, *The St. Helena*, p. 126, Marchand, *In Napoleon's*, p. 484.
430 O'Meara, *Napoleon*, Vol. I, p. 199.
431 Ibid., p. 208.
432 Gourgaud, *St. Helena*, p. 126.
433 Marchand, *In Napoleon's*, p. 490.
434 Ibid., p. 490.
435 Abell, *Recollections*, p. 189-190.
436 Ibid., p. 173-174.
437 O'Meara, *Napoleon*, Vol. I, p. 245-246.
438 Marchand, *In Napoleon's*, p. 495.
439 Ibid., p. 495.
440 Ibid., p. 497, Montholon, *History*, Vol. II, p. 482-484.
441 Ibid., p. 497-498, Montholon, *History*, Vol. II, p. 484-487.
442 Montholon, *History*, Vol. II, p. 478-480.
443 Gourgaud, *St. Helena*, p. 180.
444 Ibid., p. 163.
445 Ibid., p. 199.
446 Ibid., p. 203.
447 Ibid., p. 217-218.
448 Marchand, *In Napoleon's*, p. 504.
449 Gourgaud, *The St. Helena*, p. 233.
450 O'Meara, *Napoleon*, Vol. II, p. 26.
451 Marchand, *In Napoleon's*, p. 508.
452 Ibid., p. 506.
453 Ibid., p. 508-509.
454 O'Meara, *Napoleon*, Vol. II, p. 73.
455 Ibid., Vol. II, p. 73.
456 Ibid., Vol. II, p. 79-80.
457 Marchand, *In Napoleon's*, p. 513.
458 Ibid., p. 513.
459 O'Meara, *Napoleon*, Vol. II, p. 84.
460 Ibid., Vol. II, p. 83.
461 O'Meara, *Napoleon*, Vol. II, p. 201-202.
462 Ibid., Vol. II, p. 207-208.
463 Montholon, *History*, Vol. III, p. 1.
464 Balmain, *Napoleon*, p. 113-114.
465 Ibid., p. 145.
466 Gourgaud, *St. Helena*, p. 236.

[467] Ibid., p. 242.
[468] Gourgaud, *St. Helena*, p. 313.
[469] Ibid., p. 313.
[470] Ibid., p. 321.
[471] Ibid., p. 321.
[472] Ibid., p. 321-322.
[473] Ibid., p. 323.
[474] Ibid., p. 326.
[475] O'Meara, *Napoleon* Vol. II, p. 230.
[476] Ibid., Vol. II, p. 176-177.
[477] Montholon, *History*, Vol. III, p. 12.
[478] Marchand, *In Napoleon's*, p. 518.
[479] Abell, *Recollections*, p. 228-231.
[480] Balmain, *Napoleon*, p. 168-169.
[481] Montholon, *History*, Vol. III, p. 20-21.
[482] Abell, *Recollections*, p. 233-235.
[483] O'Meara, *Napoleon*, Vol. II, p. 235.
[484] Ibid., p. 236.
[485] Ibid., p. 237 footnote.
[486] Balmain, *Napoleon*, p. 178-179.
[487] Ibid., p. 170-171.
[488] Marchand, *In Napoleon's*, p. 522, O'Meara, *Napoleon*, Vol. II, p. 236-237.
[489] Ibid., p. 522.
[490] Ibid., p. 523.
[491] Montholon, *History*, Vol. III, p. 30.
[492] O'Meara, *Napoleon*, Vol. II, p. 245.
[493] Marchand, *In Napoleon's*, p. 524-525.
[494] O'Meara, *Napoleon*, Vol. II, p. 247.
[495] Ibid., p. 246-247, Dr. O'Meara was never successful at obtaining the letters.
[496] Ibid., p. 247.
[497] Ibid., p. 247.
[498] Ibid., p. 247.
[499] Marchand, *In Napoleon's*, p. 527-528.
[500] Ibid., p. 528-529.
[501] Ibid., p. 530.
[502] Marchand, *In Napoleon's*, p. 533.
[503] St. Denis, *Napoleon*, p. 195-196.
[504] Marchand, *In Napoleon's*, p. 555.
[505] Ibid., p. 557.

[506] Ibid., p. 557.
[507] Ibid., p. 558.
[508] Balmain, *Napoleon*, p. 197.
[509] Montholon, *History*, Vol. III, p. 91-92, Marchand, *In Napoleon's*, p. 571.
[510] Marchand, *In Napoleon's*, p. 564.
[511] Ibid., p. 564.
[512] Ibid., p. 565.
[513] Montholon, *History*, Vol. III, p. 93.
[514] Marchand, *In Napoleon's*, p. 572.
[515] Montholon, *History*, Vol. III, p. 97-98.
[516] Marchand, *In Napoleon's*, p. 582-583.
[517] Antommarchi, F., *The Last Days of the Emperor Napoleon*, Henry Colburn, London, 1825, p. 60.
[518] Ibid., p. 583-584.
[519] Ibid., p. 584.
[520] Ibid., p. 585.
[521] Ibid., p. 393.
[522] Antommarchi, *The Last*, p. 68.
[523] Ibid., p. 69.
[524] Ibid., p. 69-70.
[525] Ibid., p. 72-73.
[526] Antommarchi, *The Last*, p. 84-86.
[527] Ibid., p. 86.
[528] Quack doctor.
[529] Ibid., p. 119-120.
[530] Ibid., p. 120-121.
[531] Balmain, *Napoleon*, p. 223.
[532] Antommarchi, *The Last*, p. 122-123.
[533] Ibid., p. 123.
[534] Ibid., p. 160-161.
[535] The name of the little girl.
[536] Ibid., p. 161.
[537] Marchand, *In Napoleon's*, p. 590.
[538] Ibid., p. 590-591.
[539] St. Denis, *Napoleon*, p. 219.
[540] Antommarchi, *The Last*, p. 260-261.
[541] Marchand, *In Napoleon's*, p. 591.
[542] Ibid., p. 592.
[543] St. Denis, *Napoleon*, p. 209-210.
[544] Marchand, *In Napoleon's*, p. 592.

[545] Montholon, *History,* Vol. III, p. 112-113.
[546] Antommarchi, *The Last,* p. 292-293.
[547] Ibid., p. 293.
[548] St. Denis, *Napoleon,* p. 211.
[549] Ibid., p. 205-206.
[550] Antommarchi, *The Last,* p. 293.
[551] Gorrequer and Reade were officers/secretaries to Governor Lowe.
[552] Antommarchi, *The Last,* p. 294.
[553] Ibid., p. 296.
[554] Marchand, *In Napoleon's,* p. 610-611.
[555] Ibid., p. 612, St. Denis, *Napoleon,* p. 238-239.
[556] Ibid., p. 594-595.
[557] Ibid., p. 595-596.
[558] Ibid., p. 598.
[559] Ibid., p. 608.
[560] Antommarchi, *The Last,* p. 326-327.
[561] Ibid., p. 327.
[562] Marchand, *In Napoleon's,* p. 617-618.
[563] Ibid., p. 618.
[564] St. Denis, *Napoleon,* p. 241.
[565] Marchand, *In Napoleon's,* p. 621.
[566] Antommarchi, *The Last,* p. 379-380.
[567] St. Denis, *Napoleon,* p. 250-251.
[568] Montholon, *History,* Vol. III, p. 139-140.
[569] Ibid., p. 136-137.
[570] Marchand, *In Napoleon's,* p. 631.
[571] Montholon, *History,* Vol. III, p. 147-148.
[572] Marchand, *In Napoleon's,* p. 626.
[573] Ibid., p. 626.
[574] Ibid., p. 628.
[575] Montholon, *History,* Vol. III, p. 155.
[576] Bertrand, Henri-Gratien, *Napoleon at St. Helena,* Doubleday & Company, Inc, New York, 1952, 46-47.
[577] Ibid., p. 47.
[578] Ibid., p. 124-125.
[579] Montholon, *History,* Vol. III, p. 158.
[580] Ibid., p. 160-161.
[581] Ibid., p. 163.
[582] Antommarchi, *The Last,* Vol. II, p. 54.
[583] Marchand, *In Napoleon's,* p. 637.

[584] Ibid., p. 639.
[585] Bertrand, *Napoleon*, p. 137.
[586] Ibid., p. 127.
[587] Marchand, *In Napoleon's*, p. 640.
[588] Ibid., p. 640-641, Bertrand, *Napoleon*, p. 199.
[589] Montholon, *History*, Vol. III, p. 151.
[590] Marchand, *In Napoleon's*, p. 642.
[591] Ibid., p. 643.
[592] Ibid., p. 643.
[593] Montholon, *History*, Vol. III, p. 168-169.
[594] Ibid., p. 169.
[595] St. Denis, *Napoleon*, p. 264.
[596] Montholon, *History*, Vol. III, p. 172-173.
[597] Bertrand, *Napoleon*, p. 130-131.
[598] Ibid., p. 207.
[599] Montholon, *History*, Vol. III, p. 173.
[600] Marchand, *In Napoleon's*, 644.
[601] St. Denis, *Napoleon*, p. 267.
[602] Ibid., p. 645.
[603] Ibid., p. 645.
[604] Antommarchi, *The Last*, Vol. II, p. 81.
[605] St. Denis, *Napoleon*, p. 271.
[606] Bertrand, *Napoleon*, p. 141.
[607] Ibid., p. 150.
[608] Antommarchi, *The Last*, Vol. II, p. 92.
[609] Montholon, *History*, Vol. III, p. 176-177.
[610] Bertrand, *Napoleon*, p. 176.
[611] Montholon, *History*, Vol. III, p. 183,189.
[612] Ibid., p. 203.
[613] Ibid., p. 183,186.
[614] Marchand, *In Napoleon's*, p. 665.
[615] Ibid., p. 665.
[616] Montholon, *History*, Vol. III, p. 194.
[617] Antommarchi, *The Last*, Vol. II, p. 115-117, Marchand, *In Napoleon's*, p. 656-657.
[618] Ibid., p. 120.
[619] Ibid., p. 120, Bertand, *Napoleon*, p. 163.
[620] Ibid., p. 126.
[621] Bertrand, *Napoleon*, p. 197.
[622] Ibid., p. 199.

[623] Ibid., p. 201.
[624] Ibid., p. 204.
[625] Ibid., p. 181.
[626] Bertrand, *Napoleon*, p. 205-206.
[627] Ibid., p. 206.
[628] Ibid., p. 206.
[629] Antommarchi, *The Last*, Vol. II, p. 131-132, Montholon, *History*, Vol. III, p. 209-210.
[630] Bertrand, *Napoleon*, p. 209.
[631] Montholon, *History*, Vol. III, p. 204-205.
[632] Marchand, *In Napoleon's*, p. 673.
[633] Antommarchi, *The Last*, Vol. II, p. 132-133.
[634] Marchand, *In Napoleon's*, p. 673.
[635] St. Denis, *Napoleon*, p. 270.
[636] Bertand, *Napoleon*, p. 229.
[637] Ibid., p. 308.
[638] Antommarchi, *The Last*, Vol. II, p. 144.
[639] Montholon, *History*, Vol. III, p. 215
[640] Ibid., p. 213.
[641] Antommarchi, *The Last*, Vol. II, p. 153-154, Montholon, *History*, Vol. III, p. 216.
[642] Montholon, *History*, Vol. III, p. 215.
[643] Ibid., p. 215.
[644] Bertrand, *Napoleon*, p. 234.
[645] Marchand, *In Napoleon's*, p. 687.
[646] Ibid., p. 687.
[647] Montholon, *History*, Vol. III, 221, Marchand, *In Napoleon's*, p. 691.
[648] Bertrand, *Napoleon*, p. 235.
[649] Antommarchi, *The Last*, Vol. II, p. 161.
[650] Ibid., p. 169.
[651] Ibid., p. 171.
[652] Ibid., p. 173.
[653] Ibid., p. 177-178, Marchand, *In Napoleon's*, p. 695.
[654] Bertrand, *Napoleon*, p. 235, Antommarchi, *The Last*, Vol. II, p. 174.
[655] St. Denis, *Napoleon*, p. 280.
[656] Bertrand, *Napoleon*, p. 235.
[657] Marchand, *In Napoleon's*, p. 694-695, St. Denis, *Napoleon*, p. 282.
[658] Montholon, *History*, Vol. III, p. 225.
[659] Marchand, *In Napoleon's*, p. 695.
[660] Bertrand, *Napoleon*, p. 237, Marchand, *In Napoleon's*, p. 697.

[661] Bertrand, *Napoleon*, p. 238.
[662] Marchand, *In Napoleon's*, p. 698, Bertrand, *Napoleon*, p. 239.
[663] St. Denis, *Napoleon*, p. 289.
[664] Marchand, *In Napoleon's*, p. 709.
[665] Bertrand, *Napoleon*, p. 244.
[666] Montholon, *History*, Vol. III, p. 237-239.
[667] Marchand, *In Napoleon's*, p. 747.
[668] Gregory, Desmond, *Napoleon's Jailer*, Associated University Presses, Inc., New Jersey, 1996.
[669] Marchand, *In Napoleon's*, p. 746.
[670] Weider, Ben, and Forshufvud, Sten, *Assassination at St. Helena Revisited*, John Wiley & Sons, Inc., New York, 1995.

www.ingramcontent.com/pod-product-compliance
Lightning Source LLC
Chambersburg PA
CBHW072121290426
44111CB00012B/1737